# Amado Muro and Me

Robert L. Seltzer

TCU Press

Fort Worth, TX

Library of Congress Cataloging-in-Publication Data

Names: Seltzer, Robert, author.

Title: Amado Muro and me : a tale of honesty and deception / Robert L. Seltzer.

Description: Fort Worth, Texas : TCU Press, [2016]

Identifiers: LCCN 2016012856 (print) | LCCN 2016016074 (ebook) | ISBN 9780875656366 (alk. paper) | ISBN 9780875656434

Subjects: LCSH: Seltzer, Robert–Childhood and youth. | Seltzer, Chester E., 1915-1971. | Mexican American authors–Biography. | Authors, American–20th century–Biography. | Fathers and sons—United States–Biography. | Journalists–United States–Biography.

Classification: LCC PN4871 .S44 2016 (print) | LCC PN4871 (ebook) | DDC 070.92/273 [B] –dc23

LC record available at https://lccn.loc.gov/2016012856

TCU Press
TCU Box 298300
Fort Worth, Texas 76129
817.257.7822
www.prs.tcu.edu
To order books: 1.800.826.8911
Designed by Barbara Whitehead

All photos from author's collection.

To Christopher Aaron and Katherine Elizabeth,
whose souls shine with the spirit of the grandfather
they never knew.
To Roxanna Ramirez, EdD,
a wise, talented, and sensitive woman.
And to the
San Antonio Chapter of the
Autism Society of Central Texas.

# Contents

# Foreword

There has been some debate about Amado Muro's authenticity, ever since his stunning stories started winning passionate readers who quickly became big fans.

How dare he? How dare an Anglo writer named Chester Seltzer write as a Mexican named Amado Muro?

Well, why not? He cared so much about the worlds he described, he entered into them heart, soul, and name.

Extend this ethical question to all the fiction ever written. What if we could only write as ourselves? All the plays, all the movies, all the texts in which a man writes as a woman, a young person writes as an elder, an urban lad impersonates a farmer, a grounded writer-of-screenplays launches to Mars.

Okay? Not okay? Since when does an imagination have boundaries? And what about actors? How dare they? Perhaps the dispute lay with the fact that Seltzer/Muro actually presented himself behind an invented "other" self—his empathy for the people and places he wrote about was so engaging and immense he actually changed or channeled a new persona.

More recently there was a debate when a singer (Lana Del Rey) changed her name and musical style midstream. Could anyone still stand to listen to her? Yes. Over the course of a career, a musician plays with many bands. Is one more authentic than another? A dancer embodies many roles. A poet speaks for people he/she has never met or lived among. An Asian writer in New York describes life as an African American in the Deep American South, though he has never even been there. Does he have this right of imagination?

Amado Muro had the same right of "otherness" as any artist does—the question is practicing one's craft with love and care. Was he exploiting the people he wrote about or loving them more? Read his stories for the answer.

—Naomi Shihab Nye

# Author's Note

The past is a treacherous landscape, with reality often vanquished by our *memories* of reality—a dynamic that holds true with this book. I did not set out to deceive, but in instances where I may have gotten a date or locale wrong, I went with my memory, not the facts, subscribing to the philosophy that our recollections of what happened are more vibrant, more real, than what actually *did* happen.

I did not have a notebook and pen in hand, for instance, when my father spoke to me, conversations I described in this book. But I can still hear his voice, the ring and cadence of it, and the words came back to me just as clearly as when he uttered them all those years ago. What I heard, in my mind, was more meaningful than any transcription might have been. My father spoke to me, and he speaks to me still. The same is true of the descriptions of the home where I lived and the school that I attended. I see them still, just as sharply as I did as a ten-year-old boy. Whether those descriptions would hold up to any empirical investigations, I cannot say. But what I saw as I traveled backward in my mind was real.

I also changed the names of key figures in this story, particularly those of the school kids. I recognize that children can evolve into far better—or at least different—adults, and I wanted to give those characters the benefit of the doubt. I may have condemned too harshly in some cases and praised too lavishly in others. Changing the names, I think, protects the innocent.

In addition, I left out key characters in my life. I left them out because, while they were important to me, they were not important to the tale I was telling. What follows is my story, which is mostly about me and my father. My dear brother Charles is three years older than me, an age gap that seems more pronounced when you are preteens. Kids live in their own worlds at that age, and we were no different. For that reason, I did not include Charles in this tale. I also recognize that he may have his own story to tell, if and when he elects to do so.

# Acknowledgments

I would like to thank award-winning author and editor Marcia Hatfield Daudistel, without whose help and support my manuscript might have remained in a dusty box in my closet; Shannon Kanorr, a great friend and researcher who helped me uncover details about my father I never knew; Robert Richter, another great friend who was unwaveringly kind and positive about the unpublished chapters he read; Bruce Davidson, yet another close friend—and my boss—who once encouraged me to use the pronoun "I" when writing personal columns, advice that helped me in my attempt to be unflinchingly honest in this memoir (as Harry Crews said in his wonderful memoir, *A Childhood: The Biography of a Place*, "Only the use of *I*, lovely and terrifying word, would get me to the place where I needed to go"); Jaime Castillo, yes, another great friend and former colleague, who provided encouragement and support in the early stages of this project; Rus Bradburd and his creative writing students at New Mexico State University, who offered valuable advice as the manuscript started taking shape; Cleveland native Joe Maxse, an old friend from my sports writing days, without whose help I might never have found the home where my father was reared; Elroy and Phoebe Bode, two wonderful and supportive friends; Naomi Nye, the poet and novelist who was kind enough to write the appreciation of my father that graces this book; the talented staff of TCU Press, including Dan Williams, Kathy Walton, Melinda Esco, Rebecca Allen, Susan Hicks, and Molly Spain, all of whom made this a better book than it was when they first laid eyes on it; the McCabe Library at Swarthmore College in Swarthmore, Pennsylvania, which provided me with information about my father and his prison years; Bakersfield, the town that formed me and the town I grew to love, albeit not as much as El Paso; and, lastly, the subject of this book—the old man—who raised the literary bar so high that I realized, early on, that the joy would be in striving for it, not surpassing it.

To all these people, I owe a debt of gratitude I could never repay.

# Introduction

The best thing about time—the passage of time—is that it erodes the inconsequential, the things that do not matter. It sandblasts the bullshit. I love my father more now than I did when he was alive, and for that I am both sad and grateful—sad that I did not love him as much as I should have then, grateful that I do now.

The old man died when I was sixteen, and during the brief time I knew him, I focused on the mundane, as kids tend to do. One thing that aggravated me—stupidly, in retrospect—was his work ethic. Ensconced on the sofa, he wrote constantly, his notes scattered on the floor in front of him, as he searched for just the right word, just the right phrase, for his short stories.

If his perfectionism aggravated me, however, it also fascinated me, for I could sense his inner struggle. I pictured his mind as a musty old attic, and I could see him rummaging through every nook and cranny, hoping to find a treasure in the dark, dusty corners. Those treasures were the words, the perfect words, to describe what he wanted to say. He worked on his short stories for weeks, sometimes months, at a time. The attic yielded its treasures grudgingly.

Another thing that aggravated me was that he did not just write his short stories; he lived them. And that compelled him to be away from home for long stretches, stretches during which I missed him and needed him. A kind of latter-day Jack London—without the money or celebrity—he rode the rails throughout the Southwest, writing about men who never saw the good times that followed the Great Depression. The stories were heartfelt and lyrical, but they exhibited a compassion toward others that should have been directed toward his family—or so I thought at the time. I think differently now. It took me a while to reach that understanding.

The old man was an amazing writer, his sentences bursting with poetic clarity. He was shy and awkward in social settings, but his prose was pure, unselfconscious. And, while I recognize my bias, I think he wrote some of the most beautiful sentences I have ever read, including this passage from "Mala Torres":

> After lunch, we camped on a grassy bank near the Guanajuato Bridge where the Parral River was brown and swift and deep with quicksands making little whirlpools on the surface. The river bank was a nice place to be. The sound of the wind in the cottonwoods was like a gentle rain, and doves teetered nimbly on the branches and opened and closed their wings. Beyond the stone bridge, Parral looked like a mirage city with its low-built homes and broad, quiet squares colored by stone-bordered flower beds.

After he died in 1971, he began to receive the recognition he had shunned while he was alive. He had written short stories under a pseudonym, Amado Muro, and readers assumed this Ohio native, the son of a powerful journalist, was a Mexican. Once the truth emerged, the *New York Times* called him "the Pale Chicano." Larry McMurtry, in a review of his posthumously published short story collection in the *New York Times Book Review,* praised my father for his fluid writing and generous spirit.

"Seltzer loved Northern Mexico, its people and their language; he worked hard at getting something of the flavor of Chihuahua Spanish into English, and to a degree he succeeded," McMurtry wrote.

> The well-brought-up young man from the prominent Ohio family dropped out far enough, for the space of a few stories, to turn himself into a Mexican boy, a symbolic Chicano. In the most beautiful of these stories, "Sister Guadalajara," we find him with his friend Pug Nose Gallardo, sneaking off from school to visit the Street of Crazy Women in Parral.

The *New York Review of Books* was equally generous in its praise. In an issue with a special supplement entitled "The Chicanos," Harvard historian John Womack Jr. referred to him as the "funniest, brightest, most moving, accomplished and prolific Mexican-American writer." He called him a "veritable Isaac Babel of the Southwest."

As my father gained posthumous recognition, some Chicano literary figures expressed their disdain at his attempt to create a Latino persona. How could an Anglo, they said, depict the dreams and frustrations of a group to which he did not belong? How?

It was a question I had never asked myself. Yes, my father was an Anglo, born and reared in Cleveland, Ohio, but his critics did not know him as I knew him. They did not know about his love for Mexico—and Mexicans. And they did not know about his commitment to his craft, the short story. A man may fool the public, but he cannot fool his family, and there was never a hint of deceit in the pride and affection he expressed for the land he seemed to adopt.

As my beloved grandmother told me, a man who is born a "gringo" does not have to die a "gringo." Other literary figures seemed to understand, even though they had never met him. And while his critics were passionate, so were his defenders.

"To be honest, my initial reaction to the case of Amado Muro was one of suspicion," Jennifer Alvarez Dickinson—an English professor who has taught at universities throughout the Southwest, including the University of Texas and the University of New Mexico—wrote for a paper in a graduate seminar in 2000:

> What was he trying to hide? What did he hope to get out of this 'hoax'? At the time I read the article [by McMurtry], the fact that authors often use pseudonyms did not come to mind, a practice that I regularly accept as a creative or practical gesture, nothing more. The issue seems to be one of race and power—an author exerts a measure of power in representing a group that has traditionally had limited opportunities for self-representation, especially if the author speaks as one of the disenfranchised. But in our fear, are we not rigidly defining experience by ethnicity? The stories of Chester Seltzer are, for the most part, sensitive to and repre-

> sentative of a form of Chicano experience. I would then argue that, despite Seltzer's upbringing, his collection of stories written as Amado Muro are in fact Chicano literature, a category whose flexible boundaries reflect the very impossibility of delineating hard and fast rules of inclusion or exclusion.

I started writing this book in the mid-1980s. Like the old man, I was a perfectionist, but I lacked his doggedness—or his talent. I put the manuscript aside. It was to be a story of love, patience, and wisdom—qualities he possessed in abundance, qualities that helped me cope with the racism I experienced when I was ten. I wrote three chapters, and then the story, along with my ambition to write it, unraveled. I had my own attic, and the search for the right words proved too much for me.

Then something happened to rekindle not only my determination to finish the book, but also the memories of the trauma that prompted me to write it in the first place. It was 1993. I was a sportswriter for the *Philadelphia Inquirer.* I wrote about boxing—a dream job—and one of the fighters I covered routinely was Julio Cesar Chavez, the junior welterweight champion then regarded as the greatest boxer in the world, pound for pound. As a Latino from El Paso, Texas, I was one of the few sportswriters in the country who could interview the great Mexican fighter without a translator.

I was in Las Vegas to cover a Chavez fight at a hotel-casino. The place was packed, filled with drunks, gamblers, and boxing fans, people whose interests—and activities—sometimes overlapped. I attended the weigh-in one afternoon, and afterwards, I found myself in the same elevator as the great champion, now dressed in street clothes. We were discussing the fight, in Spanish, when a group of gamblers crowded into the elevator. There were six of them. They carried plastic cups in each hand, beer in one, poker chips in the other.

Avoiding the stampede, we moved to the rear of the elevator. The gamblers, unaware that the champion was standing behind them, started talking about the upcoming fight. One of them referred to Chavez as a "wetback." Chavez knew little English, barely enough to say "Thank you very much" at the end of each press conference. But he recognized the term *wetback*. He looked at me. Then he shook his head in dismay, as if to say, "I could shut his mouth with one left hook, but it would not be worth it."

One morning, about a year later, I walked into the sports department at the *Inquirer*. I dropped my notebook onto my desk, and the sports editor poked his head out of his office. He called out to me.

"Hey, you fucking wetback."

I walked out the door without answering him. He followed me. I took the stairs—the office was on the fourth floor—and I could hear his footfalls behind me. I was out on the street before he caught up to me, panting and sweating.

"Robert, what's wrong?" he asked.

"I don't like being called a fucking wetback," I said simply.

I forget his answer—I think he said he was joking—but I never considered filing a complaint with human resources, and several months later, still distraught over the incident, I resigned from the *Inquirer*, leaving a great newspaper to return to my hometown of El Paso, which I had left seventeen years before. I told one of the top editors, Robert Rosenthal, of my decision. A great newsman and a great man, period, Rosenthal tried to persuade me to stay. But I had made my mind up, and he wrote me a wonderful letter of reference, for which I will always be grateful. That was in 1995.

The two "wetback" comments reminded me of an incident years before, the incident that inspired me to start writing the story in the mid-1980s. That incident is the subject of this book, which deals with racism and how a father helped his son cope with it. I learned how to write "fast" as a boxing writer, but I did not write this book so much as live it—or relive it—and as one memory sparked another and another and another, I kept going back to rewrite, add, or supplement. That damned attic.

This book explores two cultures through one family: my father was Anglo, my mother Mexican. It covers one year in the relationship between me and my father, whose sensitivity and compassion helped me through a painful but enlightening experience. It was 1964, and when we moved from El Paso, Texas, to Bakersfield, California, I encountered racism for the first time. I was ten years old.

Chester Seltzer, who overcame cultural barriers through his understanding, was uniquely qualified to guide me during this difficult period. My father was from Cleveland, my mother from Chihuahua. He followed his wanderlust to the border, where he met my mother. They fell in love in El Paso—a man who was embracing a culture, a woman who was escaping it. She came to this country when she was a little girl, brought here by parents fleeing the chaos of the Mexican Revolution.

It was from this perspective, as a man who saw bridges where others saw barriers, that my father helped me deal with the racist attitudes I was experiencing for the first time. The trouble came in the form of a classmate who haunted me throughout the school year. . . . But I am getting ahead of myself. This book tells that story.

1

# The Surfboards

The blinds were cracked, and needles of sunshine landed on my desk.

When I saw the school for the first time, I thought it was a military base—St. Francis Elementary, a facility with classrooms that looked like barracks. There were no lobbies, no hallways connecting one room to another. You entered the classrooms from the outdoors, as if each room were a separate entity, with its own set of rules and regulations—and its own set of punishments for violating those rules and regulations. Catholics were big on punishment.

Built to resemble the Spanish missions along the Pacific Coast, the school boasted none of their grandeur or allure. It fronted Palm Street, a quiet street in a quiet neighborhood. As modest as the tract homes that surrounded it, the school covered a square block, most of it consumed by the playground, a vast area pocked with occasional clumps of grass.

Outside, on a patch of grass in front of the main office, a holy man greeted the students and teachers every morning, rain or shine. He was short and frail, his robe cinched by a rope at his waist. It was St. Francis. The kids loved the dark gray statue. It was austere but comforting. The saint held his arms in front of his chest, and a bird lounged in the bowl formed by his palms. Real birds would land in the bowl, crowding their poor, earth-bound cousin, but it was all right with St. Francis. He welcomed every creature, real or not—an example that some of the children, despite their affection for the saint, failed to follow.

September, 1964. The start of the school year. I was in the fifth grade, a ten-year-old boy sitting in a dark classroom, unaware that the world—my world—was about to change forever. It was noon. Mrs. Chaney always turned the light off before lunch or recess, and whenever I skipped lunch, whenever I stayed in the classroom, I never turned it back on.

It was sunny and crisp outside, summer giving way to fall, and while the other children ate their hot dogs or bologna sandwiches in the auditorium, I sat at my desk, drawing surfboards on the covers of my textbooks. I depicted them from all angles, horizontal, vertical, even upside down, as if a monstrous wave had capsized the flat, tiny boards on the oceans that were my book covers. I had never surfed, had never wanted to surf, but I loved the Beach Boys, who sang about surfing—and surfer girls—with a passion that captivated me. And so I drew the surfboards.

Five minutes before the next class, another child walked into the room, fresh from lunch. Randy Reed turned on the light. Then he sat behind me. It was his assigned seat, which meant he would sit behind me every day that year. Randy Reed was a blond kid, so big and tall that whenever he stretched his legs, his feet would emerge under my desk, his shiny penny loafers getting chummy with my worn penny loafers.

"You're doing it again," I told him, lifting my head from my book covers. "You're kicking my legs."

Randy Reed wore braces, which was bad enough, but he also wore a retainer, which looked like a bridle on his horsey teeth. He was the ugliest kid in class—big teeth, big ears, big flat-top—but nobody made fun of Randy Reed. Nobody made fun of Randy Reed because he was big and tall and mean.

"Please stop it," I said, feeling silly for saying *please* to a kid my age.

Randy Reed and I were alone in the classroom, waiting for the next class to start, one kid with his surfboards, the other with his retainer. He stood up, scraping his ankles against the bottom of my desk as he struggled to his feet. Then he peered over my shoulder.

"Goddamn it!" he screamed.

Randy Reed tore all my book covers, all my surfboards, the one I was drawing and the ones I had already drawn. When he finished, he stood by my desk, his shoulders heaving from the exertion. I looked up, and he seemed miles above me, as if he were peering over the rim of a well.

"There!" he yelled. "There! Goddamn it!"

Too stunned to react, a participant shocked into becoming a witness, I saw him scatter the torn covers across the classroom, shreds of brown paper fluttering to the floor. What was wrong with him? He kept screaming at me, the retainer catching the spit from each cuss word, but I could not understand him. I could not understand *anything.* He was so furious that he started to gasp. Then, finally regaining his breath, he spoke calmly, almost tenderly.

"The Beach Boys aren't for you," he said, smiling. "The Beach Boys aren't for fuckin' beaners."

When he finished the rant, he returned to his desk, kicking the torn book covers as he sat down. I looked at the clock above the blackboard. It was 12:30. Almost three hours to go before the final bell. The other children started to file into the classroom, unaware of what had happened. I stared straight ahead.

We must have seen each other—maybe even talked to each other—before that incident, but I recall none of those encounters. Randy Reed and I did not meet. We collided. And all I remember is the collision . . . and everything that happened afterwards.

Would it get worse? I asked myself. I answered my own question. Trouble was coming. I could sense it, sense it just as surely as a guilty child knows when the *nalgada* is coming, the spanking. What was I guilty of? If I was guilty of anything, it was not knowing what made me guilty. There was a Spanish phrase my grandmother liked to use, a phrase that reflected resignation in the face of looming disaster. *Que friega.* It was one of those terms that seemed untranslatable, but years later, when rough, everyday speech started to invade Hollywood, I would hear movie characters complain about their jobs or spouses, tortured men who sighed that life was a "bitch." Well, a *friega* was a bitch. My grandmother would have understood.

We had moved from El Paso, Texas, to Bakersfield, California, about a month earlier—my father, my mother, and me. Until that moment with Randy Reed, I never knew I was a "beaner." A beaner? I never knew I was a Mexican-American, much less a beaner. We were all the same in El Paso—or at least most of us were. We were beaners or wetbacks or greasers. But nobody ever called us that, not in El Paso. We were among our "own kind" there, free of labels and stereotypes and Randy Reed. I had heard of kids in public schools who got swatted for speaking Spanish, but that never happened at Holy Family, the little Catholic school I attended in Sunset Heights, maybe because most of the nuns were Mexican or Mexican-American. I wanted to run away, return to my family, my holy family, in El Paso.

By 2016, Latinos would represent almost 50 percent of the population in Bakersfield, with Mexican-Americans serving on the school board and the city council. They would have a voice, and they would use it, and the voice would be neither proud nor shrill. It would be normal, ordinary, because Mexican-Americans—in the eyes of many, not all, but many—had gone beyond the hyphenation. They had become Americans.

But this was 1964. Latinos comprised less than 20 percent of the population in Bakersfield. And that figure was even lower at St. Francis Elementary School. I was the only one. There were three others at St. Francis Junior High, two of them twins, but that facility was on the other side of town, miles from the barracks that were St. Francis Elementary.

In Bakersfield, we lived in a rental house on Brundage Lane, one of the busiest streets in town. We lived in a rental home in El Paso, too, a duplex. But I never called it a duplex or a rental; I called it a home. The rental house in Bakersfield—I never referred to it as a home. It was lime green, the paint on the plaster façade flecked to resemble the scales on a fish. The house had a front porch, just like our home in El Paso, but it was smaller, and there was no brick wall around it. And no El Paso beyond it.

My mother never decorated the rental house, not the way she had in El Paso. There were no nature portraits on the walls, no porcelain figures on the tables. She bought a coverlet for the sofa one day, but only because the old man, sitting there for hours at a time, burrowed a hole into the fabric, and my mother did not want the landlord to spot the yawning fissure during one of his occasional visits to the house.

"Randy Reed called me a beaner," I told my mother that evening.

My mother wore casual clothes at home. She called them house dresses. They looked like bed sheets trimmed to match her dimensions, short and plump, with a hole cut out for her head. My mother dressed up when she went out, but she had never learned how to drive, and she regarded almost every journey beyond the front door as "going out"—a trip to the grocery store, a ride to the newsstand, a walk to the mailbox.

"He called me a fuckin' beaner," I said.

My mother was wearing a house dress that day, black with white polka dots.

"*Ay, Roberto,*" she said. "*No hables así.* Don't talk like that."

"Well, that's what he called me, Mom," I said.

She told me to stand up to him, to call him names that would be just as cutting to him as beaner was to me.

"Call him a hamburger," she said. "Call him a hot dog. Those are American foods."

I was outraged.

"That's stupid!" I yelled.

Then I remembered something my father had told me.

"Mom, when you got married, Dad said you drove from El Paso to San Diego for your honeymoon."

"Yes," she said. "We did."

"Well," I continued. "Dad said you had to look and look and look for a hotel that would take you, because you were a . . . a . . . a . . . Mexican . . . and they didn't want any Mexicans staying there."

"Yes, that's true," she said softly.

"Well, San Diego is in California, and Bakersfield is in California, and now *we're* in California," I said. "Why would Dad bring us to this state, this *pinche* (damned) state? Why?"

"Ay, Bobby, that was a long time ago, almost fourteen years," she said.

"Well, I don't want to be here," I said. "California is stupid!"

My mother stared at me, a slight smile splitting her plump face, as if she knew I was right. That was the only opening I needed—that smile. I asked her for a favor. A small favor. I asked her to change her name, from Amada to Amanda, so the kids at school would not know I was Mexican, forgetting that my dark skin was a bigger giveaway than her first name.

"Please," I said, almost crying. "Please . . . Please . . . Please . . . "

Getting nowhere, I stopped pleading, but only for a moment.

"P . . . P . . . P . . . Por favor?"

I tried another tactic.

"Then let me go to the public school," I said. "I'm sure there are other Mexicans there."

My mother did not answer me. She went to the kitchen, leaving me alone in the living room, where I waited for a response. I heard the pots and pans clanging in the kitchen. She was making dinner.

# 2

## The Sage in Boxer Shorts

The old man was a writer, but I thought he wrote letters for a living, as in the letters of the alphabet. I pictured him in a first-grade classroom, practicing his cursive until his wrists ached. It was not until later that I realized he arranged all those letters into words that could touch your soul.

"What does your father do for a living?" my friends back in El Paso would ask.

"He handwrites."

"Really?"

"Yeah."

"Oh."

My father worked on the sofa in the living room, wearing nothing but his boxer shorts, in good weather and bad, his chin slumped onto his bare chest as he wrestled with letter after letter, word after word, sentence after sentence. He wrote slowly, tearing up every piece of paper that did not satisfy him, until the crumpled sheets were piled as high as the coffee table in front of him. When a phrase stumped him, which was often, he would frown and palm his bald head. My father wrote day and night. He had insomnia.

He stood about five foot nine, and my mother called him *El Chaparro* behind his back. I always wondered why. He did not seem short to me. One day, in a burst of uncharacteristic defiance, I told my mother she should call him *El Pecho*, The Chest. My father could bench press 240 pounds, and he sometimes asked me to spot him during his workouts at the YMCA, even though the barbell weighed more than twice as much as I did. *"Uuuggghhh,"* he would grunt with every repetition. The weight lifting did not make him taller, but it made him bulkier and, to me, his strength overshadowed his height. Whenever he walked into a room, his chest seemed to enter about five seconds before he did, heralding, like a fierce trumpet blast, the arrival of El Chaparro.

My father also jogged, running in his street clothes and street shoes, perhaps because he regarded gym clothes and tennis shoes as extravagant, even decadent. His purity produced some unpleasant side effects: His feet were full of blisters, his shoes full of holes. El Chaparro did not seem to mind either.

El Chaparro had another nickname, one he bestowed on himself—the old man. It was part of his self-deprecating wit, an attempt to make sure the ego never outgrew the man. The old man—*el viejo.*

"What are you writing?" I asked the old man.

It was Saturday morning, the day after I discovered I was different.

"I'll let you see it when I'm finished," he said. "I promise."

"Okay," I said.

It was a cool, breezy morning, the kind I loved. I left the old man on the sofa, writing and smoking his KOOLS, the smoke curling above the sentences he had just composed. I ran outside, the screen door banging behind me, and I jumped on my bicycle, a black Bridgestone. My mother and father promised to buy me a red Schwinn, a superior brand, some day. I shrugged and said "Okay," but deep down, I did not care. I loved my black Bridgestone.

Focused on the asphalt below, I chased the shadows as the morning clouds headed east. It was a game I loved to play—me versus the clouds. Sometimes, I won; sometimes, the clouds won. But even when I triumphed, I conceded defeat in one area: I could outrace the shadows, but I could not maintain the pace forever. I was a sprinter; the clouds were marathoners.

Chester Seltzer in the 1930s.

When I returned home that afternoon, my father asked me if I had "gone on a wander."

"Huh?" I asked.

"Ireland is like Mexico—full of poets," he said. "Did you go on a wander?"

He smiled.

"Did you wander? Did you roam? That's the phrase the Irish use—'going on a wander.' . . . Beautiful, isn't it?"

"I guess," I said, shrugging.

Then he showed me the short story. *Chingele*. Damn. Captivated by the shadows on the asphalt, I had forgotten his promise to let me read it. The story was written on long yellow paper, with the handwriting so sloppy that I could barely make it out. This was not the smoothly flowing cursive that I had assumed was his stock and trade; this was a mess. But the words—the words—were something else. The words flowed, even if the handwriting did not, and I ruffled through the yellow pages until I read every word, my eyes narrowed, my forehead corrugated like a tin roof.

It was a story about a hobo and a dog—a dog that, believe it or not, was blue. The hobo loved the dog, taking him wherever he went, although it was unclear whether he led the dog or the dog led him. It did not seem to matter, not to the hobo . . . and not to the dog. As the story ended, the hobo turned down a handout from a Good Samaritan, asking for something else instead—a little food for Blue.

> He was walking down the street with his stringy gray hair hanging down over his eyes, wearing no socks, a toe sticking out of his right shoe, and his heels pushing out of both of them. He had a whittled cane in his left hand and attached to his right hand was a chain with a small dog at the end of it. He stopped and looked at me. ("Blue")

"I liked it," I told my father, thinking this was the grandest praise I could offer him.

My father smiled, his hazel eyes glowing, and it was then that I realized he was special. We were beginning to study scientists and inventors in school—men like Newton and Galileo and DaVinci. Men who were smart because they could prove everything they said was true, with things called theorems. Well, writers were smart, too, but they were smart for a different reason. They were smart because they could not prove a damned thing. Writers were wise, Mrs. Chaney told us, and you had to trust them, believe in them. My father was a great writer, a dedicated writer. He once spent a week writing a single sentence.

"I have a novel in me," he would tell my mother. "And, one day, I'll write it."

How many weeks would it take? I wondered. After the old man let me read the short story, he typed it on his Underwood typewriter, converting the messy cursive into neat print. He kept the typewriter on the dining room table, and whenever he finished typing a story, he would slide the machine to the center of the table, where it remained until it was time to type his next tale. Other families had flowerpots or fruit bowls as the centerpieces of their tables. We had an Underwood typewriter.

My mother said he should have married his words. His *pinche* words, she called them. It was hard to argue with her, especially when the only world he cared about was the world he created through his short stories. I loved my father, the sage in boxer shorts. But did I *believe* in him? I wondered if my mother had told him about Randy Reed. I wondered if *I* should tell him. I wanted to; I wanted to ask for his help, and I *would*. I knew I would. But I was not sure I could trust him. It was hard to count on a father if you did not know where he was going to be from week to week.

# 3

# El Gringo

My mother told him.

The old man never outed her. But I knew she had discussed my humiliation with him. I knew it.

A week after the incident, armed with the certainty that he knew what had happened in the classroom, I got bold. Very bold. I asked the old man a question, a simple question, one I had wanted to ask him since the afternoon Randy Reed destroyed my surfboards.

"Dad, why am I a Mexican?"

"You know why," he said softly.

"Tell me again," I said. "Please."

And so he did. He told me a story I had heard hundreds of times before. But, this time, I listened.

They were born thousands of miles, and one culture, apart—my father in Cleveland, Ohio, my mother in Chihuahua, Mexico.

"I guess we were supposed to meet, your mother and me," he said.

Jesus and Amada Muro left Chihuahua in 1916, fleeing the chaos and poverty of their homeland during the Mexican Revolution. They were part of an exodus the *El Paso Herald* described as a "spectacle of despair." The revolution grew from noble ideas, expressed by men tired of bowing to greed and complacency, but when the rebel leaders overthrew Porfirio Díaz, the cruelty and corruption that sparked their rebellion found a new home, under a new leader, then another new home, under another new leader. And so it went—hope and longing crushed beneath the boots of each subsequent regime.

The revolution turned into civil war, with many of the rebels reduced to looters, scavengers, thugs in uniform. *What happened to the noble cause of the revolution?* the Muros wondered. And what would happen to Chihuahua, their beautiful Chihuahua, once ringed by hills that watched over their town like guardian angels? Look at our city now, they told themselves. Look at it. The hills, now wreathed in gun smoke, remained, but the guardian angels had vanished.

"The Revolution created as many problems as it solved," Manuel G. Gonzales would write in *Mexicanos: A History of Mexicans in the United States*. "Massive destruction, the result of pillage, looting, and burning, was everywhere, especially in the areas west and north of the capital."

A gray dust settled over the city, now fetid with death and corruption. Thousands died—men, women, children. The townspeople buried them in makeshift graves, each marker composed of two sticks bound with rope to resemble a cross. Friends, neighbors, loved ones, rotting in the soil beneath them. Chihuahua, their beautiful Chihuahua, was turning into a graveyard.

"I see a great, rich country . . . being smashed to chaos by a handful of child-minded men playing with the tragic tools of death made possible by modern technology," Jack London wrote in *Jack London Reports*, a collection of nonfiction that included war correspondence from Mexico.

> From garret to basement, the dwelling of Mexico is being torn to pieces. . . . The stay-at-home American listens to the slogans uttered by the various leaders of this anarchy and makes the mistake of conceiving the leaders in his own image and of thinking that "Liberty, Justice" and a "Square Deal" means the same to them as they mean to him. Nothing of the sort. In the four centuries of Spanish and Mexican

Alita, my grandmother, as a young woman before the Mexican Revolution.

> rule, liberty, justice, and the square deal have never existed. Mexico is a republic in which nobody votes. Its liberty has ever been construed as license. Its justice had consisted in an effort at equitable division of the spoils of an exploited people. . . . And so it is with all the rest of the bombastic and valorous phrases of the Mexican. . . .

Decades later, Amada Muro told me they had been landowners in Chihuahua—secure, comfortable, and happy. She spoke of her native land with pride and regret, knowing that her home was no longer a physical landscape. It was a memory, just a memory, vital but intangible—and more remote than the stars and planets.

My father said the Muros were never landowners, never wealthy. Then why did Amada Muro lie? Jesus Muro was a laborer, and he struggled to make a life for his family, and the further those days receded into the past, the more Amada tried to retrieve them. Amada was not lying, the old man said; she was resurrecting her hopes and dreams. The revolution devastated her homeland; she was not about to let it destroy her vision of the life she wanted there.

When the Muros fled the destruction, they did not go far. They reached Juárez, and they crossed the Rio Grande, and then they stopped, their search for a new home going as far as their love for an old home would take them. The family settled in South El Paso, so close to the river that they could witness the mayhem across the border from the rooftops in their new neighborhood. The Muros opened a small grocery store in the heart of the barrio, a store where fruit baskets lined the walls and red chiles dangled from the ceiling. The family lived in a three-room apartment above the store, between the Colón Theater and the Sacred Heart Church.

"At every turn you come upon ruins—houses riddled with bullet holes or breached with shot and shell . . ." Ernest Peixotto wrote, describing Juárez in an article for *Scribner Magazine* in 1916. "A public library razed to the ground, a mere heap of stones; a post office badly damaged; and, opposite the Juárez monument, a brick building, roofless with gaping windows and walls. . . ."

The Muros were safe in El Paso, but their physical security could not shield them from the emotional burden of seeing their homeland in flames. They focused on their children, one boy and four girls, including a sweet, dimpled child who was no bigger than a sack of *nopalitos*—two-year-old Amadita, named after her mother. The apartment had no bathrooms; the community restroom was outside, at the end of the complex, and during the winter, the kids tried to hold it as long as possible, for fear of freezing in the *agachado*.

There was only one bedroom, and everybody slept there, everybody, the *padres* and the *niños*. There were two beds, each one pushed up against a wall, the head of one bed meeting the foot of the other, an L that left little room for bedroom furniture. Not that it mattered; they *had* no bedroom furniture.

In the winter, the family would gather around the stove, the flames from each burner glowing blue and orange in the dank little kitchen. Amadita never forgot those days. Never. As an adult, she would turn up the heater the minute the temperature dipped below eighty.

"Our new home," the mother and father would say to each other, their voices filled with pride and regret.

Amadita was bright, personable and plump, so plump that her dimples broadened along with her face.

"I could pour a shot of tequila in those dimples," her father joked with her.

She graduated from Bowie High School, but she never went to college. The family was poor, and she went to work, finding a series of office jobs downtown, only a few blocks from their home in South El Paso. Then she got a job as a public relations assistant for American Airlines, a job that suited her personality—charming and outgoing. The office was in the lobby of the Paso del Norte Hotel, a downtown hotel that featured a circular bar where Butch Cassidy and the Sundance Kid, the western outlaws, used to hang out.

Born in Cleveland, Ohio, my father arrived in El Paso thirty years after the Mexican Revolution, another stop in what would be a lifelong odyssey—an odyssey as grueling as it was adventurous. It was 1946. He was thirty-one years old, but he had seen more of the country than men twice his age, and he had seen it from a unique perspective, traveling across the land by car, bus and freight train. My father described these experiences, quiet, poignant stories about the homeless men and women he met on the road—"Blue," "Something About Fieldhands," "Night Train to Fort Worth."

> I stood up to look out at the prairie then, and I could see the ground slipping by in a long streak and every little while a telephone pole would flash by. The moon was up close in the sky and it was white and cold and lopsided, and it looked

My mother in the late 1940s, before she met my father.

like I could touch it with a long stick. ("Something About Two Hoboes")

The stories were lyrical but understated, so warm and casual that they read like entries in a journal. Most of the tales were published in literary quarterlies. Some were cited in *Best American Short Stories*. The honors meant little to my father. We never celebrated the awards, never even mentioned them. He said writing was like gardening. You planted the seeds, and you watered the ground, and one day, poking through an empty patch of soil, a flower would begin to blossom. The words were his flowers; they were also his rewards. My dad came from a family of writers—his grandfather was a novelist, his father a newspaper editor—but, while he embraced the calling, he rejected the celebrity the calling could create.

While he marveled at the language, the old man derided Shakespeare for writing about subjects he could not have experienced or understood. A play about a Roman emperor? A Danish prince? *Really?* He also condemned Steinbeck and Hemingway, writers he had loved, for losing their way in the twilight of their careers, their art undermined by their fame and celebrity. The old man set out on a different path, writing about what he lived, with little regard for money or fame.

"Where did you get this strange idea?" a man once asked him.

"What strange idea?"

"Well . . . " the man said, "this idea that there's something wrong with being comfortable, that it's a . . . a sin . . . a type of sin."

"From Tolstoy."

"Oh, yeah? Well, where can I get a hold of this Tolstoy guy?"

"That might be a little hard," my father answered.

"Why?"

"Do you have a Ouija board?" my father asked him.

"Huh?"

"Tolstoy's dead," my father said.

In 1890, about twenty-five years before the old man was born, the US Census declared the American frontier officially closed. The Indian Wars were over, and six western states were admitted to the Union, with only four to go in the Continental United States—Utah, Arizona, Oklahoma, and South Dakota. It was a vast territory that shrank daily, thanks to a railroad that swallowed miles faster than you could say "Union Pacific."

My father knew his history, but he did not care what the US Census declared in 1890. The frontier was still there, still beckoning him to see new landscapes and savor fresh experiences, both here and abroad. So, after graduating from high school in 1932, he traveled to Mexico, lured by *The Treasure of the Sierra Madre*, a novel he loved so much that he could recite chunks of it.

He traveled on the cheap, hitchhiking and hopping freight trains. And whenever he ran out of money, he stopped to work the fields, picking potatoes in Idaho and beets in Illinois. It took the old man three weeks to reach Mexico, and two seconds to fall in love with it—its people, its culture and, because he started learning the language during his travels, its literature.

My father rode a freight train through Zacatecas, and it was the most beautiful country he had ever seen, its hills studded with pine trees—row after row, one on top of the other, like the terraces in a Spanish villa. He sat in the boxcar, his knees tucked under his chin, his arms wrapped around his ankles. The air was cool and crisp, and the world rushed by with a sensuous rhythm, each scene reduced to a rectangular snapshot as he gazed through the open door of the boxcar. He dug his chin into the cleft between his knees, fascinated by the landscape whizzing past. Mexico on rails.

On his way back to the United States, the old man stopped in Ciudad Chihuahua. He ordered breakfast at a sidewalk café one morning. It was seven o'clock. Overcast. The clouds as thick as battle smoke. He thought of the Mexican Revolution, the same revolution a woman and her family had fled about twenty years earlier. As he waited for his breakfast that morning, the clouds parted, revealing the serrated peaks of the hills surrounding the city.

"*Las lomas* (the hills)," he told the waiter, testing out some of the Spanish he had learned on his trip.

The waiter smiled.

"Las lomas," the waiter repeated.

The old man had arrived the night before, when the hills were faint outlines, oily smudges in the dark sky. He smiled, pondering the contrast between night and day. The waiter took his order. What a beautiful country, the old man told himself, staring at the hills. About five minutes later, the waiter served his breakfast.

"*Su almuerzo* (Your breakfast), *señor*," he said.

Three red enchiladas topped with two fried eggs—yellow eyes on a red face.

"Gracias," my father said, proud of the little Spanish he had picked up on his journey. "*Muchísimas* gracias."

But when the waiter left, the old man reverted to English.

"Chester Seltzer," he told himself. "You are the luckiest man in the world."

When Chester Seltzer returned to the United States, he enrolled at the University of Virginia in Charlottesville, the school founded by Thomas Jefferson. He majored in journalism, which was considered less prestigious than English. Some of the students looked down on him for choosing such an unworthy discipline. The stuffiness annoyed him. One day, going through the cafeteria line, he ordered two fried eggs, and when he sat down at the table, he slid the eggs onto his mashed potatoes—two yellow eyes on a creamy face. Then he devoured them. The other students were aghast.

Fed up with the snobs at Virginia, he dropped out of school, but after a year back in Cleveland, he decided to give college another try. He enrolled at Kenyon College in Gambier, Ohio, where two famous poets served on the English faculty—Randall Jarrell and John Crowe Ransom. He majored in journalism at Kenyon, too, but nobody looked down on him for it, and he enjoyed the English courses, even though Ransom, one of his professors, was infamous for his harsh tone with the students.

He liked Kenyon better than Virginia—the students, including another poet, Robert Lowell, were friendlier, more easygoing—but college was not for him, and he dropped out a semester before he was scheduled to graduate. Maybe he realized that education, *real* education, transcended the classroom. Or maybe he was traumatized by Ransom, who wrote a succinct comment in the margins of a paper the old man had written:

"Mr. Seltzer, this paper shows a strange combination of genius and illiteracy."

My father enjoys the weather in Miami, where he was a sportswriter in the late 1930s.

Following his aborted attempt at getting a college degree, he returned to Cleveland, and then he hit the road again, this time landing in Miami, where he worked as a sportswriter at the *Miami Herald*. Then World War II broke out, and he thought about Mexico, the land he loved, and the more he thought about it, the more he wanted to follow the path of a family he did not even know—the Muros. And so he did, but unlike the Muros, he launched his journey from the North instead of the South, heading back to the Southwest, first to San Antonio, then, after several years, to El Paso—the two US cities that reminded him the most of Mexico.

The story captivated me, and as the old man talked about his past, I got lost in the music of his language . . . and the beauty of his adventures. To experience a foreign land—and to love it as your own—was amazing. I did not seem to love my land, Bakersfield, much less a foreign land with strange people and strange customs.

I thought I was paying attention to the old man, but the more he talked, the more I focused on the topics that intrigued me. The freight trains, the scenic vistas, the strange meals in Chihuahua and Virginia. I could not get either breakfast out of my head, the image of those fried eggs sizzling in my imagination.

But there was a dark turn in the story, a detour into a menacing alley. I was too enthralled by the rest of the story to catch it. But it was there, vague and unsettling, lurking among his descriptions of the trains and the landscapes and the meals. What was it? Would I ever find out? Would I ever want to?

After the detour, the dark turn, the tale moved to El Paso, where he found work as a reporter for the *El Paso Herald-Post* in 1946. He loved journalism, but his wanderlust trumped his dedication. He was working on a story one day, and before it was half-finished, he grabbed his coat and, without explanation, walked out the door. He left the story on the typewriter cylinder. His colleagues never saw him again.

He was bound for Europe, a merchant marine sailing on a tramp steamer. He saw Greece, Italy and Portugal, but it was the getting there that exhilarated the old man. The Atlantic was remarkably placid, but there were times when the ship would pitch, and the water would climb, and the craft, before he knew it, would be sitting on a mountain of water—a cliff of foam and froth that raged higher and higher. Then the water would drop, and the ship would drop with it, and the old man, gazing at the vast horizon in front of him, would smile. *Damn*, he said to himself. The rising and falling—he loved it.

The high seas, however, did not always represent high times. Drudgery often trumped adventure, especially when the men were on sanitation detail, which they rotated. The crew accepted the tasks stoically, and that included the old man, who happened to be mopping the deck during a stop in Greece, the land of Ulysses.

The freighter was anchored about a quarter mile from shore. A quarter mile—so close that the old man felt he could wade his way to land. The islands beckoned, but work proved a stronger—albeit uglier—siren, shackling him to his mop and bucket.

Shoving his bucket across the floor one morning, the old man stumbled into the forecastle, where he interrupted an important meeting between the captain and a group of affluent Greeks. The captain ordered him out, and as the old man left, shaken by his blunder, he spilled soapy water on one of the guests. Damn. The guest was kind, but the captain screamed at the old man, embarrassing him in front of the group. My father left quietly, only to vent his anger later, through a poem he showed one of his mates, Louie, who posted the verse on the bulletin board:

With an ice pick for a pillow and a straitjacket for a bed
He'll lie supine as his keepers gently massage his head
For he is not a normal man, he delights in discord and strife
And a lunatic asylum is the proper stage for his life.

Louie, an oiler, did the old man no favors. The poem was anonymous, a harmless piece of paper tacked onto the bulletin board, but it was not harmless to the captain, who recognized the author behind the words. He reacted swiftly and decisively, putting the old man on latrine duty until the freighter docked in New Orleans twenty-five days later—twenty-five days of cruelty the old man would never forget.

When he returned to El Paso about a year later, he got a job as an English teacher and football coach at Sacred Heart Elementary, a Catholic grade school in the same neighborhood where a girl named Amadita had been raised thirty years before. He bought the football players a set of barbells, and he taught them how to lift the weights with the proper leverage, so they would not sprain their backs or legs. The kids hit the books and the barbells with equal fervor.

They met in the circular bar at the Paso del Norte Hotel, a few blocks from the Segundo Barrio where he worked as a teacher. He ordered her a highball, and he fell in love, although it took more than a cocktail to persuade her to go for *El Profesor,* who seemed rough and shabby, even in his suit and tie. How much more did it take? It was her family that provided the final push, albeit unintentionally. The Muros—most of them—branded him a gringo, and at least partly to annoy them, she said yes, yes, she would marry him. Her mother approved, and her father, who had died of polio in 1940, would have given his consent as well, she knew. It was her brother and sisters who scorned her decision. They called the old man *el pinche gringo,* but she did not care about them. *Que se vayan a la chingada.* They can go to hell. So they got married.

It was a simple, poignant story—a story I had heard hundreds of times, always from my father. How Chester met Amada. The tale was never embellished, never ornamented with pathos or sentimentality—not that I would have recognized those traits at my age. And it always ended with his proposal and her acceptance. That was it. End of story. "*Punto total,*" as my grandmother, the original Amada, would have said. If I wanted the rest of the story—the drama that lay beyond their "wedding" before the Justice of the Peace at the County Courthouse in El Paso—I had to supply the missing details myself, from stories my mother and grandmother had told me about the old man.

My father worked as a teacher and reporter, but he lived like a migrant worker, sometimes leaving a job after a few months, his wanderlust overpowering his responsibility. Or was it that his wanderlust was his responsibility? It was not a question he pondered. When the need arose—when he *felt* that the need arose—he moved on. And we, my mother and I, moved on with him—or after him.

They got married in 1950, and I arrived four years later. El Paso was our base. No matter where we moved, we always returned to the town on the US-Mexico border. We never settled down. Not really. Even when we stayed in a town for years—El Paso, Las Cruces, Dallas, El Paso again—our home was never his home. The old man worked as a newspaper reporter in every town—his teaching career cut short by his love for journalism—but he would leave for days or weeks at a time, depending on whether he had vacation time coming. He traveled by freight train, taking a notebook and a jug of water, usually an old Clorox bottle my mother had washed to get rid of the poison. I asked if he would take me with him, one day, and he said he would, but that day never came.

After Chester and Amada got married, he adopted her maiden name as his pseudonym. Amado Muro. He loved the name, loved the sound of it. Amado was gentle, and Muro was bold, a beautiful combination. And it was an honor, he said, to assume the name of his wife and mother-in-law.

The first name meant *beloved*. Was there any other language that could inspire such a lovely name? the old man wondered. He thought about English words and their Spanish equivalents, sky and *cielo*, love and *amor*, dirt and *tierra*. In almost every case, the Spanish word seemed more powerful, more exquisite. And when you heard the word, you did not just hear it. You saw the country from which it sprang; the heart from which it breathed; the soul from which it soared. English had Shakespeare, Shaw, Whitman, and Twain, and they were great writers, all of them. But when the language itself is poetic, it nurtures the lyricism that resides in every human breast, the old man said. Shakespeare, Shaw, Whitman, and Twain developed their voices, and their voices happened to be in English. But

My father and mother stroll down a street in downtown El Paso in the early 1950s.

Lorca, Fuentes, and, yes, even Cantinflas, the great Mexican comedian, had a head start, for they wrote and spoke in Spanish, and Spanish was fertile soil for the work of poets, novelists, and screenwriters.

When the old man sent his short stories to literary quarterlies, he signed his name Amado Muro, telling the publishers he was a laborer who wrote as a hobby. It was a gentle ruse, intended to focus attention on the words, not the man who wrote them, for beyond the name and identity, something else changed, the subject of the stories. He began writing about Mexican villagers, many of whom clung to their past despite moving to the United States. Some of the characters were illiterate; others were well-read—self-educated experts on the literature of their homeland. All spoke with the passion and eloquence of poets, and while the old man continued to write in English, he captured the flavor of their speech with a respect that indicated he was one of them—regardless of where he was born. Chester Seltzer was Amado Muro, but I would not realize that until later, and when I did, it was thanks to my beloved Alita, the original Amada Muro.

My father was comfortable speaking both English and Spanish. We were visiting a news stand in South El Paso one day, and a Latina woman bumped into him on her way out of the store, saying "excuse me" in broken English. The old man said, "Don't worry," followed by "*No tenga cuidado,*" and she smiled.

One day, the old man took me to the main plaza in Juárez, a park shadowed by the great cathedral, Our Lady of Guadalupe, a stone structure with two towers topped by crosses. We met a man in the park, a painter in the middle of his latest work—a deer staring at us from the canvas on the easel. The painter was short and frail, and his arms ended at the elbows, which he pressed together to wield his brush. He had suffered an industrial accident years before, but he had learned how to substitute his elbows for hands, and he dismissed any suggestion that he was handicapped.

"*Pa que necesito manos?*" he asked the old man. "*Tengo mis codos.* Why do I need hands? I have my elbows."

They spoke for about thirty minutes. The old man took notes, and the painter waved his arms as if he were splashing paint across the canvas. I looked from one to the other, fascinated by the conversation between these two men.

"I am thinking of describing him in a story," the old man told me afterwards.

"Dad," I asked, "how does he do it?"

"How does he paint without arms?" the old man responded. "I don't know, Beto. But I think part of the answer has to do with his huge heart."

The old man loved music. He owned a vast record collection, and except for the occasional Count Basie and Dizzy Gillespie, most of the albums were in Spanish. His favorites were Jorge Negrete, Pedro Infante, and José Alfredo Jiménez. They were also movie stars, suave but rugged, and their voices boomed from the record player, turning the living room into a Mexican village—vibrant, emotional, proud.

I loved them, too. My favorite was Negrete. He sang a song called "*Cucurrucucu Paloma*, Cooing Dove," and he stretched *Cucurrucucu* into so many syllables that I thought his chest would explode before the final "cu." I thought the Beatles expanded the word "do" in "All I Gotta Do," but this was different; this was breathtaking. *Hijole.*

"Beto," the old man told me one morning in Bakersfield. "One of these days, I want you to read *The Futile Life of Pito Perez* by José Rubén Romero. You're way too young now, but one of these days. . . . Will you promise me?"

I wanted to laugh. The name *Pito Perez* sounded like Pito Peterson, one of our mean neighbors in El Paso. I stifled my laughter.

"Yes, sir, I will," I responded with feigned solemnity.

Before Chester and Amada got married, my mother thought he was eccentric, even weird, but she never imagined—*nunca, nunca, nunca*—that he would dismiss what others, including herself, considered the most important elements of happiness: comfort, security, money. The old man talked about his ideals, his sensitivity toward *los de abajo*—the disadvantaged—but she never thought his compassion would lead him to travel the same roads, wear the same clothes, experience the same hunger, as the poor. She thought they were words, just words, ideas that lost their meaning as soon as they left his mouth. *De los dientes para afuera*—lip service.

Then they got married, and everything changed. The old man still discussed the poor, just as he always had, eloquently and passionately, but now the words gave birth to actions, and the actions upset her. The discussions led to journeys, the journeys to short stories. My mother said he deceived her, but deep down, she knew the truth: she had deceived herself. And it mortified her. She should have seen it coming. The old man always returned, but by embracing the poor, he was embracing their poverty—and forcing us, his wife and son, to embrace it with him. If only he would focus on the newspaper business, advance to a position as an editor, maybe, just *maybe*, he could get somewhere, as his father had years before.

He followed a dream, and the dream paid the bills, but my mother wanted more. Not a *lot* more. She was not greedy. She just wanted what the old man seemed to detest—comfort. If you gave the old man a typewriter and a roof over his head, everything else was an extravagance.

The arguments were always about his writing or his trips. They approached these battles differently, my mother and father. She was bombastic, and he was cool, but his anger was no less intense for its civility. The old man contained his anger, but it was there, below the surface, and I could sense it churning and bubbling. It scared me more than the eruptions that came out of my mother. I knew what she was thinking; I could not always say the same about the old man. And sometimes, when his outrage overcame his elegance, he would respond with a fiery "Goddamn it," and then the anger would subside, and I would breathe easier.

One night, after one of his freight train trips, he came home late. It was wintertime. We were living in El Paso. He had walked home from the rail yards, about three miles away, and he was tired and dirty, his notebook sticking out of his back pocket. The door was locked. He knocked. No answer. My mother, Alita, and I were asleep. He knocked again. Still no answer. The old man decided to sit on the porch, as cold and lonely as he was on the freight train he had just left. He stayed there all night.

"I was on the porch all night," he told my mother the next day.

"I know," she said.

And that was it. No arguments, no recriminations. As with his short stories, the old man knew that some arguments had natural endings. There was no need to prolong them.

The old man traveled with the poor and homeless, chronicling their lives and aspirations, and when he returned home, he would talk about his experiences, sometimes for hours. He was held for vagrancy during a trip to Big Spring, but the cops let him go after they checked out his story that he was a journalist in El Paso. The old man told me all these stories, and I hung on every word. These tales, these story hours, helped me discover something about the old man. The very components of happiness that the poor craved—comfort, security, stability—were the ones he shunned, if only temporarily. The old man led two lives, Chester Seltzer at home, Amado Muro on the road. He could slip from one identity to another, sometimes seamlessly, sometimes explosively, the fireworks depending on whether my mother was angry about yet another trip, yet another abandonment. But, no matter how long his freight train journeys lasted, the old man always came back to his home, his family. We were his safety net. And he was ours.

After we moved to Bakersfield, where he found a job with the daily newspaper, the *Californian*, I thought about my friends in El Paso. Did any of them have a father whose office was the open road? No. And yet, while I knew the old man was different, different from the other dads, anyway, I never thought his work—his life—was so strange as to be unique. He was just the old man, and his calling was just his calling. But, *chingele*, he was gone so often, so damned often, that I had to cope with his absences, cope with them somehow, and I did it the only way I knew how—with my mind.

No matter where he went, no matter how many miles he strayed, I was always with him, transported to his side by my imagination. I was with him in Sweetwater, Tucson, and Barstow. I was with him in Bisbee, Tucumcari, and Riverside. I was with him in Lubbock, Flagstaff, and Colorado Springs.

I was with him in hobo jungles, sprinting as the freight trains thundered down the tracks, the boxcars lurching with every curve. We ran alongside the trains, waiting for the right moment to jump into the empty boxcars. It was an art. You had to pick the right boxcar—and the right spot on the right boxcar. And never jump between cars. Never. That was the first rule. If you did, you could end up on the tracks, a bloody, mangled meal for the first vulture to notice your corpse.

I was with him in the boxcars, our hands clasped across our knees, fighting the icy blasts of December or January or. . . . Some of the tramps, clinging to the old days, hid among the rods that connected every car, from the locomotive to the caboose. The rods were underneath the train, inches above the ties and rails, and you had to hang on with the grip of a python. One sweaty hand, and it was all over; the old man knew of hobos who slipped to the tracks, ground to death by the huge, callous machines above them. So he—and I—took the safer route, in the boxcars.

I was with him winter and summer, and no matter what the season, the world seemed to rush past us. If we were sitting in a boxcar, we could not view the scenery without getting dizzy. The landscape flashed by with hypnotic speed. Life on fast-forward. My father called it "balling the jack." The only constants, the only static objects, were the sky and, if you were in the desert of Texas, Arizona, Colorado, or New Mexico, the mountains. They were the anchors, the linchpins; they let us know that, no matter how fast we thought we were going, the familiar land was still out there, ready to embrace us—or kick us in the butt—the moment we jumped off the freight train.

I was with him when the freight trains stopped in town after town, our bodies still vibrating from the constant rumble under our butts—the grinding wheels, the churning gears, the shaking earth. I was with him in rescue missions, eating beans and stew that tasted like wet cardboard. Mission slop. Each town was the same. San Antonio, Phoenix, Riverside—all the same. The freight trains did not pass through the "good" parts of town. They passed through the dirty, rotten sections, each one a giant grease stain filled with bars, flophouses, and tattoo parlors.

Most of all, I was with him when he took out his notebook, transcribing the colorful words that flowed out of the colorful characters, the real-life people who ended up on the pages of his short stories. All kinds of people—black, white, brown. People like the man who requested a handout for the dog, Blue. The old man made them feel comfortable, so comfortable that they never noticed the notebook, the frantic scribbling, as he recorded every sentence, word for word, just as they uttered it. So this is what the old man does, I thought, captivated by the process: He listens, and he writes, and he turns the jottings in his notebook into something beautiful and wondrous. He turns them into short stories; he turns them into literature.

> He hitched himself closer to the fire and hunched his shoulders a little, pulling his overcoat collar higher around his throat. Beside him, Rails stared numbly into the shadows that jumped and wavered with the changing flames. The full white moon had risen and was coming over the prairie looking like it rested right upon the sand swells, and it made everything look like silver except in the shadows. ("Hobo Jungle")

Whenever he returned home, my father would describe his journeys—the freights, the interviews, the towns where he landed. I listened attentively, massaging my thighs in rapt wonder, as if the stories were campfire tales. But the rich details, the vivid descriptions, I did not need them. I did not need any of them, because I had been with him, right there with him, on the very adventures he was describing; thanks to my powers of invention, I was a seasoned and robust traveler.

Then one day, after we moved to Bakersfield, I realized he would never take me with him, not until I was older, and I was at the age when I did not want to wait for tomorrow, much less a tomorrow that might never come. I kept traveling with him, in my imagination, but these journeys were less fanciful, more bitter. I was no longer a companion; I was an observer, a detached, lonely traveler who wanted the trip to end. And the more my father wandered, the more these feelings grew. I did not want a gifted, passionate author. I wanted a father.

Whenever I grew bitter about his absences, I thought about the gap in his story, the "dark turn" between San Antonio and El Paso.

Why did he have to leave so often? I guess his absences were the dark turns in my story.

The old man finished the tale of how he met my mother.

"Do you know what racism is?" my father asked.

"Racing?" I asked, thinking of Bob Hayes, the US sprinter who had just won a gold medal in the Olympics. "Uhhh, yeah, I think so."

My father laughed gently. He always chuckled when I mispronounced words, my ten-year-old tongue struggling with adult terms and phrases. Once, when I referred to Hannibal and the Carthagenians as "Hannibal and the Carthage Injuns," he laughed and laughed, hugging me so fiercely that I felt like a wrestler trapped in a half nelson.

"No, racism," he said. "Racism."

He laughed again, and then he asked me if I wanted to go for a ride the next day, and I said yes.

"Okay," he said. "Now get to bed."

4

# The Dark Turn

The hole in the story crept into my dreams that night, and I had trouble sleeping.

Focused on the meals in Chihuahua and Virginia—one a genuine pleasure, the other a subtle *chinga tu madre* (screw your mother) to the snobs at the university—I missed the shift in the narrative, the detour into a dark corridor. The old man was describing the eggs, and then he was describing a hard time in his life, a time when he was lost, encaged, his bitterness growing every day.

Between San Antonio and El Paso, my father got into "a little trouble," but I was still in Chihuahua, emotionally if not geographically, and while he discussed the problem, I was thinking of the hills and the waiter and the breakfasts that looked like a face. I wondered if I should ask him to repeat himself, but he was caught in the momentum of his storytelling, and by the time I realized the mood had darkened, it brightened once again, and I let the moment pass.

I let it pass, but why did I let it pass? It was a question that would haunt me throughout the year. I was paying attention—or thought I was paying attention—when the old man told me how he met my mother, but I was so captivated by the tale that I stopped listening and started daydreaming, and it was during the reverie that I missed the shift in his story. How I sensed this shift, when I was so distracted, is something I cannot explain to this day. Maybe it was his tone.

Maybe it was his expression. Whatever the reason, I knew he had told me something bad and disturbing. And so, whenever something bad or disturbing happened that school year, I would think of the gap in the story.

The gap—I would come to think of it as the dark turn, although I never used that term to describe it. I never used any term to describe it, maybe because the sensation was too vague, too ephemeral to affix a name to it. . . . It was just something I sensed, the kind of anxiety that grips you when the clouds gather and the sky darkens, and it would emerge without warning, usually when the old man said or did something that reminded me of our conversation that evening.

As the days and weeks passed, I thought about asking the old man to repeat that part of the story. But what would I find out if I did? Would I find out that the old man was as lonely and fragile as I was?

5

## The Ring of My Dreams

The old man loved his crummy car.

It was a 1960 Rambler, a box on wheels. Standard transmission. Tan interior. Powder blue body (almost four years off the assembly line, it seemed more powder than blue, the California sun having blasted the paint into a dull smear). The dashboard was warped and dusty, and the springs poked through the upholstery on the front seat, which explained why the old man drove so funny, raising first one cheek, then the other, to keep from becoming a human shish kebab, his flesh speared by the coils under his rump.

"Get in," he said.

We took off in his shabby little car, driving up Main Street, toward downtown. I did not know where we were going, and he would not tell me. He just drove, constantly shifting in his seat to find his comfort zone.

"Do you see that man on the street corner?" he said as we approached one of the department stores downtown.

He pointed to a man waiting for the light to turn green at the crosswalk.

"Yes," I said.

"Notice the shirt he's wearing?"

It was a weird shirt, with ruffles upon ruffles, a doily with buttons.

"Yes, I see it," I said.

"What do you think of it?"

I hesitated, afraid that it was a trick question, afraid that a wrong answer would banish me to my room for the rest of the weekend. A dark turn loomed.

"Well?"

"I don't like it," I finally blurted out.

My father smiled.

"Neither do I," he said.

I was relieved; my room would not become a weekend gulag, after all.

"What do you think of the man wearing it?" my father asked.

Ay Dios mio. I had no sooner answered one question than he hurled another one at me, this one more treacherous than the first. What could I do? What could I say?

"I don't know."

My father smiled again.

"Of course, you don't," he said.

I was relieved—but confused.

"You don't know, because it wouldn't be right to judge a man because he's wearing an awful shirt," my father said.

He shifted in his seat.

"It's the same way with the countries that people are from," he said. "They might be from Mexico or China or Africa, but that doesn't make them bad, and it doesn't make them good. You have to judge them based on something deeper than their skin color or where they come from."

"Like what?" I asked.

"Well, like how they treat other people."

"Oh . . . ," I said. "Does that mean Randy Reed is bad?"

He kept heading north, away from downtown Bakersfield.

"Yes, it does," he said, finally. "But it doesn't mean he's all bad. And it doesn't mean he'll stay bad forever. . . . Give him a chance."

I did not want to give him a chance. I wanted to hurt him. I wanted to find out what his surfboards were—and destroy them.

"Okay?" my father asked.

"Okay," I answered.

He kept driving, heading toward North Bakersfield, where the neighborhoods got uglier and uglier, until we reached the area that everybody called "the bad part of town."

"What's that?" I asked, pointing to a brown brick building with a hand-painted sign in front—GYM.

That was all—just GYM.

"Let's go see," my father said.

We parked in front of the building, and we went inside, crossing the threshold into another world, a modern-day gladiator school. Fight posters lined the walls, and kerosene heaters glowed from three corners of the room, even though the temperatures had not dipped below 80. It was mid-September. Was my mother in charge of the heating?

And then there was the ceiling—the ceiling was almost breathtaking. It was so high that, whenever the fighters stopped pounding the heavy bag, the chain kept rattling, swinging back and forth, back and forth, as ominous as a hanging rope. The creaking was the backbeat to the punching—one-two, one-two.

I looked around, sinking into a heavy green chair that reminded me of the seats in the Rambler. I gazed at a poster of Sonny Liston, the former heavyweight champion, his head shaved, his arms raised as if he were brandishing truncheons, not fists. And then I watched the fighters in the ring.

It was beautiful. I had never seen anything like it. This was not street fighting, two beasts bashing each other until one collapses, so motionless that a cop could draw a chalk outline of his body. No, this was different. This was a ballistic ballet, a series of dance steps in which one false move could mean the difference between scoring a knockout and suffering a knockout. The fighters pivoted delicately, dipping their shoulders to find an opening. And when they found it, they threw their combinations—short and sweet and solid.

"That's the way," a man yelled up to one of the boxers in the ring. "That's the way. Yardstick him! Yardstick him! Come on. Come on."

From his spot on the floor, the man mimicked the dance in the ring—the feints, the jabs, the backpedaling.

"Time!" the man yelled, and the two boxers stopped sparring, tapping each other on the chest with their oversized gloves—a sign that things were back to normal, that they were "friends" again.

"That's the way," the man repeated to his fighter, a tall, thin man with straight black hair sopping with sweat.

"Very sweet," my father told the fighter, whom he seemed to know. "*Muy dulce*."

Before I realized what I was doing, I dashed to a corner of the ring, reaching up with my right hand and yelling, "That's the way—very sweet." The fighter looked down and smiled, spitting his mouthpiece into a white bucket on the canvas. Then he tapped my hand with his glove.

"*Muy dulce*—very sweet," I repeated.

"Thank you" he said, his dark skin glistening with sweat. "*Gracias*."

"*De nada*."

On the way home, I thanked my father for taking me to the gym.

"Dad, that fighter, the one I, uh, shook hands with, does he live here, in Bakersfield?"

"Yes."

"Oh," I said, smiling.

I thought he had come from another town, maybe Delano or Barstow.

"Why?" the old man asked.

"What's his name?" I asked, ignoring the question.

"Cruz . . . Cruz Ortega."

I smiled again.

"He's Mexican?" I asked.

"Yes, he's Mexican."

That night, in my bedroom, I thought about the dark turn in the story about how my father met my mother. And I thought about Randy Reed. Was the old man telling me I had to stand up to Randy Reed? To fight him? I stood in front of the mirror on the dresser, trying to throw the same combinations I had seen the Mexican throw in the gym. I let out a menacing sound with every punch I hurled, a *whooosh* that represented a rush of air, as if my blows were faster than the wind. We never returned to the GYM, although every once in a while, my father would ask me if, one of these days, I wanted to go back. I would always say "yes," but for some reason, we never did. It did not matter, because I could see the Mexican every day, throwing those lightning-swift combinations, in the ring of my dreams.

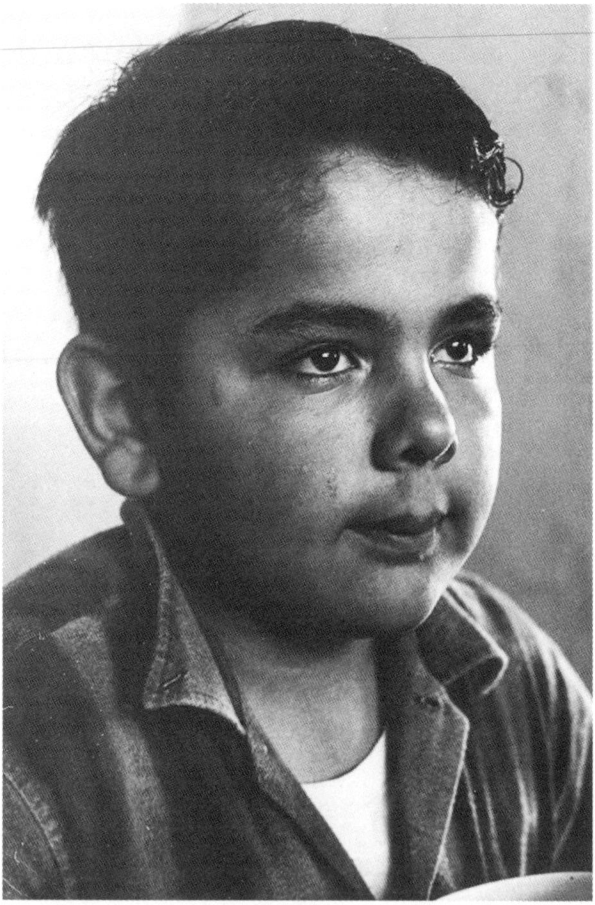

Me as a fifth grader in Bakersfield.

## 6

# Beyond Reach

She sat next to me that year, just a few inches to my right, so close that only my fear and shyness made the distance unbridgeable.

Rachel Olsen. Beating up Randy Reed was one of my obsessions; admiring Rachel Olsen was the other. I had fallen in love before, but the women were always larger than life, their eyes and lips glowing from the big screen. My first love was Marilyn Monroe, as beautiful as she was unattainable. I saw *Some Like it Hot*, on *Saturday Night at the Movies*, when I was nine years old.

When I saw Marilyn, I felt a mysterious stirring in my body, part of me growing and, then, solidifying. I looked down, and I saw a little steeple rising from my shorts, stout and solid and unexpected. My first sexual experience—arousal. It felt delicious.

Rachel Olsen was different. There was no lust involved, no fantasies of carnal pleasure. She was too sweet for that, too sublime and exquisite. Brown hair, blue eyes, full lips—lips so soft and tender that they looked like the product of delicate brush strokes. She was a Renaissance painting come to life.

She was also the smartest girl in class, the perfect counterpoint to Randy Reed. She got As in everything, including a subject they called the "new math." Not knowing what the old math was, we were not sure what made the new math new. But, whatever made it fresh and vital, she was good at it, better than anyone else.

"Hi, Robert," she would say every day. That was it. "Hi, Robert." But the greeting, so perfunctory on the surface, was so lyrical in my heart.

One morning, we were sitting at our desks, silently reading a poem by Henry Wadsworth Longfellow—our first English assignment of the day. She looked up, turning to her left, and I could sense her eyes on me, not looking at me, but on me—on my nose, my cheeks, my heart. I felt scared, desperate, unable to breathe. Why was she looking at me? Did she like me? Did she like me as much as I liked her?

Then, gaining the courage to span the chasm between our desks, I decided to look up. I felt as if I were peering through a keyhole—without the protection of the door. I gulped. I met her gaze, but her gaze did not meet mine. She was not looking at me. She was looking at the next assignment on the blackboard, an essay by Ralph Waldo Emerson.

I sank into my chair, receded into my body—humiliated and defeated. Then the bell rang for recess, and I felt liberated; no one had seen me make a fool of myself, least of all Rachel Olsen. As my classmates scrambled to their feet, I breathed heavily, relief smoothing the frown on my face. My hidden love would remain hidden. . . . Or would it?

Randy Reed emerged, standing over me with an ugly leer on his face. I thought about the dark turn in the story the old man had told me. Then I shivered from a fear I neither recognized nor understood.

Randy Reed glared at me, his gray eyes burning, and then it hit me: He knew I was in love with Rachel Olsen. He knew. Crawling into my psyche, he rummaged through the archives of my mind, and he found it; somehow, among all my wants and needs and desires, he found it—the file that contained my love for this beautiful girl. The thought terrified me. It terrified me, because I knew what it meant: Rachel Olsen was just another surfboard, beautiful but beyond reach.

## 7

# My Alita

The worst thing about Bakersfield—besides Randy Reed—was that my Alita was a thousand miles away.

I loved my Alita, short for Abuelita. Her real name was Amada Muro, the name she gave my mother. Alita was in her late eighties, fragile but feisty, with a vocabulary spiced by the occasional—sometimes more than occasional—*cabrón* (jerk) or *huevos aguados* (weak-kneed—literally, sagging balls) or *chinga tu madre* (screw your mother). Of all the Muros, except my mother and one of her sisters, she was the only one who embraced the "gringo," my father.

In El Paso, my father and grandmother would sit on the porch at dusk, savoring the sherbet colors that smudged the night sky—the pinks and oranges and purples. They talked about her *tierra*, about Emiliano Zapata, the revolutionary, and Mario Moreno, the beloved comic more commonly known as Cantinflas. And, as they talked, passion ignited their faces, making their eyes glow like tiny bonfires as darkness settled over the city.

"*Tu papa es medio enojon—en veces—pero es muy noble,*" she would tell me. "Your father has a slight temper—sometimes—but he is very noble."

My Alita and my father, separated by forty years and two cultures, but united by something stronger—a desire to bridge those gaps. They did it subconsciously. Yes, it just happened. It just happened because they wanted it to, their cultural differences evaporating in the warm glow of their humanistic impulses. It was a relationship—and an attitude—that said *ya basta con* geography—enough with geography—for both were Mexican, one by birth, the other by choice. It was as if my father, by virtue of his love and passion for Mexico, had been granted honorary citizenship by an agency more powerful than any immigration office. My Alita recognized his fealty to Mexico, and she loved him for it.

When the old man fell in love with my mother, he started writing under the pseudonym he had derived from her maiden name. Chester Seltzer became Amado Muro. He wrote most of the stories in first person, creating a false identity that none of his readers suspected. My father did not set out to fool anyone, however; he embraced the culture so wholeheartedly, writing from the perspective of a Mexican, that he seemed to morph into Amado Muro. Nobody appreciated that transformation more than my Alita; after all, she was the original Amada Muro, and rightly or wrongly, she regarded the pen name as a tribute to her character, integrity, and loyalty.

Was my father more Mexican than my grandmother? No. But, as a child, I always thought he was more Mexican than my mother. It was not just that he learned to speak Spanish—or that he loved Jorge Negrete, while she idolized Trini Lopez, the US pop singer who recorded a lame cover of "La Bamba." That was part of it, but the main reason was that he embraced a society whose poverty and hardships my mother had been trying to flee. Yes, Alita escaped the brutal conditions in Mexico, too, but she did it for her children, not for herself.

I never knew my grandfather, Jesus Muro. He died of polio, stricken when he was forty. It was about fifteen years after the family had fled Chihuahua. My grandmother started running the grocery store in South El Paso, with the help of her kids, including Amadita, the girl who would become my mother.

After Jesus Muro died, Alita hung his portrait on the wall behind the counter in the grocery store, a portrait she would keep in her bedroom years later. Jesus looked like a matinee idol—thick moustache, wavy hair, fierce pride. Pride is not a physical characteristic, but you could sense it in his eyes, which glowed with an intensity that reminded me of Negrete, the singer who became a movie star.

"*Alita, porque se murio de polio?* Why did he die of polio?" I asked my grandmother one day, years later, before the move to Bakersfield.

I reminded her that they had developed a pill to prevent polio. I had swallowed one myself. It was sweeter than candy. They were passing them out at Jesus and Mary Church one Sunday morning, after mass. The kids lined up for blocks, waiting for the pink sugar cubes that contained this mysterious medicine.

"Ay, Robertito," she said, smiling through her tears. "*Como te quiero.* Oh how I love you."

In El Paso, we lived in a tiny duplex, the front and back yards as sparse as the desert around them. Alita moved in with my mother and father after they got married. She would sit in a chair by the living room window, quietly smoking pack after pack of Lucky Strikes, her thin, hunched shoulders draped in a black shawl, winter or summer. She was our sentry during the day, eager and committed.

Whenever one of my friends bounded up the cement steps to the front door, she would announce his arrival by describing his primary characteristic. If he was short, she would call out, "*Aqui esta el vecino del piso.* Here is a boy so short he is neighbors with the floor." Or "*Aqui esta el chaparro.* Here is Shorty." If he was fat, it would be "*El gordo*—Fatty." And, if the poor boy embodied two such traits, he would get a double dose of her nicknames: "*Aqui esta el chaparro gordo.*" And if, God forbid, he had three distinguishing brands—including, for example, slovenliness—it would be: "*Aqui esta el chaparro gordo mugroso.*"

No matter how early I arose, Alita was always up before me. I would stumble into the kitchen, still rubbing the dreams from my eyes, and she would ask, "*Como quieres tus huevos?* How do you want your eggs cooked?" And before I had a chance to answer, she would say, "*Estrellados, verdad?* Sunny side up, right?" I would always say "Sí," regardless of how I really wanted them cooked.

Alita and I watched television together, both of us listening intently to every word, every sentence, every song; during the commercials, I would translate whatever transpired in the segment before. Her favorite shows were *Bonanza, I Spy,* and *The Man from U.N.C.L.E.* We would watch them on the portable Magnavox in her room, away from the prying eyes of the old man, who banned me from watching violent shows on TV. But her favorite program was one the old man would endorse—*The Andy Williams Show.* I had trouble translating "Moon River," the hit tune Williams sang on his show, uncertain whether to call it "La Luna del Rio" or "El Rio de la Luna." She called him "El Willie," and, every Christmas, she would buy me a present inspired by the singer—a brown sweater with gold buttons, the kind he and the Osmond Brothers, the kid singers he championed—wore during the more relaxed segments of his program. I had stacks of the sweaters in my dresser drawer, each one a little larger than the last.

At nighttime, after my translating services in front of the television set, I would nestle in my blanket, waiting for my grandmother to enter my bedroom. She visited me every night, and I remember that rich, nutty odor that old people seemed to emit, especially my Alita. I loved the smell. I loved the nightly ritual. And I loved her.

Alita would pull a folding chair up to my bed, leaning forward to tell me dark stories about ghosts and spirits. My favorite was "*La Llorona,* The Weeper," an enigmatic woman in life—and a frightening one in death. She was tall and beautiful—qualities she used to flirt her way out of poverty—but she married a man who was equally shallow, a handsome, decorated soldier who prized her beauty above her character. He forced her to stay at home, making her tend to their three children, while he cheated on her with a callousness that grew over the years. She was no longer a wife, a mother, a woman; she was a keepsake, and her drop in status—from an object of affection to an object, period—devastated her.

"*Pobre mujer,*" Alita would say, recounting the story. "Pobre mujer. Poor woman, poor woman."

Still a young woman, the beautiful wife felt old, desiccated, entombed. It was unbearable. One night, desperate with unhappiness,

Alita, standing in front of Mundy Park in Sunset Heights, my old neighborhood in El Paso.

she took her children to the Rio Grande, its usually placid waters pounding the banks on either side. It was a cold, rainy night, and the wind was so fierce that it shrieked, Alita said, like a lunatic. The woman stood there with her children, quietly, stoically, knowing that the darkness around her would soon become eternal.

*"Brincó en el rio, y todos se murieron—todos,"* Alita said. *"Y ahora, cuando oyes alguien llorando en la noche, es La Llorona, triste porque*

*mato a sus niños.* She jumped into the river, and they died—all of them. And today, when you hear someone crying in the night, it is the Weeper, crying because she killed her children."

One night, after another retelling of "La Llorona" story, I was more scared and anxious than usual. I saw a connection between the old man and the heartless general. Not that the old man would cheat on my mother. Or mistreat her. But he was away from home so much, chasing his short stories on some freight train, that I feared my mother, desperate and lonely, would carry me to the banks of the Rio Grande one wind-swept night. I expressed my concern to Alita.

"*Ay, mi'jo*, Oh, my child," she said, hugging me.

After telling me these haunting stories, she would lead me in prayer—a strange mixture of the profane and the sacred. I did not mind. I always found the "Our Father" more comforting, more exalting, in Spanish.

*Padre nuestro que estás en los cielos, santificado sea tu nombre,*
*venga tu reyno, hagase tu voluntad,*
*asì en la tierra como en el cielo.*

When we moved to Bakersfield, my grandmother stayed with one of my aunts in El Paso. But I thought about her all the time. I thought about her stories and her cigarettes and her failings as a short-order cook. And I wondered what she would tell me if I asked her for advice about how to deal with Randy Reed.

"*Que debes de hacer?*" she would probably say, exasperated, her silver hair drawn into a tight bun. "*Con ese cabrón, huevos aguados, hijo de su chingada madre? No le hagas caso.* What should you do? With that weak-kneed jerk son of a bitch? Don't pay attention to him."

# 8

# The Old Man

One afternoon, about a week after our trip to the gym, my father told me a story about a boy who lived in the Midwest, a teenager. It was a short story, but the length of the tales never mattered to me. If the old man was the storyteller, they were all epic.

The teenager walked up a hill one morning, and when he reached the crest, he was on top of the world, as close to eternity as he would ever get. It was breathtaking. And there, from the hilltop, he took it all in, the sky above, the lake below—a broad silver band shimmering in the early morning sunlight.

The boy had stood on this spot a hundred times before, and he would stand on this spot a hundred times after. But none of those experiences could rival this moment, this sliver of time frozen in his memory—and in his heart. And, each time he talked about that morning, he described it the same way, the morning he witnessed something beautiful, something sublime, something eternal.

That was it. End of story. The boy was my father, and the lake was Lake Erie. It was part of his city, part of his life. My father loved Cleveland. I could tell. He described it as though it were his Oz—magical but real.

My father called himself "the old man," a term he intended to be both endearing and self-deprecating. But there was some truth in it. He lived in the past, reveled in its musty odor, its tenacious grip, for it refused to let go of him—and, yes, he refused to let go of it. The old man gave me impromptu quizzes on mythology and ancient civilizations every day. Who was Hector? Who was Hannibal? What was the Roman name for Zeus? How many labors did Hercules perform? Where did Achilles get pierced with an arrow?

But it was the Cleveland stories I loved the most, the stories from his childhood. They were the real myths, the tales freighted with humor and drama and joy. And no matter which story he related, the best character was always the town itself—big and raw and majestic, the backdrop for all his youthful adventures.

By 1964, Cleveland—the Cleveland my father knew and loved—was disappearing. It was facing problems, some financial, others social, and in a few years, it would become a punch line, a city that other cities disparaged. The Cuyahoga River would burst into flames in 1969, a fire ignited by the toxic chemicals dumped into the water by manufacturing companies. Residents fled to the suburbs, and between 1930 and 1969, the population dropped from 900,429 to 505, 616. Comedians called the city "the mistake by the lake."

In 1930, however, Cleveland was still Cleveland, raw but vital, with adventures on every corner. God made sure the old man would be born in Cleveland, arranging the comings and goings of all his ancestors so that they would end up in Northern Ohio—or so I thought. The town and the man were made for each other.

The family lived in a Tudor-style house in Lakewood, but his real neighborhood was the town itself, all of it, from one end to the other. Cleveland was not the center of his universe; Cleveland was his universe. He never expressed this thought, not directly, but he never had to. When he talked about his hometown, he was so passionate that I fantasized about my own life as a parent. Would El Paso, not Bakersfield, become my Cleveland when I became a father? Would I regale my children with stories from my youth? I hoped so.

Cleveland was rough and gritty, with buildings that were massive but inviting, each one a monument to the tough, hard-working men who built them. These men, many of them, were immigrants. They came to seek a better life in America, but they did not just seek it;

At about age four, long before he started reading
Leo Tolstoy, my father pretended to be a soldier.

they built it, brick by brick. The evidence was everywhere—the Cleveland Trust, the Terminal Tower, the Higbee Company, the Public Library. And, in the middle of town, a rugged flower sprouted from an unlikely garden, the Soldiers' and Sailors' Monument on Euclid Avenue, with its majestic tower lancing the Midwestern sky. They built that, too.

The old man entered every building with a sense of discovery, as if he were experiencing it for the first time. His favorite? The public library, a squat building with a helmeted sentry above the entrance, a bust of Athena. She was the goddess of war and wisdom—the old man never explained the connection between the two—and he called her the Lady of Literature.

The minute he walked inside the library, he would pause a few feet from the heavy wooden door, savoring the sweet but musty odor of all those books. It was sublime, the smell of genius. Tolstoy, Chekhov, Dostoevsky, Turgenev. Their words were rich, pungent, profound.

If the landscape was raw and vibrant, so were the people. The old man loved them. They came from all over—Lithuania and Hungary, Czechoslovakia and Germany, France and Italy. And they brought their homelands with them—customs, languages, religions. Everything but the soil. They turned their neighborhoods into Little Hungary, Little Lithuania, and Little Italy.

In some of the neighborhoods, the Catholic churches offered masses in Hungarian, Lithuanian, and Italian every Sunday morning, and every Sunday morning, among the celebrants from the old country was a celebrant from the new country, the old man. He was Protestant, not Catholic, and he spoke English, not Hungarian or Lithuanian or Italian, but he loved those languages; he loved them because they were bold and clear and authoritative, and because they made the word of God sound like the word of God.

In the poorer neighborhoods, the kids transformed paved roads into asphalt parks, construction projects that required only one building material—imagination. They turned broom handles into bats and rubber balls into baseballs, spheres that looked like pellets compared to real baseballs. Home plate was a manhole cover. And the outfield fences? Well, there were no outfield fences, so a home run was any ball that hit a designated landmark or, in the worst-case scenario, broke a window. The street was not League Park, the 22,000-seat home of their beloved Cleveland Indians, but it was as close as you could get without grass and seats and fans. You could almost hear the cheers, the triumphant roars, swelling from the sidewalks as the kids whacked their crummy balls with their crummy sticks.

After hours of hitting, fielding, and running, it never failed: The kids, bursting with energy in the first inning, faded at just the right time, when the rich odors started sailing from their kitchen windows—goulash, spaghetti, egg noodles. The smells gave them their second wind. And as the sun dropped, leaving red wounds across the sky, the boys rushed home as if trying to beat out a ground ball to short. After they finished eating, the fatigue returned, and they shuffled outside, lolling on the stoops or curbs of their apartment buildings until nightfall. And then, if it was spring or summer, they slept on the fire escapes, eyeball-to-eyeball with the street lamps and telephone wires. The old man lived in a different environment, a softer environment, but during his jaunts across the city, he saw these kids, and he envied their freedom, their sense of adventure, sleeping under a ceiling that stretched for miles and miles, a vast canopy needled with golden lights.

That was Cleveland, the town he loved. I had never seen the town, never experienced its rich heritage, but I loved it, too. It was part of my emotional landscape.

One weekend afternoon, when the old man was quizzing me about mythological figures, I grew distracted, just as I had during the dark turn in his story about how he met my mother. He asked me who Atlas was, and instead of stuttering and feigning bewilderment—something I did to heighten the tension—I answered immediately. Atlas, I said, carried the world on his back. The whole pinche world. And then I shrugged, as if to suggest that I could shoulder the same burden. Big deal. *No es gran cosa.*

"What's wrong?" the old man asked.

"Nothing," I said.

"What's wrong?" he repeated.

"Well, I'd rather hear a Cleveland story," I said finally.

And so he obliged. He told me a story. And, as he told me the story, I breathed the same air he breathed, in Cleveland, all those years ago.

The old man loved to wander the streets of Cleveland, sometimes by foot, sometimes by streetcar. He saw wondrous things, and he saw horrible things, he said. And one of the most horrible came during the Great Depression, when mob figures were the most successful entrepreneurs in town.

It was 1930. Cars—a term derived from rail cars—crowded the roadways, replacing the horse-drawn wagons that had carried milk, bread, and cheese only a few years earlier. The hit song was "On the Sunny Side of the Street," and one of the top movies was *All Quiet on the Western Front*, an antiwar film that made $3 million at the box office. Men wore suits to prizefights, lending a genteel air to venues that boasted all the gentility of a barroom. One of the fighters they saw was Johnny Risko, the popular Cleveland heavyweight who fought a man he outweighed by about thirty pounds, welterweight Mickey Walker; Walker won.

The old man was fifteen, and he stepped off the streetcar one afternoon, ready to roam the downtown he loved so much. He saw two men approach each other on a street corner; both wore black, double-breasted suits, one of them with a colorful handkerchief blossoming from his coat pocket. Mr. Handkerchief stuck his arm out, as if about to shake hands with the other man, but it was not a hand he was extending. It was a gun. Mr. Handkerchief started firing. The other man collapsed to his knees, as if genuflecting; then his upper body crashed onto the sidewalk, his head twisting as it hit the concrete. Mr. Handkerchief walked away, briskly but casually. My father saw the murder, and he vomited, and years later, when he recounted the story, you could sense the horror—and the bile—coming back.

Then he told me another story, this one more traumatic, more life-altering. Before my father could become an old man, he had to become a young man, and the transition from childhood to manhood, rough and unexpected, occurred one afternoon in a downtown diner. It was set, like the other tale, during the Great Depression. A Saturday. He met his best friend, Whitey Bimlap, and the two boys walked the streets without purpose, but, then, that was their purpose, for the greatest freedom was to act without having to act, to move without having to move.

Cherishing a Saturday afternoon together, the two boys stopped at a diner on Euclid Avenue—Clark's Lunch Shop. The place was packed, but they found two empty stools at the counter, a spot sandwiched between two hulks who burrowed into their food like earth movers. My father and Whitey were starving, but their appetites were bigger than their pocketbooks. Much bigger. They were penniless. But Whitey had a plan.

When they finished their meals—my father a hamburger, his friend a grilled cheese sandwich—Whitey jumped off the stool, retching and groaning. He bent over, his head nearly scraping the floor—a pathetic figure folded in half, a flower with a weak stem. Then he started screaming.

"She . . . she . . . she . . . " he stammered, pointing at the young waitress behind the counter. "She spit on my sandwich! I saw her! I saw her!"

The manager rushed out from the kitchen.

"What seems to be the problem?" he asked.

"She spit on my sandwich!" Whitey screamed, still groaning.

"Okay, you two fellows can go on now," the manager said, escorting them to the door.

Then they heard him scream at the young waitress.

"And you," he said. "You're fired."

Just like that, she was gone. And with barely a shred of evidence. The manager let two boys—one a pint-sized Paul Muni, the other his silent accomplice—rage, fume and plot their way out of paying for a meal. Whitey had feigned illness, but when they hit the sidewalk, my father felt truly sick, his heart burdened by the injustice he helped perpetrate. The two teenagers conspired their way into a free meal, but they cost an innocent woman her job in the process. It was during the Great Depression, my father repeated, and most people were hurting. Was the young woman a single mother? Was she taking care of a handicapped aunt? Was she working her way to a better life in California? My father would never know. The young woman was a mystery, a nameless victim.

The stories were so stark, both of them, that they reminded me of the dark turn in the story he told me the day after the surfboard incident. And I wondered how these experiences helped shape the man my father became. Here was the old man in larval form, adventurous but sensitive. Was his compassion for the poor and needy born on this Saturday afternoon? Did a lifetime of dedication spring from a moment of guilt? I never asked him, but I would always wonder if the cruel trick in the diner led to his social conscience.

"Try not to have fun at the expense of other people," he told me, finishing his tale.

"How will I know?" I asked.

"You'll know," he said.

He looked at me for several seconds, and I looked down.

"And don't be mean to anyone," he said, finally.

"Dad," I said, pausing.

"Yes?"

"Are you saying that I shouldn't be mean, like Randy . . . "

"Yes, don't be mean like Randy Reed," he said.

"Okay," I said sheepishly.

9

# The Detonation

The creatures were waiting.

Dusk filtered through the cottonwoods, and shadows pooled on the sidewalk, creating eerie images that morphed into monsters—hideous blobs eager to suck the entrails out of my body. I thought about the detour, the dark turn in the story about how my father met my mother. I looked up at the old man. He smiled at me, draping his arm around my neck, as we continued our march through the treacherous landscape. Was the old man aware of my anxiety, on that dark, desolate street, unstated though it was?

I knew the old man understood. I knew because every Halloween he would tell me about the night—the night he went to see the stage version of *Dracula* at a Cleveland playhouse. It was 1932, a year after the movie had terrified audiences throughout the world. The old man was seventeen, and he loved the film, loved its subtle creepiness, its haunting atmosphere. And he loved the way Bela Lugosi, the star of the film, injected a sense of dread into his speech, stretching every syllable till his voice sounded like a creaking door: "G-o-o-o-d e-e-e-v-e-n-i-i-i-n-g."

Lugosi reprised his movie role on stage, and he was scarier in person, his skin more ashen, his eyes more piercing, his presence more threatening—so threatening that the danger did not dissolve when the play ended. Not for the old man. When he walked out of the theater, he saw creatures spring to life, mutated from the shadows he passed on his way back home. Was that Dracula—the vampire himself—lurking at the next intersection? The old man picked up his pace, stumbling along the curb, as far away from the trees and shrubs as possible. It was, the old man said, one of his first lessons on the power of imagination.

As the old man and I walked through the tree-lined street in Bakersfield, the monsters disappeared, banished by a father who understood the frailties of youth. The old man knew what it was like to be entombed by your fears. With a simple gesture—putting his arm around my neck—he accomplished the impossible: he turned the sidewalk, shadows and all, into a safety net, making the rest of the walk a warm, pleasant experience. I was glad he was there, with me, not on some freight train thundering to Stockton, Salinas, or Modesto. It was a weeknight, but we were headed toward school, about six blocks from the house we rented on Brundage Lane in Bakersfield.

It was open house at St. Francis Elementary School, and Mrs. Chaney greeted the parents with more warmth and enthusiasm than she showed their sons and daughters during the day. Mrs. Chaney was our homeroom teacher. She was short and dumpy, with a body that seemed segmented into thick layers of fat—a human caterpillar.

A humorless disciplinarian, Mrs. Chaney wore tight skirts that made her look like a matador—without the smooth, subtle curves. And those eyes, always bloodshot, always bulging. Even when she squinted, her eyes bulged. The problem was simple—too much eye, not enough eyelid. Those big, black, malignant orbs dwarfed the lids, which looked like curtains that were too small for their windows. That was Mrs. Chaney. Maybe she started life as a shadow on the sidewalk, a sliver of a silhouette, and maybe she morphed into our homeroom monster.

Mrs. Chaney thought she was smarter than the kids, but the kids possessed a cunning that transcended intellect. It also transcended decency—or what Mrs. Chaney regarded as decency. Whenever she grew bored with the daily lesson, she would launch a mini-sting, trying to entrap the devious students in her midst.

One afternoon, about a week before the open house, Mrs. Chaney tried one of her stings. She walked out of the classroom, telling the students she would be back in ten minutes. Somehow, the class clowns knew what she was up to; she was heading to the main office, where she would turn on the intercom to hear who was talking, who was misbehaving, who was defying her authority, back in the unattended classroom. Bad move.

About two minutes after she left, Gregory Bukowski, the biggest kid in class, lifted Wendell Wilson, the smallest kid in class. Bukowski looked like a circus strongman performing a military press. Carrying his cargo toward the blackboard, the big kid angled the little kid so that his butt hovered in front of the loud speaker—a human cannon aimed at the unsuspecting disciplinarian in another wing of the school. The rest of the students watched this strange turn of events, their hearts racing with delight.

Flailing in the air, Wilson grunted and grimaced, his face turning red from the effort to detonate. Bukowski, teetering every time his freight shifted, steadied himself in front of the loud speaker. The tension was excruciating. It was like watching a tightrope walker. Would he make it? Could he make it? Then it came, the moment we anticipated with such fiendish delight—an explosion so wet and thunderous that it seemed to splatter onto the loud speaker. The class erupted into laughter. Bukowski dropped Wilson, and both kids scurried to their desks, trying to assume choirboy poses before the homeroom teacher returned.

I was no choirboy. With the detonation still echoing in my mind, I laughed so hard that I had to close my mouth and grab my sides. The laughter, unable to flow out of my mouth, seeped through my nose, producing a squeak that sent a tingle down my spine. I shivered violently. The squeaking continued. I stifled my laughter, and as I lowered my head, a monstrous sneeze started to build in my nose. I covered my face, and I sneezed, and then I sneezed again and again—eruptions that rivaled the splattering on the loud speaker only moments before. I could have played "Cucurrucucu Paloma" with my nose, holding the notes as long as the great Jorge Negrete. After the final sneeze, I withdrew my hands from my face, and my palms were dripping with *mocos*—snot. Please, Lord, I said in a silent prayer, do not let Rachel Olsen see it. *Please.*

I looked to my right. Rachel Olsen smiled, and I smiled back, so caught up in the hilarity of the moment that the awkwardness I would normally feel melted away. None of the other students noticed my *mocos*—not even Randy Reed.

We sat there, waiting. Mrs. Chaney would return eventually, and when she did, we would be sorry for the explosion. We would all be sorry, even though only two of us were responsible—Wendell Wilson and Gregory Bukowski. One boy fired the weapon; the other aimed it at the loudspeaker. But no matter who the culprits were, we would all pay. We waited, and the silence overwhelmed us. I looked at Rachel, and Rachel looked at me, but the smiles had vanished from our faces; when the executioner approaches, the condemned lose their sense of humor. For once, I felt like part of the group.

When Mrs. Chaney returned, she walked slowly, each segment jiggling as she headed toward the center of the classroom. Then she stopped abruptly, her eyes popping out like musket balls—dark and malevolent and eager for retribution. She was about to speak—or scream—when the clock rescued us; the final bell rang, and the kids took off like racehorses.

That was Mrs. Chaney during class time, a different creature from the one who greeted her visitors during open house the night my father walked me to school. She was warm and personable with the parents, a disciplinarian transformed into a hostess. It made me sick.

"Hello, Mr. Seltzer," she said, greeting my father as we arrived for the open house. "And hello to you, too, Robert."

10

# The Odyssey

My father saw through her artifice, her cheap attempt to curry favor with the parents—a ploy as conspicuous as her bulging eyes. Not that my father needed those bulging eyes, or the cloying attitude that went with them, to detect her insincerity. Not at all. My father was like an x-ray machine, able to bore through the veneer of civility. My mother and grandmother called this talent an *ojo clinico*. What did he see inside Mrs. Chaney? He never said, but I could tell by his body language—the way he rocked back on his heels, as if ready to execute a quick retreat—that he found her a little unpleasant, a little off-putting. Did he see her as I did—a creature that emerged from the shadows of a vivid imagination? Mrs. Chaney, homeroom monster? I was sure he did.

"Robert seems to be a very bright boy," she told my father. "But . . ."

Mrs. Chaney let her "but" hang there—an axe suspended inches above the neck of a condemned man.

"But . . . he seems so, well, detached," she said. "He refuses to interact with the other children."

My father took it all in, stroking his chin as if to digest her wisdom.

"I see," he said.

For days afterwards, I would repeat those two words to myself—"I see." They were so vague, so gloriously noncommittal. They could have meant anything, from deep concern to deep bewilderment, but my father invested them with so much profundity, stroking his chin the whole time, that the homeroom teacher seemed satisfied. When my father said, "I see," Mrs. Chaney seemed to respond, "Yes, Mr. Seltzer, yes, I can tell that you do."

If there was a night when I wanted my father to be noncommittal, it was this night. At home, an hour before the old man and I walked to school, my mother had threatened to rip into Mrs. Chaney at the open house, demanding to know why she allowed the students to call her son a . . . she could barely utter the words . . . "a fucking beaner." Who did they think they were? *Malditos desgraciados.* Disgraceful bastards. My mother fumed, remembering slights from her own childhood, and the more protective she became, the less protective I wanted her to become. I was mortified. If I knew anything, it was the dynamics of parental interference: Being assaulted by Randy Reed was bad enough; being defended by my mother was worse.

"I don't know why we had to come to this . . . this pinche pueblo in the first place," she told my father. "You . . . you with your white skin, you don't know what it's like. You can't . . . "

"Don't talk to me about my white skin," he responded calmly. "My white skin has guaranteed me nothing. At least nothing that is important to me. You can be lily white, you can enjoy all the advantages in the world, have what other people dream of having, and still be an outsider. I know that's no consolation to people who have truly suffered for their . . . their . . . skin color. But don't tell me I don't know what it's like."

"Ay, pobre gringo."

"I'm not feeling sorry for myself . . . I live the way I choose to live. I'm just trying to explain to you, if you'll let me . . . "

*I'm not feeling sorry for myself.* The words jarred me, and for an instant, there it was again, staring me in the face, the dark turn—the gap in the story the old man was telling me after the surfboard incident. Something happened to him, something bad. What was it? And then my mother shattered my reverie.

"You're trying to explain it to me?" she screamed, her round face, framed by short black hair, turning red. "Don't explain it to me. Explain it to your son. I'm going to that open house, *y me voy a bailar a la cabrona de la Chaney . . . Ha de creer que llegué en la troca de alfalfa*. I'm going to teach that jerk Chaney a lesson. She must think I arrived on the alfalfa truck."

I yelled at my father.

"Dad, please tell her not to . . . ," I began.

The old man interrupted me, and I knew why. He hated to hear pronouns when I referred to my mother. It was a sign of disrespect, he said.

"Your mother is not a 'she' or a 'her,'" he would say. "Your mother is your mother, and that's what you should call her."

I had tried to correct myself before he could reprimand me, but it was too late.

"Please tell my mother not to," I pleaded. "This will just make it worse. They'll think I'm a sissy."

Then I used a word my father hated.

"They'll think I'm a *joto* (queer)."

My father looked at me; then he looked at my mother.

"Amada . . . ," he started.

Every time my parents argued, I would drop my religion textbook onto the coffee table, leaving it open to the chapter on divorce. Divorce. I hated the word, the schism it denoted, the misery it implied. It even seemed divorced from itself, one word tragically, and irrevocably, split into two—Di-vorce. It was also a sin, as egregious as any of the transgressions listed in the Ten Commandments. . . . So I would leave my religion book on the coffee table, hoping they would see the admonition against divorce. If my parents did not care about their vows—or their son—maybe they cared about their eternal souls.

There was no religion textbook handy that night. It was in my bedroom. I could have run to the room and rushed back with the book, but I was caught in the crossfire of their argument, and I wanted it to be settled now—divorce or no divorce.

"Amada," my father repeated.

I expected my mother to launch into one of her periodic tirades. When she cussed, she cussed in two languages, mixing her "*cabrónes*" with her "son of a bitches," and the result was frightening—a great, strangling waterfall of profanity that threatened to flood the household. She spewed like my Alita, but what seemed charming in my grandmother seemed offensive in my mother, perhaps because old age invests everything, even obscenity, with great flair and humor. Or perhaps it was because Alita always directed her invective at individuals outside the family circle. Whatever the reason, my mother was a boiling receptacle of hostility, and it had only one outlet—her mouth.

But this night was different. This night, she tightened her lips, and the vitriol stayed inside her, churning in her guts. She looked at my father, and then she spoke.

"Bueno," she said finally. "You two go to the open house by yourselves. I'm afraid I'll say something I'll regret. I'll wait for you here."

So we walked to school alone, a father and his son, braving the monsters outside and the monster inside. Which was worse? All I knew was that the monsters outside evaporated; the monster inside remained where it always was, in front of the classroom.

"I'm glad you understand, Mr. Seltzer," Mrs. Chaney said, discussing my behavior with the old man.

"I do," my father responded solemnly.

Before we left the classroom, I checked out a book from the makeshift library behind her desk—a tiny shelf loaded with classics. I picked an illustrated edition of *The Odyssey.* Mrs. Chaney smiled until I handed her the copy. *The Odyssey* was a classic, and she appreciated its lyricism, but this edition was too much for Mrs. Chaney. The sirens graced the cover, their silhouettes unclothed and unrepentant—as bold and stark as the Cyclops. It was artistic, but to Mrs. Chaney, it must have looked like one of those nudie magazines at the newsstands.

"Here," she said, gruffly handing me the release form, even though my father was standing by my side.

As we left the classroom, another set of parents and kids walked by.

"Hello, Mr. Seltzer," Randy Reed said. "Hi, Robert."

As Randy Reed walked past my father, he sneered at me. I looked down. And then I looked at my father.

"Was that Randy Reed?" my father asked as we stepped outside the classroom.

"Yes," I said. "How did you know?"

My father ignored the question.

"Remember I told you that Randy Reed wasn't all bad?" my father asked.

"Yes," I answered.

"Well, I still think that's true . . . " he said.

The pause hovered in the air—first ominous, then excruciating.

"But, as far as his relationship with you is concerned, I do think he's all bad," my father said, finally.

Another pause.

"Does that make sense?" he asked.

"Yes," I said.

I lied.

# 11

# The Monkey Bars

Dangling from the monkey bars on a sunny morning, I savored my topsy-turvy view of the world, the ground and the sky trading places in a moment of sublime contradiction—up was down; down was up.

It was the next best thing to space travel, this feeling of suspended animation. The trees looked more serene, more stately, from this angle, their leaves stirring so gently that they resembled underwater plants. And then there were the noises, the everyday noises—the singing birds, the laughing children, the honking cars. They seemed distant, muted, as if a thick veil separated me from the rest of the world. *Aaahhh.* It was like living in a snow globe.

As I hung upside down, my knees folded across the top bar, I focused on the blackbirds perched on the wooden fence. There were dozens of them. Maybe hundreds. They just sat there, as quiet and motionless as lawn ornaments. Or did they just stand there? In reality, they neither sat nor stood, for like the ten-year-old boy who was transfixed by them, they were hanging upside down. Or so it seemed.

In the middle of a bustling school playground, the monkey bars were my refuge, my holy place. They protected me from Randy Reed. Not physically, but psychologically. The bars were my emotional fortress, open to the elements, but closed to the barbs that wounded my psyche. I felt safer upside down than I did right side up. "*No le hagas caso,*" my grandmother would have told me. "Don't pay attention to him." The monkey bars were my way of following her advice, unspoken though it was.

Randy Reed was the instigator, the destroyer of my surfboards, but his hostility inspired some of the other kids. They started calling me "Mex," "beaner," "spic" and "chili." The chili stood for chili beans, even though Mexicans ate refried beans, *refritos*, not chili beans. Everyone knew that. *Pendejos*. Idiots.

I had stopped asking my Mom to change her name and, thus, my identity, knowing that a simple name change could not lighten my dark skin or my dark blood, for surely my blood was as dusky as my skin. I was a Mex, after all, and the darkness seeped from the inside out, making me a beaner forever. Or so I thought.

One day, my father asked me about the kids who were mean to me. That was his word, mean, for I never characterized their behavior. I merely described it, coldly and clinically, trying to stifle my emotions out of fear that, if I let them loose, they would burst out of my eyes . . . as tears.

"Who are the kids that are mean to you?" he asked.

"Who are the kids?" I repeated.

"Yes," he said. "Their names."

I gave him names. Reed and O'Sullivan, Hornacek and Damiani, Gorteski and Nelson and . . . I paused, unable to remember all my tormentors, but he had heard enough. He shook his head sadly.

"What's wrong?" I asked.

"Most of those kids are minorities, the grandsons or great-grandsons of immigrants," he said. "Their ancestors suffered from the ignorance—and arrogance—of others. . . . Every group has reason to be proud. You . . . you have reason to be proud, Beto. Don't let them take that away from you. Those kids should know better."

But they did not know better, so when I was at school, I quarantined myself. I did everything alone. I ate alone. I studied alone. I rode my bike alone, to school in the morning and to the rental in the afternoon.

Our classroom was at the end of a barracks-like building, with a narrow dirt path separating us from a cyclone fence on the western edge of the school property. Sometimes, when we were not in class or in recess, I sat there, by myself, on that cold, dirt floor. I ate there. I read there. I stared at the fence there. The isolation was oppressive, and it could not have been more complete, more definitive, than if I had been a visitor from another galaxy.

I was alone on the monkey bars, too, but it was a different type of isolation, an isolation I enjoyed. The bars set me apart, but they did not set me apart in their world. They transported me to another world, a world I loved, a world where I wanted to be alone—liberated and happy.

On the morning I dangled upside down, I was focusing on the blackbirds when the school bell rang. With my knees still draped across the top bar, I executed a sit-up in mid-air, pausing for a second, just a second, before flipping backward onto the soft soil of the playground. A perfect landing. *Chingele,* as my grandmother would say, a term that could be positive or negative, depending on the circumstance. *Chingele,* a positive *chingele.* For this was a perfect landing—smooth and effortless. But, no, it was not perfect. I looked down, and I saw two pairs of penny loafers on the ground, mine and . . . he was standing in front of me, so close that his breath congealed on my face.

"God-damned Chili!"

I would grow to stand about six foot three and weigh about 215 pounds, but my growth spurt came years later, and when I was ten, I was a frail, brown sapling—short, skinny, and scared. Too scared to retaliate. I was a book cover, something to be destroyed and discarded.

Randy Reed stood there, his body coiling in anger, and I could see my surfboards, shredded into scraps of paper, fluttering in front of me again. I felt a thud, and I saw him step back, withdrawing his hand from my face. Was it his right hand? I wondered. I stared at him for several seconds. Then I felt something warm in my mouth. I swallowed my blood.

The other kids gathered around us. My haven had turned into a theater, and I was on stage by myself. Everyone was staring at me—

dozens of kids from each classroom. Rachel Olsen bowed her head, whether out of compassion or disgust, I could not tell.

As I surveyed the crowd around me, the blackbirds took off, all of them, their wings flapping with a percussive fury. I looked up, the blood leaking from my mouth. The sound grew louder, more insistent, and as the birds wheeled across the sky, they drew a black curtain over the horizon, plunging my sanctuary into darkness.

*No le hagas caso.*

# 12

# Long Tall Sally

For a ten-year-old boy, the night was mystifying—scary one minute, comforting the next.

How was that possible? How could nighttime embody such jarring contradictions? The paradox haunted me, but there it was, too powerful to deny.

If you were out on the street, without your father or your friends, nighttime was frightening—a long black cloak that wrapped you in doubt and uncertainty. As night fell, the familiar world vanished, its sun-kissed landscape snuffed by a giant shadow, unbidden and unwanted. Trees became monsters and stop signs became aliens, silhouettes that seemed solid and palpable despite the darkness.

Inside, away from the streets, it was a different story. You were safe inside, sheltered from the demons unleashed by the night. But it was not the roof over your head that proved so comforting, so enchanting; no, it was the psychological canopy, the canopy provided by sleep.

And so it was that on Wednesday—the day after my tumble from the monkey bars—I woke up refreshed and happy, a surge of joy I had come to expect every morning. Why? It made no sense, but no matter how many chili beans the kids hurled at me in class, the nighttime always cleansed the spic, washing away all the humiliation and anxiety. Safe in my bed, wrapped in my comforter, I was visited by unseen angels . . . phantom therapists. It was mysterious—and sublime.

Fresh from a restful sleep, I would rub the dreams from my eyes, reaching for the radio on my nightstand, a beige, clunky Westinghouse that looked like a Geiger counter. I would tune the radio to my favorite rock 'n' roll station. If I was lucky, the DJ would be playing the Kinks or the Beach Boys or the Rolling Stones. But if I was really lucky, he would be playing the Beatles, and if I was luckier still, he would be playing a rave-up by the Beatles, one of those shouters that threatened the structural integrity of my bedroom.

*He saw Aunt Mary coming . . .* Paul McCartney, the lead singer on "Long Tall Sally," pronounced Mary with a long a, as in Hades—a word I learned from the tales the old man told me. The word sounded cool, almost brazenly cool. *MA-ry*. It was always neat when you heard adults break the very rules of grammar and pronunciation that you were forced to obey. *MA-ry*. Long *a*.

Long *a* or short *a*, the lyrics befuddled me. They were beyond the grasp of my fifth-grade libido, still in its nascent stage, despite my appreciation for "older women" like Marilyn Monroe. It was the same with "(I Can't Get No) Satisfaction" by the Rolling Stones.

I sensed something different about the lyrics in "(I Can't Get No) Satisfaction," something urgent, something menacing. But I never connected the menace or urgency to sexual frustration—or to the menstrual cycle that created the sexual frustration. I was in the fifth grade; if I had made the connection, they would have promoted me to the freshman class at Harvard. Still . . . there was something about those lyrics, something I wanted to discover. I asked the old man what they meant. He told me to "shut up"—one of the few times he was ever harsh with me. Why? What was he shielding me from?

Whatever the Beatles or the Rolling Stones were singing about, it was the music, not the lyrics, that truly captivated me. The music—chaos with a chorus, mayhem with a melody. It was one of the reasons I embraced the morning, knowing that a twist of the dial would unleash a torrent of raw, vibrant rock 'n' roll—the only sound better than the diaphanous silence of dreams.

No matter how uplifting the music, however, reality always aborted the joy. And so it was on the day after my tumble from the monkey bars. I stumbled down the hallway, humming "Long Tall Sally," and when I reached the bathroom, I stared at the mirror. It brought me back to reality; it brought me back to the dark turn in my story. I stood so still that my reflection looked like a portrait.

There it was—an image frozen in all its disturbing nuances, dominated by those big, ugly, purple lips. Were they filled with helium? I kept staring at my reflection, driven by a macabre fascination with the by-product of that punch. I hated Randy Reed more than ever; his fist was a surgical instrument, and it performed reconstructive surgery on my face, enlarging my lips to a size that was as compelling as it was grotesque.

The evening before, my mother had made a fuss about my swollen lips, and when the old man got home, he asked me what happened, and I told him my tumble from the monkey bars was just that—a tumble. He looked at my face, studying me with the cool intensity of a diamond appraiser. Does it hurt? he asked. Just a little, I said. Then I explained what happened. I was hanging upside down, my knees folded across one of the bars, when the school bell rang. The other kids dashed to their classrooms, leaving me behind, stranded on monkey-bar island.

Instead of bending my way back up to the bars, the way I usually did, I decided to slip to the dirt, softly and gently, thinking I could catch my fall with my extended arms. But I was wrong. When I straightened my legs to unhook them from the bar, I fell swiftly, my face crashing to the earth before I could cushion my fall.

"Ouch," my father said, as if he could feel the pain I had experienced that morning. "I'm going to tell you something you may already know: You need to be more careful. If you keep performing stunts like that, you're going to end up hating those monkey bars. You don't want that, do you?"

"No," I said softly

And now it was the morning after, and there I was, in front of the mirror, staring at my face. I smeared a capful of Groom & Clean onto my hair. My father walked by, pausing in the corridor. He looked at me, and he looked at the tube of Groom & Clean, and he started laughing.

He chuckled because a few mornings earlier, the old man had grabbed the same tube of Groom & Clean, which sat next to the Pepsodent on the bathroom counter. There was only one problem. My father was bald; he used to joke that, if his face were a map of Mexico, his hairline would be in Juárez—*El Norte*. He needed Groom & Clean the way I needed Aqua Velva, the after-shave lotion—"Because there's something about an Aqua Velva man," the seductive blonde sang in the television commercial. But there he was, squeezing the goop onto his toothbrush, never noticing that the peppermint odor had been replaced by the sweet smell of hair grease.

"Goddamn it, Bobby," he had screamed, rushing out of the bathroom, his face twisted into an ugly frown as he tried to spit out the hair grease.

But on the day after the monkey-bar incident, he laughed, and I laughed, both of us remembering the Groom & Clean fiasco, and then he asked if I was okay. I said "yes," that my lips did not hurt, even though they were still bruised and bloated. He smiled, and as he was about to leave, I resumed my fascination with the image in the mirror, and he stopped smiling.

"Are you sure you're okay?" he asked.

"Yeah."

"Sure?"

"Yeah."

"Okay, then," he said. "Remember, be more careful."

The old man left for work, and I returned to my face in the mirror. I stared and stared and stared—not just for minutes, but for days. I studied my face—my helium lips, my brown eyes, my black hair, parted on the left and slicked with Groom & Clean.

And then slowly, after a few days, the helium—and the purple hue—drained from my lips. I looked like Robert again. The lips seemed normal, and my self-absorption, like the swelling that inspired it, disappeared. Would my anxiety—and my disappointment with myself—evaporate so easily?

13

# The Granadas

Separated by age and background, we bridged the gulf through twin obsessions. The old man had Cleveland; I had El Paso. He had his memories; I had mine. *El viejo y el chavalo*—the old man and the kid. The symmetry was cool.

The funny thing—funny and sad?—is that I was sustained by memories before I had memories. I was ten years old; my backlog of experiences was shorter than I was. But no matter: There I was, a pint-sized version of the old man, nurtured by the photo album in my head—picture after picture of an idyllic past that stretched almost a thousand miles behind me, from Bakersfield all the way to El Paso. I thought about Randy Reed all the time. He was everywhere—in my dreams, my fears, my classroom. But he was not in my hometown. And the longer we stayed in Bakersfield—and the more I stewed about Randy Reed—the more I thought about El Paso.

And the great thing about El Paso was that, deep down, we both had it, my father and I. It was my real home, my birthplace, but it was his adopted home. And because he chose it—rather than it choosing him—he may have loved the town with a fervor that was greater than my own, even though his wanderlust led him periodically to other towns, including Bakersfield.

Was El Paso idyllic? Probably not. But distance blurred the negatives, turning the bad into good and the good into better. The hazy past offset the clear present, just as it had for my beloved Alita after she moved from Chihuahua to El Paso. And so I remembered.

I remembered Alita, her stern demeanor tempered by a sly humor that was mischievously youthful. I remembered her laughter, echoing from a deep well of joy and pleasure. And, yes, I remembered her quick wit and quicker tongue, weapons she wielded to assault my friends, sometimes venomously, sometimes good-naturedly.

"*Ay, Bobby, tus amigos huelen a baño publico.* Oh, Bobby, your friends smell like a public bathroom," she would tell me.

I remembered the Frontera Swimming Pool in South El Paso, the cool water making you forget that it was surrounded by hot desert. And I remembered the *helado* vendors who would not let you forget. All day, from morning till dusk, they rode around the park that surrounded the facility, pedaling those contraptions that were part bicycle/part freezer—appliances on wheels. The old men wore gray pants and white shirts, their dark faces weathered by the blistering sun, and whenever they smiled, their wrinkles deepened into trenches. They never ran out of popsicles—or smiles.

"*Helados,*" the vendors would yell. "*Helados de todos sabores.* Ice cream in all flavors."

One afternoon, I asked for an orange creamsicle, and when the vendor opened the freezer, I reached in with both hands, scraping the ice along the steel wall. I rubbed the shavings on my face, patting my cheeks to make sure I had coated every inch. *Aaahhh.* The vendor grinned.

"*Te voy a cobrar por el hielo tambien.* I'm going to charge you for the ice, too," he said, laughing.

I remembered the sunsets—sunsets so spectacular that God must have poured buckets of paint onto the clouds. A celestial Jackson Pollock, favoring spontaneity over technique. No matter where you were, no matter what you were doing, the sky beckoned, compelling you to marvel at its colorful face, its fierce beauty.

"*Mira.* Look," Victor Serrano, one of my friends, said one evening, pointing at the sky.

Standing on a hill overlooking our homes, we interrupted our "sword fight," a battle in which our weapons were two smooth sticks that surveyors had planted into the soil near a construction project.

"Mira," he repeated, holding his sword by his side.

The sun dropped, and we looked up, transfixed by the daily miracle—sunset in El Paso, the sky glowing with the soft, creamy colors of dusk. It was beautiful. And then, after a few minutes, it came, the paradox that thrilled us every evening: The lower the sun sank, the brighter the sky flamed—reds, oranges, and purples clashing in the sky, each color taking on the shape of the cloud it illuminated, as if the day were hanging on, refusing to die, refusing to be swallowed by darkness. And, as the sun descended, the temperature dipped, evaporating the sweat on our cheeks—the coolest, sweetest sensation in the world.

"Mira," Victor said for the third and final time.

I remembered the alleys. Ah, the alleys. Like station wagons and transistor radios, they began disappearing in the 1970s—remnants of an era booby-trapped by progress.

Realizing that alleys consumed space—and profits—developers started jamming houses into each other, with none of those damned alleys in between. The result? Backyards melded into backyards, forcing neighbors to put up fences for privacy. Homeowners got their privacy, but they lost something in the bargain—the charm, mystery, and allure of the alleys. I was lucky. Those damned alleys were still around, still part of the cultural landscape, when I grew up.

Why were alleys so important to me? They were like streets . . . but for kids—unlit, unpaved, and, best of all, unsupervised. Parks were for organized activities—baseball, football, kickball—but alleys . . . alleys were for the pursuit that kids loved best: mayhem.

We lived on Prospect Avenue, an avenue in name only. The street was about a mile long, maybe less, stretching from the gully on the west to the Safeway Supermarket on the east. It was located in Sunset Heights, one of the oldest neighborhoods in town, an area partitioned between rich and poor, sprawling houses on one block, ramshackle duplexes on the next. If anyone, or anything, undermined these class divisions, it was the alleys—a network of open-air catacombs, as intricate as the streets themselves, where status and money meant *mierda,* crap, as Alita would say. In the alleys, the kids were equals, rich and poor united by a single goal—*travesuras.* Mischief.

We had a pomegranate tree in the backyard, the only vegetation amid the dirt and brush, and when the fruit ripened in the fall, we would shake the branches until the *granadas* dropped like tiny paratroopers. They were rich and juicy, exploding with seeds that dribbled down our chins with every bite. Alita told us they were poisonous, but since none of the kids died, we kept on eating them, spitting out the seeds as if they were spent shells from a machine gun.

And then one afternoon, we found out about the dog. They discovered him in the alley, about a block from the gully, his body so limp that it looked like an empty sack. Was he hiding in there, inside the sack, a smaller version of his old self, laughing at the neighbors who gathered around his body?

He was a German shepherd—four, maybe five years old. His name was Apache . . . *Pobre Apache.* He belonged to a family on Porfirio Diaz Street, just a few blocks from Prospect Avenue.

The Guerreros had no kids, so they adopted Apache as the child in their family. And Apache adopted us. We took him out for walks, and we marveled at his ability to retrieve rubber baseballs, the kind with those goofy red seams meant to simulate stitches; darting this way and that, he was quick and agile, slicker than any infielder in the major leagues.

Apache was a mature canine—lean, sturdy and active, his growl marking him as the best watchdog in the neighborhood. But he retained the features that endeared him to all the kids: the big, brown, liquid eyes of a puppy. Apache was *familia.* . . . Apache was, well, Apache.

There was no blood, no sign of trauma, in the alley. But he was dead, just the same, his bark silenced forever, lost within the folds of his baggy skin. Pobre Apache.

"*Miralo,*" Alita said. "*Muerto. Se enveneno.* Look at him. Dead. Poisoned."

It was the pomegranates, she said. The pomegranates killed Apache. And we believed her. We believed Alita, the neighborhood coroner; her admonitions, once so empty and comical, now buttressed by forensic evidence. That limp body. We could not think of the dog without thinking of the fruit that killed him. *Envenenado*.

"Dad, did the *granadas* kill Apache?" I asked my father one day.

"Is that what your grandmother told you?"

"Yes."

"Well, then?" he said, refusing to undermine Alita.

It was not malice or insensitivity, but we were kids, and as time passed, our sadness passed with it. Pobre Apache devolved into pobre nosotros, poor us, our thoughts centered on our activities—or absence of activities—for while children can be vibrant and passionate one minute, they can be dull and listless the next, their sense of adventure stymied by their lack of imagination. We were no different. So we would sit around, as sluggish as iguanas, asking the same old questions and hearing the same old answers:

"What do you wanna do?"

"I don't know. What do you wanna do?"

It was as if our imaginations had melted in the desert heat. Then one afternoon, congregating in my backyard, we saw a pomegranate drop, and this time it was not because we had shaken the tree, for we had disavowed the fruit a long time before. This granada fell on its own, plopping onto the dirt in the middle of my backyard. I stared at it, enraged, my sense of loss returning, boiling in my guts. That fruit killed Apache. I picked it up, and I hurled it at the trashcan, rattling the lid as the missile ricocheted onto the ground.

Then something weird happened; instead of relief, I felt tension, excitement. I stared at my friends, and my friends stared at me, and we scrambled toward the tree, shaking the trunk until the fruits dropped, one by one, each granada transformed into a moist, juicy projectile. *Chingele*.

We picked up the granadas, gathering them into the folds of our T-shirts, which we stretched into makeshift pouches. There were five of us. We looked like farm workers, but these fruits were not destined for market; they were destined for mischief. As soon as we filled our pouches, we raced into the alley, our arms folded across our stomachs to keep the granadas from spilling.

Looking for anything we could turn into a bunker—a trashcan here, a cactus there—we scattered across the alley, each kid flying in a different direction. Then we released our pouches, letting the granadas fall to the ground in little, menacing heaps. The granadas turned into grenades. We let them fly, filling the desert air with juicy bombs. *Hijole*. Most of them missed, proving that enthusiasm is no substitute for accuracy.

After ten minutes of warfare, there was one granada left. And it was mine. I flipped it into the air, watching it drop into my hand with a soft, delicate thud. Then I did it again and again, each time flipping it higher and higher. I felt like an executioner. My friends watched, their anxiety growing with every toss. Which kid would I target?

I picked Marco, the slowest kid in the group, his stubby legs no match for the wicked ferrets among us. Pobre Marco. He took off, his *longjas*—belly fat—jiggling with every step. I fired, but the release felt wrong from the start, its arc higher than I had intended. Much higher. Marco kept running, but before he knew it, the missile soared past him—past his stubby legs, his jiggling longjas, his anxious yelps. *Pendejo*. Idiot. Eluding the object one second, he was pursuing it the next. The rest of us burst into laughter.

When he recognized this bizarre role reversal, he stopped, and the world seemed to stop with him. The air turned heavy, languorous, and we saw everything up close, in slow motion. The granada sparkled in the sun. It kept soaring, its ascent so slow that each rotation revealed a flash of green here, a flash of red there. This slow-motion climb was fascinating. But when would it end? And where?

A car door slammed. Pito Peterson, one of our neighbors, emerged from his red Chevrolet, panting from the effort to extract his squat body from the shiny interior. And then it happened. The slow-motion world disappeared, replaced by a burst of reality, as swift as it was unexpected. We should have seen it coming. The granada kept spinning, faster and faster, a missile searching for ground zero.

It whistled through the air—a whooosh followed by a splaaat. Peterson staggered backwards, his face dripping with juice, seeds, and hostility.

"*Chavalo cabrón!* Little jerk!" Peterson yelled, somehow singling me out as the marksman of the bunch.

"*La Migra!*" my friends screamed, using the phrase that equated every threat to the arrival of the immigration police, a phrase we used regularly, even though we were all US citizens.

I sprinted home, my heart filled with a crazy mixture of fear and delight—fear that I was in trouble and delight that I was in trouble. I wanted to laugh and cry at the same time. And, as I raced home, Peterson lumbered behind me, an older version of Marco, his jowls flapping from the effort to catch me. I turned back, and there he was, staring machetes at me.

"*Chavalo jodido!* Fucking kid!" he screamed.

As I sprinted home, I felt energized, propelled by the thought that the old man would save me. He would rescue me from this bearded old ogre. *Ándale, cabrón!* Take that, you jerk! But as I cleared the last hill on my way to the duplex, I remembered, and for a moment—just a moment—I hated the old man and his freight trains.

The old man was gone that weekend, gone on one of his journeys to Big Spring or San Angelo or Fort Worth. He kissed me good-bye that morning, and I giggled when his stubble scoured my face. It was a Saturday. He said he would be back by Tuesday, and I said "good," but when he tried to kiss my mother good-bye, she sniffed and said, "*Vete.* Get out." The scene flashed through my mind as I tried to flee Pito Peterson. The old man was in Big Spring or San Angelo or . . . He would have saved me from this crazy neighbor, I knew he would, but the old man was gone, and there was no freight train in the world that could get him back in time to rescue me.

I kept running. As I scurried to the backyard, my heart leaping out of my mouth, I saw Alita standing by the wooden gate in the backyard, a Lucky Strike dangling from her hand. She was waiting for me.

"*Vete adrento*. Go inside," she told me.

Peterson arrived, puffing and sweating; the exertion—and anger—turned his pores into a sprinkler system.

"*Ese muchacho*, that boy . . . " he started.

Alita cut him off.

"*Ese muchacho* . . . " she said, pausing to correct herself. "*Bobby no te hiso nada*. Bobby didn't do anything to you."

Alita pronounced Bobby, with a long O, as in "low."

"*Bobby no te hiso nada*," she repeated. "*Yo vi todo. Estava jugando con sus amigos, nada mas*. I saw everything. He was playing with his friends—nothing more."

Alita turned around, leaving Peterson with a mouthful of words and nobody to hurl them at.

"*Vemos si se envenena el viejo maldito*. Let's see if the old jerk gets poisoned," she said, hugging me as she walked into the house.

And then she smiled at me.

"*No le hagas caso*. Don't pay attention to him," she said.

Alita saved me—God bless her—but I would have given a bucketful of granadas if the old man had been there instead.

14

## Bobo and Jack

I hated myself for lying to the old man about the monkey bars. But it was better to be devious with the old man than to be honest with myself. The humiliation would have been more painful than any punch to the jaw.

The folly of my ploy—my lie—was that I could fool everybody but myself. I knew what had happened. I was there, on the playground, taking the punch I would feel for the rest of my life. And, no matter how many lies I concocted, no matter how many schemes I devised, I could never erase the ugly truth: I had failed to stand up to Randy Reed—for the second time. First with the surfboards, then with the punch. And what made the lie worse was that I knew, deep down, how to deal with Randy Reed: tell the old man what had happened. Seek his advice. . . . Seek his advice, then follow it. . . . It was that simple. As a kid, the old man was tougher than I was—more rugged and thick-skinned. He would have known how to conquer Randy Reed; I knew that. But I could not bring myself to tell him the truth.

And then, two weeks after the monkey bar incident, Randy Reed did it again. It was after lunch. I was alone in the classroom, just as I had been the day he shredded my surfboards. He strolled into the classroom, and as he walked by, he bumped into my desk, jostling the book I was reading, our literary anthology. He was wearing his retainer, but bridle or no bridle, there was no controlling Randy Reed, the two-legged beast. He looked at the open page.

"O. who?" he asked.

It was a short story by O. Henry—"The Gift of the Magi." Randy Reed stared at me, but I dismissed his question with an empty stare. Then I went back to my story, leaving his question hanging in the stale air of the fifth-grade classroom.

"O. who, chili?" he asked again.

I ignored him. The story was mesmerizing, more potent than Randy Reed. Then the story succumbed to a greater force. I felt . . . a jolt . . . in my leg. Randy Reed kicked me in the shin. It felt as if he had plunged a knife into my bone. The pain shot up my leg, advancing like a forest fire that ignites tree after tree in its path. First, it struck my shin, then my calf, then my thigh. It did not stop until it hit my psyche, and that was the worst hurt of all. . . . I should have jumped out of my desk, grabbed him by the collar and . . . but I just sat there, quietly, stupidly. Randy Reed smiled.

As I rode my bicycle home that afternoon, I tried to concoct another lie, but how many times could I tell the old man that I had fallen from a monkey bar? I was no O. Henry when it came to telling tales.

I streaked down the alley, waving at Mr. Cotton, who managed the Texaco station next door, and for the first time that day, I smiled. I was no O. Henry, but I did not have to be. Not today. The attack left a bruise, but it was on my shin, and nobody had to see it—not my mother, not my father. Not anybody. My pants would conceal the evidence. I was so worried about manufacturing a lie that I forgot I did not have to—not this time. *Pendejo.*

"Hi, Mom," I said when I walked into our rental home.

My mother was making fried chicken, one of her gringo dishes.

"Hi, Bobby," she said, wiping her brow with her apron.

"Is Dad in town?" I asked her.

"Of course, he is," she said. "What kind of a question is that? *Que estas loco?* Are you crazy?"

"Well, you never know with him," I said.

"Bah!"

The door busted open. It was the old man. He was like a big, shaggy sheepdog, unable to do anything quietly or discreetly—a delicious irony considering he demanded what my mother called *la paz de los muertos*, the serenity of the dead, when he was writing. The old man was home from work. He was wearing what he termed his "office outfit"—brown slacks and white shirt, with a tie that dangled from his collar. It was red and white, with diagonal stripes, and it looked like a candy cane hanging from his neck. He had loosened it on his way home from the *Californian*.

The tie was a noose around his neck, but the pants and the shirt were just as bad; they seemed at least one size too small, making the old man look like a big sausage in a small casing. . . . And then there was the belt; the belt was too long. It looked fine until it reached the final loop in his pants, and then the tongue had nowhere to go. Maybe the old man had lost weight. Maybe my mother, who bought all his clothes, thought he had a bigger belly than he did. Whatever the reason, the belt was about six inches too long, so whenever the old man walked fast, which was often, the tongue of the belt flapped wildly, up and down, back and forth, like a severed extension cord that set off sparks with every gyration.

"Hi, Beto," he said, plopping onto the sofa in the living room. "How was school?"

I frowned.

"Bad?"

I shrugged.

"Oh," he said, stroking his chin. "Well, if you're not answering me, that can only mean that it wasn't bad, and it wasn't good. It was just . . . somewhere in between?"

I smiled. It could have been "bad" because Randy Reed kicked me in the shin, but there was no physical evidence of his assault, at least none that the old man could detect, so that meant my day was bad but not that bad. How did he know?

"What is your mother making for dinner?" he asked, changing the subject.

"Fried chicken," I said, speaking for the first time.

Taking his cue from me, the old man resorted to nonverbal communication. He rolled his eyes. The old man was a vegetarian, and while my mother and I ate assorted meats, including chorizo, meatloaf, and fried chicken, he stuck to bread and vegetables and "no-thank-yous" whenever someone offered him a *cacho de carne*, piece of meat.

"Oh," he said.

The old man looked at me, the silence so ominous and impenetrable that we reacted the only way we knew how—we laughed.

"Fried chicken," he repeated, puckering his face as if he had swallowed a bowl of sauerkraut.

Then, with dinner sizzling in the kitchen, the old man got serious.

"Beto, did I ever tell you about Bobo?" he asked.

He had—dozens, maybe hundreds of times—but I lied. Again. I was getting good at deception.

"Bobo?" I asked, pronouncing the name slowly. "Bobo . . . Bobo . . . No, I don't think so."

The old man was my O. Henry. He loved to tell stories about his youth, repeating them so many times, always with fresh details, that his childhood seemed more real than mine. When he was my age, he was Chess—no, Young Chess—but he was already the old man to me, a miniature version of the individual he would become, bold, daring, eager to tackle new adventures, no matter how scary they may have seemed to others. I loved hearing about his childhood, loved it so much that I begged him to repeat stories I had heard hours before. But, sometimes, he did not have to repeat them; sometimes, I could hear the stories echoing in my mind long after he recounted them. And so it was with the tale of Bobo—a tale he had told me, for the first time, about two years before we moved to California.

"Really?" he asked that evening in Bakersfield, "I never told you about Bobo? Are you sure?"

"Yes, Dad. I am sure. You never did."

The Seltzers lived near the southern shore of Lake Erie, and there were times when Young Chess stood in the front yard, dizzy over the good fortune that landed him there, in a two-story, Tudor-style house. He never took anything for granted. Why me? he thought. Why Young Chess? Did he deserve this good fortune? He knew other kids, other families, who lived on the streets, and yet here he was, in this mini-fortress—a home with two chimneys and four cupolas, each one shaped like an inverted *V*. Young Chess loved it.

Louis Benson Seltzer, his father, was editor of the *Cleveland Press*, and his mother, Marian Elizabeth Seltzer, was a stay-at-home mom who rarely stayed at home. She was involved in so many charity and volunteer efforts that she seemed as busy as her husband, who was known as the most powerful journalist in Ohio. Marian E. Seltzer had brown, curly hair, rolled back into a massive bun, an austere hairstyle that belied her warm, giving personality.

With both of his parents away from the house so much, Young Chess could do what he wanted to do—have fun. It was liberating. He felt like a latter-day Tom Sawyer, enjoying adventures that he would remember—and recount—his whole life.

It was a cool, autumn morning. Young Chess sprinted across the front lawn, a football tucked under his arm, cutting and darting to avoid the flowerbeds that served, in his solitude, as his gridiron opponents. The roses and tulips lunged for him, their petals quivering as he streaked past them, a young Red Grange, the Galloping Ghost who starred for the University of Illinois. Young Chess smiled.

It was seven o'clock, too early for his friends to stumble out of bed on a Saturday morning. But it was not too early for Young Chess. He loved the weekends, lived for them, and he was not about to miss one minute of the joyous liberation they offered, even if it meant playing alone, before his friends had vanquished sleep.

"Chess," his father asked him one evening, "what is it about the weekends you love so much? Is school that rough? You come home on Fridays with a smile that could span Lake Erie."

"Dad," he said, "you love the weekends, too. You just love them in a different way. You like to rest, and I like to play."

"Hmmm," his father responded, smiling. "Maybe so, maybe so."

On the lawn that autumn morning, Young Chess dashed for the

end zone, the imaginary line between two oak trees. He ran with a high kicking action, his knees almost scraping his chin, but as he neared the goal line, he felt a pull on his left leg, and he went sprawling, his hands shooting forward, palms up, as his face plowed the dewy lawn. Shit! He got up slowly, his face a wet, green mask. When he turned around, spitting out a blade of grass, he saw him.

"Bobo!" Young Chess screamed, tears welling in his eyes.

Bob Olson laughed.

"Fuck you, Seltzer," Bobo said. "Hey, where's the little baby's sailor suit. Sissy!"

And then he walked away.

Bob Olson was the neighborhood bully. He was eighteen, almost four years older than Young Chess and his friends. The kids hated him, and he hated the kids, but his favorite victim was Young Chess, who popularized the nickname Bobo—short for Bob Olson. He stood six-foot-two and weighed 175 pounds, and he seemed as broad as he was tall, with biceps that had to be sixteen inches around. Sixteen inches, the kids marveled among themselves. They felt guilty for admiring a boy they detested. But, dammit, they could not help it. Bobo played fullback and linebacker at University School, the private high school Chess wanted to attend the next year.

"Dad," I said, interrupting the old man. "How do you spell Olson?"

"Why?" he asked.

"Just wondering."

"Oh . . . O-l-s-o-n."

"Good," I said, relieved that Rachel and Bob could not be related because they spelled their names differently.

Later that year, during the summer, Young Chess got a job in a downtown clothing store, packing and unpacking shipments. He did not need the job, but he hated to ask his parents for money, and he swore he would never cheat another waitress out of her job. Young Chess was a stock boy, and the manager, Simon Peach, liked his attitude. He was earnest and hardworking, and of all the stock boys in the shop, he was the only one who refused to participate in the daily ritual—yelling out, when Mr. Peach was not looking, "Peach is a fruit!"

Flustered every time he heard the chorus, Mr. Peach stammered, "Wha . . . wha . . . what are you doing? Get to work—now!" He wore striped shirts and bow ties, and he plastered his hair with Murray's Superior Pomade. Young Chess wondered why he bothered. Mr. Peach was in his thirties, but he was already balding, and the hair he pomaded consisted of a few strands that looked like lonely sunbathers on his vast beach of a head.

Bobo walked into the clothing store one day, looking for a suit. The manager asked him what kind of suit he wanted. Bobo said something nice, something a girl might like. Mr. Peach riffled through the racks, and Bobo tried on suit after suit—solid, checkered, pin-striped, each one producing a scowl on a face that was already dour. And then Bobo saw it—the suit. He settled on a gray, double-breasted suit with wide lapels. No checkers. No pin stripes. Solid. It fit him perfectly, loose but not baggy, elegant but not showy. Bobo smiled. Mr. Peach asked Chess to wrap it for the gentleman. Chess took the suit, and looking back at "the gentleman" and the manager as he scurried away, put it back on the rack. Then he replaced it with another suit—same style, same color.

A week later, Chess was watering his imaginary football field—the front lawn—when Bobo and his girlfriend, Linda Carmichael, strolled down the sidewalk, hand in hand. Linda smiled at Chess, and Chess smiled back. Bobo grimaced.

"Hi, Bobo," Chess said, smiling broadly.

Bobo responded with a tortured smile. He looked uncomfortable, and not just because he had to mask his hostility toward the youngster in the presence of Linda Carmichael. The suit, which fit him so splendidly in the shop, had shrunk. What the hell had happened? The suit seemed two sizes too small, especially around the chest and arms. But it was not just the coat. It was the pants, too. They looked like leotards, forcing Bobo to walk with the short, dainty steps of a ballerina. He looked like a sissy. Chess laughed.

"Goddamn it, Seltzer!" Bobo screamed, finally realizing the awful truth.

Young Chess had switched suits in the clothing store.

"You son-of-a bitch," Bobo screamed.

Bobo minced across the lawn. It was the only gait he could execute. He went after Young Chess, but his mind was racing faster than his legs, much faster, and it had only one thought—pulverize Seltzer.

"Bob!" Linda yelled. "Leave little Chess alone."

Little Chess retreated. He stumbled, losing control of the hose. It fell to the grass. The hose squirmed, pointing upward, and the water slammed into Bobo and his ill-fitting suit.

"Bobo! I mean Bob . . . If you lay one hand on that poor little boy. . . . "

Drenched and humiliated, Bobo stopped, his lust for the girl overpowering his hatred for the boy, and Chess dashed into the house, leaving the hose squirming on the lawn, two feet from Bobo, his drenched nemesis.

"Thanks, Linda!" Chess yelled.

"You're welcome, little Chess."

Young Chess would go on to compete in four sports at University School, the same school Bobo had attended. He participated in football, baseball, basketball, and boxing, and he excelled at all four. He never became the behemoth that Bobo was, but he ran and lifted weights during the off seasons, and his arms were lean and hard, roped with the kind of sinewy muscles he admired in Jack Dempsey, the great heavyweight champion.

A grade-school dropout, Dempsey left home when he was sixteen, a teenager with only one marketable skill—the ability to beat people up. And beat them up, he did. Nicknamed the Manassa Mauler—he was born in Manassa, Colorado—the teenager hopped freight trains from town to town, participating in "tough man" contests in every saloon along the way. "I can't sing and I can't dance, but I can lick any son of a bitch in the house," he would say. Lick any son of a bitch in the house? He could and did. But Dempsey did not merely lick the sons of bitches; he did it with a fury that appalled the very fans he attracted.

If the old man loved Dempsey, it was not just because of his boxing prowess. It was because of the obstacles he overcame to display his boxing prowess. The boy developed a sensitivity for men, like Dempsey, who lived in hobo camps as they scattered across the country looking for work. Some of these camps emerged in urban areas, including Cleveland. They called them "Hoovervilles," after the president whose economic policies, many believed, contributed to the Great Depression.

Young Chess did not know the numbers—by 1933, more than 50 percent of the industrial workers had lost their jobs in Cleveland—but he knew the numbers had faces, and he saw those faces every day on the streets of Cleveland, their eyes hollow, their foreheads roadmapped with wrinkles. Even the kids seemed old and tired, as if they were halfway through lives that had just started.

The fighter reminded Young Chess of Bobo, but the comparison ended with their physiques. Dempsey was a legend, Bobo a louse. After he graduated, Bobo continued to attend the football games at University School, sauntering up to his seat moments before kickoff, so that all the students could cheer him, a hero returning to the battlefield where he had earned his glory. But nobody cared about Bobo. Not anymore. He would go to his seat quietly, head bowed, always with a new girl on his arm. Bobo had graduated from University School, and Linda Carmichael had graduated from Bobo.

The old man told me the story, and all I could think was . . . the old man had his own Randy Reed.

15

# The Hobo Jungle

A hot afternoon in Bakersfield, hot for October, one of those days fit for the gate-tenders of hell, as Alita would say.

It felt like ninety to ninety-five degrees—hot enough to turn our shirts into damp rags. Imagine a scale—Bakersfield, hell . . . hell, Bakersfield. We plodded along a railroad trestle, the old man and the kid, each of us submerged in grass that grew as high as cotton. The heat rose from the tracks in shimmering waves—stark, incandescent curlicues that blurred the landscape in front of us.

Lugging a bag overflowing with groceries, I was too short to peer over the burden, so I walked sideways, my steps so slow and laborious that I looked like a man clinging to the ledge of a skyscraper. I twisted my head to see where I was going, but the tactic backfired: Looking sideways when I should have been looking down, I stumbled along the cinder-strewn path. *Chingele*.

My father walked ahead of me, his arms bulging with three sacks of groceries. He turned around to check my progress. Then he laughed—gently.

"You can put it down if you want," he said.

I tried to set it down, but the lower I crouched, the heavier the bag became. My arms trembled, and my knees buckled. The sack wobbled in my arms, the cans jostling as I eased the load onto the ground.

"We're almost there," my father said.

He was right. I could see the smoke curling in the sky, wisps of heat that corkscrewed through the dense, hazy atmosphere. My father called it a "hobo jungle." It looked like a campsite—a shabby campsite—with clothes, blankets and utensils strewn across the thick undergrowth of grass and briars. The men were cooking hot dogs and chili beans.

The "grill" was a pile of rocks, arranged in a circle, with a fire glowing in the middle. A "patio oven," the men called it. They set a steel grid across the rocks, each rod coated with the grease of all the meals that came before.

One of the young hobos, the "chef," tossed the meal onto the grid—the dogs and beans. The beans were still in the can, its lid pried open so that it resembled a tiny vent. You could see the reddish brown goo bubbling from the heat.

The old man never took me on his freight train journeys, but this was the next best thing. I looked around. Like their surroundings, the men were rough and grizzled, with thick hair matted into greasy clumps. They sat on boulders or old pieces of cardboard, waiting for the food to cook. The chef turned the hot dogs with a thick branch. He was tall and muscular, with blond, wavy hair swept into a greasy pompadour. The other men—there were eight of them—called him "Fifi."

"Hey, Fifi, are those dogs ready yet?" one of the men yelled.

Fifi hurled a can of chili beans, unopened, at the man.

"There's your meal, you fuckin' bastard," the chef said.

The man caught the can with one hand, snatching it out of the air as though it were a pesky mosquito. He stared at Fifi; Fifi stared at him. I got scared. Then the two men started laughing.

"Hey, Chet," another man greeted my father. "Como estas?"

It was Big Bill, the leader of the group. He wore a T-shirt and overalls, and he was one of those fat men who did not seem fat. It was weird. He lumbered toward us—tall, bearded and heavy—his belly so huge that it looked like a separate entity, a watermelon swaddled in overalls. But he was not fat. He was just . . . massive. And if his body was enormous, so was his personality. His name was

Guillermo, but the other men called him Bill. Big Bill. His first name was an adjective, and his last name was a first name. Big Bill. It suited him.

"Thanks for the groceries," Big Bill said.

"You're welcome," my father answered. "De nada. How you been?"

A kid can spy without spyglasses. A kid can study the world. Or a hobo jungle. And so I did. I studied everything—the greasy hair, the dirty grill, the scary exchange between Fifi and the impatient diner. I was a babe among giants, a child peering at the world through a cracked door. It was a phenomenon peculiar to kids. Nobody—nobody—can hide in public like a child, invisible yet accessible, especially when the adults are busy.

My father knew I was there. He knew I heard Fifi call the diner a "fuckin' bastard." And he knew I was taking everything in, a pint-sized Margaret Mead among the Samoans. I was standing by my father the whole time, and whenever someone cussed, he would drape his arm around my shoulder, giving me a reassuring squeeze. Was he telling me that the language was bad, but the men were good? Was he telling me that, regardless of the bad language, I would be okay?

As I wrestled with the questions, an explosion shattered my reverie. It was percussive, but there were no drums around, just rumps. And that was it. A rump produced that sound—a rump like the one that hovered in front of the loudspeaker in the classroom at St. Francis Elementary School. It belonged to Fifi, a man whose civility, apparently, extended no further than his hairstyle.

"Goddamn it, Fifi," Big Bill roared, his eyebrows arching into thick feathers. "I'll tell you, Chet, when that boy farts, he can singe your eyelashes and rot your teeth . . . One of these days, he's gonna blow a hole clear to China, I swear."

My father rested his arm on my shoulders—again—and for the first time, Big Bill noticed me.

"Chet, I'm sorry," Big Bill said. "These men don't know how to act in front of a refined young man. My apologies."

"Big Bill," my father said, "I think my son has probably heard those sound effects before."

"Well, I apologize, just the same," Big Bill said, sneering at Fifi.

I thought about Wendell Wilson, a kid whose firepower was prosaic—one concussive blast at a time. Fifi was different. Fifi sounded like a saxophone player, bending the emissions as if they were jazz notes, low and plaintive one second, sharp and shrill the next. He was a musician—the Coltrane of crepitation—but instead of blowing air into his instrument, he blew air out of it. I wondered if Greg Bukowski could lift him.

"How are you, son?" Big Bill asked me. "I apologize for this man. He flunked finishing school."

"I'm fine, Mr. . . . "

The formality seemed silly for someone named Big Bill.

"I'm not a Mister, son," he said, extending his hand. "I'm a Bill . . . I'm a Big Bill."

"Oh . . . I'm a Robert."

"Hi, Robert. If you're anything like your dad, you must be a fine young man. *Mucho gusto*. Pleasure to meet you."

I smiled proudly, but my emotions dissolved into a tug-of-war between pride and embarrassment . . . Embarrassment won. I looked down, staring at the cinders around the fire, my eyes watering from self-consciousness. Then Fifi erupted again. I could have hugged him . . . If the aroma had not discouraged such intimacy, I would have hugged him. The blast took the spotlight off me, returning it to a man whose rump was a munitions dump. I looked up from the cinders, and my heart said what my mouth could not: "Thank you, Fifi."

When we left the camp, I asked my dad about the men in the hobo jungle. He said they were good men, rough but decent, spurned by a society that could not look past their clothes and vocabularies and, yes, digestive problems. I looked at him, puzzled.

"Their farting," he said.

Farting. My mother called it *ventoseando*. Ventilating. She could be elegant when she wanted to be.

"Oh," I said, laughing. "Farting."

As we drove home, the telephone poles flashing by quicker than I could count them, I thought about the men who lived under the stars.

"Dad?"

"Yes."

"Why do they live outside?"

"They have to."

"Why?"

"Well, they don't have jobs, for one thing," he said. "And, for another, they don't fit in well with other people, people who live in homes and have jobs. It's . . . complicated."

I felt deflated. Complicated? This was Chester Seltzer, my father, the man who could vanquish raging monsters with simple gestures, and he could not tell me why these men lived without televisions and refrigerators and roofs? How could that be?

"It's complicated," he said. "They're poor, and life has beaten them down. They don't trust most people."

There was a pause, long enough for me to count about forty telephone poles, each one flashing by with an almost hypnotic power.

"Do you want to go for a ride tomorrow morning?" my father asked.

"Aren't you taking a freight train to Riverside tomorrow?" I asked.

"Who told you that?"

"Mom."

He rubbed his face.

"I decided not to go," he said, finally.

"Oh," I said. "Sure, I'd like to go for a ride."

"Early? Very early?"

"Sure."

When we got home, I thought about Fifi and Big Bill and . . . Randy Reed. No matter what dominated my thoughts at the moment, Randy Reed was always there, lurking in the dark corridors of my mind. Randy Reed, my dark turn. He turned my brain—or was it my ego?—into an open wound, an ugly, suppurating mass of exposed, pre-adolescent nerve endings. I wanted to kick him, punch him, pound him. And, as the violent fantasies swirled in my head that night, I smiled and fell asleep.

# Night Train to Fort Worth

## *A Story by Amado Muro*

One night I got on a Texas and Pacific mainline run at Toyah with a one-legged rover nicknamed Sticks because of his crutches. When the engineer eased the train out, picking up the slack without a bump, we were in an empty with open laths about six cars behind the Big Jack engine.

A damp soft snow was falling, and we bundled up with carlining. But the wind blowing straight and steady from the northwest made us feel the snow's wetness on our foreheads. Sticks, small and spindly with a gray-streaked beard that didn't hide his sickly complexion, shivered.

"You feel the cold more when you're hungry, buddy," he mumbled apologetically.

Near Pecos the freight train thundered over a highball stretch so fast it skipped on rail joints, and the rocking boxcars hit back on their coupling pins with a wrenching jerk. We sat with our legs apart and our heads down, bracing for sudden jolts of slack, with our hips numb from the pounding. Then the train began to bounce with a staccato roll, and we stood up to ease the punishment. The double-track roadbed was speeding away beneath us, and the barren alkali land swung in a semicircle around the boxcar's metal door. Sticks lurched forward, but the train jarred him straight. He blinked owlishly, and showed his worn-down teeth in a grin.

"This boxcar's like a leaping tuna—it's got eight flat wheels and should have gone to the shops a hundred years ago," he said.

When the boxcar's jarring rattle lessened, we bundled up with carlining again and Sticks, shivering in a raveled rope sweater with the collar turned up around his face, told me he'd sold blood plasma in Los Angeles.

"My arm's like a dopehead's with needle marks—I was puttin' down twice a week there," he said. "I was blowin'n goin' though—I eat one of those fifty-one-cent meals at Jake's on the Nickel Street skid row every day and I slept warm in that tram dormitory above the Hard Rock Bar at Fifth and Wall every night. That plasma's a good deal—it ain't like the four-dollar blood banks. You can give it twice a week, and they never take the needle out of your arm. They get the plasma and then put your blood back in and give you dextrose besides. It takes about a hour—like a operation. But the last time I went to the Plasma Center they turned me down—not enough iron. It don't matter through—I'll make it better in Texas. Where there's hundreds of stiffs waiting in L.A. souplines there's only dozens in Fort Worth."

Out in the open the wind was blowing harder and the snow was getting heavier. The train was running faster, and the suction scooped up cinders from the roadbed and pelted them against the steel cars. Sticks rolled up his sleeve and showed his biceps. His arm at the elbow was pockmarked with little white dots.

"A nurse give me a bottle of iron tablets," he said. "I taken all those tablets so I'll be ready to sell blood again in Fort Worth. I'll bleach the four-dollar blood blank's finger marks off with Clorox so I won't have to wait six weeks to put down again, then make the Plasma Center too. If I'm still low on iron I'll go to Scotty's Blood Bank—they just take your temperature and a sample and don't ask no questions there. Me'n you'll fill up with Oklahoma-style black eyes when I get my passover money. You can make it in Fort Worth, buddy—you're on both feet."

He passed me a tobacco sack and one of the brown paper bags that hoboes roll cigarettes with when they run out of the regular book tissues. After that he rolled a cigarette himself, packing the tobacco carefully so no grain would fall and then guiding his lips along the edge of the bag of paper with his forefinger.

"I been on the rail all my life—I got to hear that train rolling and the wheels clicking," he said. "Hardships ain't broke me of the habit—I was born with a goin' spell and I got rambling in my blood. When I make up my mind to go with my back roll and skillet I'll ride any kind of a load. I got it from my daddy—he was a horse trader in Antlers, Oklahoma, and went around from place to place. Once I tried to get off the tracks and I worked at the pay desk in a big walk-up flophouse that had 300 wire cages. But I quit because I had to climb a section ladder and pick fruit so I could eat and sleep good—just settin' was killing me. I've gandied and sawmilled and worked on ranches too—that's how I lost my leg last year. A steer kicked me and broke it in two places."

The train's thunder rolled, and a wire fence beside the tracks took up the vibration and hummed with it. A truck passed on the narrow, high-centered highway paralleling the railroad's high embankment and there was the sound of milk bottles clattering in a tin rack. Then the roadbed turned on a banking curve and down the tracks we could see a highway town's hazy lights, clean and beautiful in the snow. The strung colored lights of this town's main street illuminated an empty, quiet thoroughfare. The stores were closed; the depot dark. On the courthouse lawn a big lighted Christmas tree glowed greens and reds and yellows. The sign at the edge of the sleeping town read: Fort Worth . . . 310 miles. Sticks compressed his lips and closed his eyes.

"After I lost my leg I tried peddling needles I bought for seven cents a box from wholesalers in San Francisco," he said. "But the Bay Area's hilly and you got to walk up eight or ten steps to a house. I got used to dogs barking and grabbing me by the britches-leg. But all that climbing with the sticks made my thigh gall me so, and my shoulders, knee, and ankle ache and hurt so much I had to give it up. After that I was hittin' it pretty rough. I was hungry and couldn't find a sleeping place so I had to carry the stick. One night I stopped to get warm in a bowling alley near Sacramento's two street skid row. But they could tell I was on the dog because I was raggedy and smelled of smoke so they run me out. After that I taken to selling my blood."

Monahans was a snow-blurred sprinkle of lights pushing toward us like a mammoth postcard. Just west of the town near an old abandoned wildcat well, the freight train took the siding to let a westbound manifest pass and we stood in the boxcar's wide doorway looking out at the mesquite-clumped prairie. The mesquite trees were thick and made a fence for a clearing on which an old derrick rose. Its timbers were gray as an old mop; away from it a little piece lay a huge wooden bullwheel with rusty bolts.

Somewhere dogs were baying. It was a vibrant, sonorous sound like the musical notes of a deep reed instrument. Wind gushed in the trees with the sound of a distant river and the tops of the cottonwoods, silhouetted against the sky, whipped and threshed like tiny Christmas trees in a storm. The rails began to murmur and after a while a locomotive's light showed, tiny as a lightning bug. It began to swell and earth trembled as if the railroad cut's sides were going to cave in and carry us under the train. Then the manifest's pounding wheels thundered and crashed and, after a long time, the red marker lights of the caboose passed. Sticks pinched off the burning end of his cigarette and, breaking the paper, poured the tobacco into a sack.

"I'm pretty well beat down, buddy, and I ought to get down on my knees for some help," he said. "But I'd rather be on my own and not on the mercy of missions. A stiff finds a little companionship running up and down the railroad tracks. On every train there's a new buddy to pal up with, and in every jungle there's a boabout going your way. I made it better during the depression though. The older you get the tougher it gets—people start calling you Pop."

The locomotive wheels spun slowly, pulling hard, and we could hear the coupling pins knocking against each other and connecting. Then the boxcars moved and the slack ran out of the drawheads. The freight train was going east again. The brown grass along the fence lines bent flat in the wind, and snow sprayed through the boxcar's latticed sides. Sticks shuddered and clenched his teeth. Beneath the white skin of his neck, the muscles were limp and trembling.

"The road gets in a man's blood, but there are times when he wants shelter and a roof over his head," he said. "I'd like to get me a little old tin and tarpaper shack near the railroad yards and just squat for a while. A hobo, when he ain't traveling, just likes to sit and watch yard engines work boxcars around."

He dropped his head to his chest and then came up straight with a shudder, jerking his closed eyes open.

"Soon's it gets warm I'll freight up to Sioux City. They pay twenty dollars a pint for O-Positive blood there," he said.

The locomotive whistle whined back through the snow.

# 16

# The Deer

My father woke me up at five o'clock the next morning, brushing my upper lip with a straw he had yanked from a broom. It was the gentlest "waker-upper" he could devise—one swipe and you were awake. He even gave it a name, as if it were one of those contraptions in a Dr. Seuss book—the sleeper tickler.

The sleeper tickler may have been foolproof, but it was not quick acting—at least not with me. One swipe and you were awake, but there is a vast difference between consciousness and coherence, open eyes not necessarily translating into open—and receptive—brain cells. So there I was, languishing between two landscapes, consciousness and coherence, my eyes awake, my brain snoozing. My father had a simple solution—another swipe with his Seussian device.

"Are you ready?"

"Yes," I said, rubbing my eyes to finish the work the sleeper tickler had started.

Shuffling down the hallway, I poked my head into their room, and my mother turned to her side, snoring softly. Was she smiling? In her sleep? She was, and as she snored, her lips looked like a pot of boiling *champurrado*, a thick chocolate drink, the part that gets sucked into the rest of the glop, plunging—then resurfacing—to expel a whoosh of steam. *Pppuuuhhh.* A little geyser. That was my mother, a profane geyser by day, a gentle geyser by night. It was such a tender sound, so calm and tranquil, that I wondered why my father always complained about it; when an insomniac finally falls asleep, I reasoned, every little noise must disrupt his sleep patterns.

As I stood in the doorway, contemplating his fragile REMS, I felt a gentle push from behind. It was the old man, directing me to the bathroom, where I washed my face and brushed my teeth. Time to go.

We hopped into the Rambler, the box on wheels, and as I rolled down the window, I stuck my head out, savoring the cool morning air on my skin. *Aaahhh.* I looked up, and the clouds were blowing so fast that the moon seemed to be racing across the sky. It was amazing—a giant lozenge propelled by a furious wind. Then I realized it was the clouds, not the moon, sailing into the dawn. It was disorienting, and wonderful.

When we passed the city limits, the clouds disappeared. The sky was pristine, as clear as a saint's conscience, and the moon stopped streaking across the atmosphere. I marveled at the stars, and when I redirected my gaze to the world in front of me, I saw another cluster of stars—the streetlights that dotted the landscape like a network of heavenly bodies. What a beautiful world, I thought. What a cool, beautiful world. This was why morning people were morning people.

"Thanks, Dad."

Holding the steering wheel with one hand, he tousled my hair with the other.

"You're welcome."

After an hour on the road, the terrain started to change, hot land giving way to green hills. The road, flat and dry for miles, climbed and narrowed, winding along tree-lined paths that seemed to darken despite the approaching dawn. Then it hit me. We were heading into the sky, the poor Rambler transformed into a rocket ship—the most unlikely vehicle you could imagine for such a journey.

I stared straight up, my head jolted back by fear and gravity, the same phenomenon I experienced on roller coasters. Except this was no roller coaster ride; this was real. The Rambler labored up the slope, its engine grinding and churning, but the higher we climbed, the more elusive our destination became. What was our destination? Could this be a mountain without a summit?

As the car headed into the horizon, I glanced out the window. A locomotive was rumbling through a deep gorge, so far below that it looked like a model train. *Ay Dios mio.* I closed my eyes, hoping my fear would disappear, but the fear remained, so I opened my eyes, and I stared straight ahead, focused on the vast, cold space in front of me.

The sky offered little perspective, providing no landmarks, no milestones, with which to measure our journey—just a vast and quiet nothingness. And the more nothingness we traversed, the more nothingness lay ahead—or so it seemed. We advanced; the sky receded. We advanced some more; the sky receded some more. The Rambler was on an asphalt treadmill, a bizarre contraption tilted toward the sky. If there were a bottomless ocean, I wondered, could there be a topless mountain—a mountain so high that it ripped a hole in the sky, allowing us to gape into forever? I turned to the old man.

"Are we leaving the earth?" I asked.

Pondering the question, the old man shifted in his seat to avoid the coiled springs under his butt.

"No, we're just visiting another layer of it," he said.

"Another layer?" I responded, puzzled.

"Well, the earth is made of layers," he said. "Valleys, seas, flatlands and mountains. We're heading into the mountains."

"El Paso has mountains," I said. "But it's not like this."

"That's because El Paso, all of El Paso, is high up, so you were used to the altitude," my father answered. "You became accustomed to it. This is different because you're used to the flatlands of Bakersfield, and now you're in the mountains, and it's a new, refreshing landscape for you."

"Hmmm," I said.

"Hmmm?" my father asked.

"Hmmm," I answered.

We might have kept *hmmming* forever, but the slope finally flattened, and the vista was beautiful—giant pines shrouded in thick clouds, their leafy branches saluting the overcast sky. The old man parked along an asphalt strip near a picnic bench. We got out, and I took a deep breath. The mist hung low to the ground, as if the Earth were breathing—soft, steady whiffs that brushed my cheeks.

The air was cool and brisk, more cloud than air, but it felt hard and brittle—so hard and brittle that I thought I could ping it with my forefinger. So I did; I flicked my finger into the atmosphere, but I struck nothing . . . nothing but air. And then, as I took a few steps toward a cove of trees, I remembered the deer.

"Dad," I shouted.

He turned around.

"Do you remember the deers?"

"I sure do."

It was in Ruidoso, New Mexico, a mountain community about 120 miles from El Paso. Alita went with us. We headed out early, just the three of us, before the pink clouds started to smudge the eastern sky. Alita sat in the back, a black shawl draped across her shoulders, quietly reciting the rosary in her lap. As the miles multiplied, so did the Hail Marys and Our Fathers.

Alita hated automobiles, an aversion that developed in 1923, when gangsters gunned down Pancho Villa in Parral, Chihuahua. The bandit—uhm, revolutionary—was riding in his car, a Dodge Sedan. If he had been on his horse, she would have hated horses.

If you pressed my grandmother, she would admit that she preferred Emiliano Zapata to Pancho Villa, who had more wives than he had bullets in his bandolier. Villa was a thug, Alita would say grudgingly. Ah, but Zapata . . . Zapata was noble, a man whose integrity was reflected in his famous statement: "*Es mejor morir de pie que vivir de rodillas.* It is better to die on your feet than live on your knees."

Still, Alita would say, Villa was a Mexican icon, and as such she owed him her respect, if not her devotion. And thug or no thug, the man died in a car. There was no argument over that.

Cheche—Alita could not pronounce Chester—tried to ease her anxiety, telling her it was not a random act, the sign of a capricious fate, which struck Villa; it was a group of assassins, and he just happened to be in a car when they struck. Alita scoffed at this logic. God targeted Villa, she responded, and the instrument of doom was a vehicle.

Villa or no Villa, car or no car, she agreed to accompany us on our trip to Ruidoso, eager to escape the hot, oppressive air of summer in El Paso. If only for one day. Focused on her beads, she never gazed out the window, never commented on the scenery, not even when we passed the glistening terrain of White Sands, New Mexico. She just kept praying, her eyes shut so tight that her forehead trembled.

"*Ya llegamos?* Are we there yet?" Alita asked, sensing that we had arrived.

As we waited at a red light near a coffee shop in Ruidoso, we saw a set of antlers gliding through the early morning air. Then we saw another . . . and another . . . and another—four in all, each set of antlers suspended in the misty atmosphere. And then the entire forms took shape, slowly and elegantly, like photographs in a tray of chemicals, the antlers melding into heads, the heads into bodies, the bodies into legs. Four beautiful deer.

Munching on the grass along the road, they cocked their heads in our direction, so still and quiet that they looked like cardboard cutouts. The light turned green, but the Rambler stayed put, and a driver behind us, apparently anxious to hit the campsites, blasted his horn.

"*Ya hombre!* Enough!" Alita yelled, putting her rosary in a small coin purse. "Cabrón."

She emphasized the *ca*, as if the accent fell on the first syllable. "*CA-brón!*"

Spooked by the horn blasts, the deer scattered into the woods, all four of them, bounding so gracefully that they seemed frozen in mid-leap—four statuettes mounted on pedestals of air.

"*Mira no mas.* Look at that," Alita said.

And now, a year later, we were in California, hundreds of miles from the gliding antlers.

"Dad?"

"Yes."

"I miss El Paso."

"I know you do."

We listened to the silence.

"I miss Alita," I said.

"I know. She misses you, too."

He looked at the trees around us.

"Do you miss your friends?"

"I do," I said.

And I did. I missed the sword fights and granada fights, the battles that began in neighborhood alleys and ended in neighborhood lore. We remembered everything, embellished everything, and no matter how grand the reality, the fiction was always better, enhanced by time and imagination. Pito Peterson? He was an ogre, fat, wild, and demented, and he chased me for miles, the granada juice sliding down his face like sweat. And Alita? She scared him off with a broom, spraying him with cuss words that would have made El Rayo Jalisco, the legendary *luchador* (wrestler), blush.

Ah, but up there, on that mountain in California, I had no need for fiction. I cut through the artifice, the baroque ornaments of childish fantasy, and I faced the reality—the sweet, lovely reality, pure and unvarnished. *Chavalos pendejos.* Stupid kids. Why did we feel compelled to reconstruct, to mythologize? Why? Maybe we mythologized the experiences that were worth mythologizing. Maybe the myth brought us closer to the moment, the reality from which the fiction blossomed. Peterson was not an ogre. But he was a cabrón. Is there any difference, really?

I could not articulate these thoughts, but I felt them. I know I did. I felt them, up there, on that mountain, among the trees and clouds and memories. And, as I stood in the mist, I thought about El Paso, poor, dusty, sun-baked El Paso, a town so old that every step forward seemed like a step backward—backward in time. I loved it.

I loved all of it, the alleys and mountains, the dawns and sunsets, the angels and cabrónes; I even loved Pito Peterson, the old, blustery ogre, because he reminded me of my hometown, my beloved hometown. After all, I told myself, the old man had Cleveland, but I had El Paso.

"Yes, Dad, I miss my friends," I repeated.

"You can make new friends in Bakersfield," he said.

I frowned.

"You can."

Whenever I made friends, they were shadow friends, intimidated by Randy Reed, the bully of St. Francis. They were sneaky and furtive, scattering whenever he approached, as if talking to a "chili" were tantamount to being a "chili." I was contagious.

"I know, Dad."

"Your lip looks better."

"It feels better."

"That must have been a nasty tumble from the monkey bar."

"Dad?"

"Yes."

"I didn't fall from the monkey bar."

"I know."

I smiled. Guilt-ridden kids (are there any other kind?) know the feeling. No matter what their transgression, no matter how grave or venial, the world is their confessional, a place where they joust with their darkest secrets, afraid to reveal them, afraid not to. . . . But the old man saw through me, just as he had seen through Mrs. Chaney during open house. He peered into my soul, peered into it before I could reveal its contents, and he saw a boy who made up a story because of guilt and shame. He spared me the agony—and humiliation—of confessing. And so I smiled.

"He's going to do it again, you know."

"I know."

"But, next time, you won't be shocked by his actions," he said. "Next time, you'll know what he's capable of. "

The old man stopped, leaving the rest of his message unstated.

But I knew what was on his mind, if not on his lips. Randy Reed could not shock me, not anymore. I had seen the worst of Randy Reed, and now that I knew what he was capable of, I would have to find out what I was capable of. God help me if I responded in a manner that caused me further shame.

"Thanks, Dad."

On our way back home, after hiking through the mountains and eating the *frijole* and *picadillo* burritos my mother had made for us the night before, we stopped at a coffee shop in Tehachepe. We sat at the Formica counter. The old man ordered us two hot chocolates.

The waitress thanked the old man and ducked into the kitchen. She was wearing a green dress and a white apron. The apron was full of coffee stains that looked like the countries on a map—brown blotches with white borders between them. She was young, in her twenties, with black hair and hazel eyes. I thought of that poor waitress in Cleveland, the one my father had victimized.

When the black-haired, hazel-eyed waitress returned, she slid the hot chocolates onto the counter, and she served me a chocolate chip cookie on a big white plate.

"You want a cookie, honey?" she asked me.

"How much are they?" my father asked her.

"You've got a cute boy there. This one's on me. The next one will cost you."

"Thank you," the old man said.

It was paradoxical—a word and concept I could not even define—but there were times when it was the happy moments that triggered memories of the "dark turn" in the story about how my father met my mother. This was one of those times. It was comforting to think about the dark turn when I was happy. It made me feel that, no matter how ominous that gap in the story seemed, there could be something to counteract it, something sublime, like this moment with my dad at a diner in the mountains. I smiled, dipping my cookie into the hot chocolate. The old man smiled, too.

"You know when a boy becomes old?" my father asked me.

"No."

"When he stops dunking his cookies into his milk. . . . Never stop dunking, okay?"

I shrugged.

"Hey, Dad!" I yelled, pretending to gag. "The waitress spit in my hot chocolate."

I smiled, trying to soften the reference to the cruel waitress trick, but the old man frowned.

17

# The Night of the Cicadas

Did the sun set in Bakersfield?

It must have. It must have descended every evening, slowly and gradually, until the sunlight crawled into that black hole we call night. But, try as hard as I can to retrieve that image from my memory bank, the vision eludes me. There is no sun plunging into the West, no lightshow flashing across the mountains. Nothing. Just a dark, empty sky.

Bakersfield had mountains, just as El Paso did—the Kern Mountains. They ringed the town, north and south, east and west. But they were smaller, more distant than the Franklin Mountains in El Paso—so distant that they seemed ephemeral, as if their jagged peaks were cloud formations. They were not a dramatic presence in the town, not for me, anyway. I was used to real mountains, mountains that seemed as near as your own front yard. The Kern Mountains were *chafa*, border slang for "trashy." You did not notice them unless you were looking toward a distant horizon, and, even then, they looked like part of a gray, murky background.

In El Paso, I would sit on the porch steps to savor the mountains and the sunsets. In Bakersfield, I sat on the porch steps to wait. Sometimes, I waited for the mailman; sometimes, I waited for the old man. My dad would park his powder-blue Rambler in the alley between the rental home and the gas station, and some evenings, when I was not preoccupied with the Beatles or the Rolling Stones on the radio,

I would sit on the steps, waiting for the old man to return from work.

One Monday evening, the old man arrived later than usual, tired from a long day at the office. He trudged up the porch steps, smacking his thigh with a rolled-up newspaper, but when he saw me, the fatigue evaporated from his eyes. The old man smiled, extending his left hand to lift me from my perch.

"Shhh," he said, pausing at the top step as I held onto his hand, spinning like a wind chime in a cool breeze. "Listen."

There was a gentle hum, a symphony of cicadas in the scrawny bushes that lined the front of the rental home.

"Listen. . . . Nice, isn't it?"

"Yes," I said, although, deep down, I thought the drone was dreary, monotonous.

We stood on the front porch, enjoying the evening, with or without the glory of a sunset. The old man smiled again. We inhaled a long stream of fresh air, let it creep into our nostrils, circulate in our brains, our imaginations. *Aaahhh.* The old man was right. It was nice. The cicadas, the air, the evening—everything was nice.

"How was school today?"

There was that question again.

"How was it?" he repeated when I failed to answer immediately.

Every evening—every evening he was in town—the old man asked me "how it went" at school. And, every evening, the question rankled. The old man wanted details—lunch, recess, what I read in English class—but I knew what he was really asking. He wanted to know about Randy Reed.

The question was touched with love, warmth, and concern—emotions I needed, even wanted. But the fact that I needed them, and wanted them, tormented me. The question forced me to confront an issue I did not want to confront. I was a lost cause. That was it—a lost cause, so inept and forlorn that only a saint could help me. True Catholics would understand.

"How was it?"

I looked at the old man. I smiled at him. He smiled back at me.

How was it? I asked myself the question he asked me. How was it? The question did not embitter me, not tonight. Not the way it usually did. You know what? I wanted to tell the old man. It was great. It was amazing. And I want to tell you about it.

And so I did. I told him all about it. It was just another day at St. Francis Elementary School in Bakersfield, California. We filed into class, and Mrs. Chaney barked out her orders, and we responded like the little toy soldiers we were.

It was Show and Tell that day. But Show and Tell with Mrs. Chaney was unlike Show and Tell with any teacher I had ever known. It was her show, her tell. Mrs. Chaney was the star, and her students were the audience.

Like the cicadas in the bushes, she droned on and on, something about a weekend trip she had made—a trip to Washington or Oregon or Northern California. One of those places. And she found a metal on this trip—or a fake metal, I am not sure which. And she called someone a fool, someone she had met on the trip, I think.

It was all a blur—the trip, the metal, the fool. Mrs. Chaney stood in front of the class, and I could see her jaws flapping with a dreadful urgency, but for all the drama, all the theatrics, all the rhetorical fireworks she was trying to ignite, I heard nothing. Nothing. Not a sound issued from that cavern of a mouth. Not a peep. Not for me, anyway. I was too distracted.

While the other children focused on Mrs. Chaney, I studied Rachel Olsen with the single-minded intensity of a scientist peering through a microscope. She sat in the next row, to my right, unaware of my attention. It was a bright, sunny day, and the blinds were pulled halfway down, allowing a few rays to seep through. The sunshine spotlighted Rachel Olsen, making her eyes sparkle like stained-glass windows. *Aaaahhh*. This was my show and tell, but it was all show, for Rachel Olsen rendered any verbal accompaniment superfluous, irrelevant. There were no words worthy of her glowing loveliness. She was just Rachel. Lovely Rachel.

I followed the arc of light, from the window to the girl, an arc that could have descended on any student, any object, but it picked Rachel. It was as if the sun knew what I knew—that a girl this beautiful deserved to be touched by something equally radiant . . . and magnificent. Dizzy but content—coherent despite my disorientation—I swirled in a vortex of mad, innocent love. My admiration set me apart from the other boys in class, for only I appreciated her beauty, her intelligence, her gentleness. *Idiotas*. All of them were idiots. They did not appreciate her, did not value what I valued. Whatever made her special made me special, too. It was magical. And, then, the magic vanished, undermined by the cruelest juxtaposition of all—the one you never expect.

Lost in my admiration for Rachel and her suitor, the sun, I turned around, and there he was—Randy Reed, his maniacal grin spreading across his horsey face. I jumped in my seat, startled by the transition from radiant beauty to brutish stupidity. He dropped a stone on my desk, an ugly stone splotched with black and yellow markings. Why did he place this piece of *mierda* on my desk? Was he taunting me?

I took the rock, cradled it in my palm. Then I smiled at Randy Reed. And, as my smile grew, so did my defiance. I fondled the stone one last time, slowly and lovingly, and then I flipped it behind my back, grinning as I heard it rattle against the radiator.

"Robert!"

It was Rachel, and she looked sick with fear.

"What did you do?" she whispered.

Randy Reed sat there smirking, content to let me stew in my own dread and anxiety. His braces—and the retainer that protruded from them—had vanished weeks before. But whatever those braces were supposed to rectify—his horsey teeth or his malignant smile—they had not improved his appearance. Randy Reed was still Randy Reed, bridle or no bridle.

"That was the fool's gold!" Rachel said.

Fool's gold. So that was what Mrs. Chaney was droning on and on about! Fool's gold. She must have discovered it on her trip to Washington or Oregon or wherever the hell she went. *Chingele*.

Mrs. Chaney lounged at her desk, perusing a copy of *Leaves of*

*Grass* as the students passed the fool's gold from hand to hand. I could hear my heartbeat—thump, thump, thump. It was as if Ringo Starr were in there, trying to pound his way out of my rib cage. I buried my head in my palms. Why me? *Pen-DE-jo.*

"Stupid chili," Randy Reed said, smiling.

Rachel Olsen scurried to the back of the classroom, three desks away, folding her skirt as she dropped to her knees in front of the radiator. Mrs. Chaney looked up from her book, her thick eyebrows arching above her reading glasses. Aware of almost every movement in the classroom, the bug-eyed monster could have spotted a lizard skittering across a field of dry leaves a hundred yards away.

"Rachel, what are you doing back there?"

"I . . . I . . . I . . . I dropped my pencil, Mrs. Chaney."

"Hmmm . . . all right."

Mrs. Chaney returned to her poetry, and Rachel smiled weakly, aware that any other student would have felt the ire of our homeroom teacher. Rachel, emboldened by her narrow escape, continued to search for the fool's gold. I felt guilty for allowing this beautiful girl to execute my rescue, but what could I do? I knew that if I had tried it, Mrs. Chaney would have aborted my mission with a thunderous roar: Robert, get back to your seat! Now!

So I let Rachel—poor, beautiful Rachel—perform the daring operation. She scuttled along the floor, her skirt hiked above her knees to keep it from getting dirty. Rachel peered under the radiator, behind the radiator, careful not to get too close—it was mid-October, and the radiators were turned on, their accordion-shaped ribs emitting a sizzling heat. And as Rachel dragged her knees across the floor, she waved an open hand inches above the tiled surface, back and forth, back and forth, scanning the area as if her palm were a metal detector. I looked from Rachel Olsen to Mrs. Chaney, and back again, hoping the girl would find the rock before Mrs. Chaney set down her copy of *Leaves of Grass.*

Twisting awkwardly, her head tilting to the left, her body to the right, Rachel stretched her arm behind the radiator, stretched it as far as she could. I watched, astounded, as the arm—it was the right arm—disappeared behind the metal contraption. The space between the wall and the radiator was tiny, and I was sure she would burn herself.

Then, after a few seconds in this clumsy position, she flashed a jewel of a smile, her eyes sparkling with the same intensity I had noticed earlier. Rachel hopped to her feet, her right hand balled into a fist. She was holding something, something small but valuable. I knew it. She skipped back to her seat, performing a quick, graceful pirouette as she approached her desk. Then she stopped in mid-twirl, right in front of me, opening her hand for the first time, as if to say *Ta-da*. There it was, the fool's gold I had flung to the back of the room only moments before. I sighed, expelling my breath in a dizzying rush of joy and relief. *Thank you*, I said silently, mouthing the words to Rachel. Then I passed the fool's gold to the student in front of me. Rachel had saved me.

"Damn," Randy Reed said.

"You know what, Dad?" I said, finishing my tale.

"What?"

"Well, when Rachel Olsen found the rock, Randy Reed was, uh, *encabronado*, pissed off," I said, wary of using a cuss word in front of the old man. "He had a sour look on his face."

"Sour?" the old man asked.

"Yeah . . . like he had bitten into a giant lemon."

"Ha!" The old man erupted into laughter.

When I told the old man the story, I left out some key details. Well, one key detail. I omitted the fact that I was in love with Rachel Olsen.

"Do you like her?" the old man asked when his laughter subsided.

"Yes!" I said with too much enthusiasm.

"Do you love her?"

The old man was always asking me questions I did not want to answer.

"It's not a bad thing. After all, she did something nice for you. . . .

Do you?”

The cicadas stopped droning, and the air stopped flowing, softly and sweetly, into my lungs.

“No,” I said

Why was I always lying to the old man?

# 18

# The Saint

From the porch steps of our rental home in Bakersfield, I could see the pith helmet floating in the air, above the shrubs and trees and flowers.

It was three blocks away, maybe four, but I could see it clearly, down to the air holes that looked like tiny eyes. It was a beautiful sight, but it trapped me in an emotional limbo. I wanted the pith helmet to advance, to emerge from the distance until I could see the man wearing it. But the anticipation was delicious, and the longer I waited, the more exquisite it became. Did I want the man to hurry, or did I want him to slow down? Did I want him to arrive, or did I want my suspense to hover on the edge of forever? Jittery with excitement, unable to answer my own questions, I sat on the steps, my toes performing an impromptu tap dance on the cement surface.

"Son, what is that mailman bringing you?" Mr. Cotton asked. "You've been staring at him for the last five minutes. It must be the greatest present in the world."

Mr. Cotton managed the Texaco Station next to our rental home. We lived on a busy street, with businesses interspersed among houses, and the gas station was so close that I could hear the cars rumble up to the pumps from our living room. The old man—my father, not Mr. Cotton—called our street an artery, and I pictured the intersection awash in blood, seeping into every corner of town. No, not that kind of artery, the old man said. Well, whatever an artery was, I was glad we lived on one. The only good thing about our neighborhood, the only thing that made the rental home bearable, was its proximity to the gas station—and to Mr. Cotton.

"Well, Mr. Cotton," I began.

"Please call me Ralph."

"Uh, okay. . . . Well, Mr. Cotton, my mother said that my Alita was sending me something special today."

"Your who?"

"Oh, I'm sorry. . . . My grandmother."

"Your grandmother, huh? Well, she must be a good grandmother if she sent you something that can get you so worked up. What's she sending you?"

"Oh, I'm not sure," I said, embarrassed that I was so excited about a package whose contents I was not even sure of.

"Well, those are the best presents, aren't they? The surprise ones."

"Yes, sir. They are."

"Ralph."

"Yes, sir, Mr. Cotton . . . Ralph."

A red Buick drove up to the pump, and Mr. Cotton waved his red bandana at me.

"See you later, son. Hope you like your present."

The pith helmet kept advancing, and as it got closer, I could see the mailman attached to it. I stood up, and the mailman smiled, withdrawing a small, oblong package from his brown leather sack. I felt the present, still inside the package. It was soft and mushy. I massaged it, squished it. The sense of delicious anticipation intensified. This was the moment. I tore the package open. The gift was mummified—an object wrapped in old newspapers that crackled as I ripped through them. And, then, there it was. A statue of a saint, his hands folded in prayer, his robe bound by a rope at his waist. I ran into the house.

"Mom, look what Alita sent me."

"St. Jude," she said, smiling.

"St. Jude?"

I knew about St. Christopher. Alita placed a statue of St. Christopher on the dashboard whenever she drove with us; it was her way of thwarting the menace that was born with the death of Pancho Villa. And I knew about St. Francis, the saint who loved the animals. The one who greeted all the students and teachers in front of my school. But St. Jude?

"He's the patron saint of lost causes," my mother told me.

"What?"

I dropped the statue, still partially wrapped in newspapers, on the living room floor.

"*Que estas pendejo?* Are you stupid?" my mother cried. "You could have broken it."

"Why am I a lost cause?"

"Ay, mi'jo, you're not a lost cause, but sometimes people go through experiences, through things that seem hopeless," she said. "St. Jude helps them. . . . Does that make sense?"

"No, it doesn't make sense," I yelled. "You told Alita about Randy Reed. You told her he whipped me!"

I ran out of the house, cutting across the gas station next door.

"Son, be careful," Mr. Cotton said, still pumping gas into the red Buick that had driven up to the pumps. "Where are you going?"

I kept running. I sprinted through intersection after intersection, twice dodging the postman I had just seen—once as I fled the rental, once as I headed back. Desperate to get nowhere, I ran so long—and so hard—that by the time I returned to the rental, panting and sweating, my body was drained of all its heat. When I rushed into my room, shivering, I discovered that my mother had placed St. Jude on my dresser, a beacon for lost causes. I turned him around, facing the mirror, away from me. I loved my Alita, but . . . Randy Reed may have kicked my ass, but I was not a lost cause. Was I?

For weeks afterwards, every time I came home from school in the afternoon, I found St. Jude facing forward, and every afternoon, I turned him around, his back toward me. I did not want to face him. I did not want to face what he represented.

This went on and on, this crazy minuet, the statue facing backward in the morning, then forward in the afternoon. It was a stalemate that could have gone on forever. Then, one day, I gave up. My mother turned St. Jude forward, and I left him there, his gaze piercing me with both compassion and approbation.

It was late October, and Barry Goldwater stickers were appearing everywhere, his balding head so luminous that it looked like a light bulb. Bakersfield loved Goldwater. Even Randy Reed, who cracked an awful joke about Goldwater and toilets, loved the Republican presidential candidate.

"What does Lyndon Johnson flush his toilet with?" Randy Reed asked. "Goldwater. Ha!"

Johnson was the president of the United States, and he was running for reelection on a campaign promise to end the Vietnam War, which had started under the previous president, John F. Kennedy.

"If he'll stop the war, he has my vote," the old man said simply.

Every time I saw a Johnson or Goldwater sticker, I thought about that night the year before, that horrible night in 1963, when I developed a hatred for a contraption that once captivated me—our television set. It was the year before we moved to Bakersfield. Alita was outside, kneading her rosary beads on the front porch. The rest of us were in the living room, my mother and father on the couch, their nine-year-old son tucked between them on the floor, his back resting against the seat cushions. Their nine-year-old son? That would have been me, of course, but I did not feel like myself. I did not feel like Beto, the nine-year-old son of Chester and Amada Seltzer. I felt confused and detached, an intruder in my own home.

The TV did not bring us images that night. It brought us the real world, the tears and heartaches that are often reduced to images. The television screen became a portal, and it opened wide, and the violence spilled into our living room, raw and naked. President John F. Kennedy was dead, cut down by a gunman—gunmen?—in Dallas

The newscast showed old footage of the president—signing bills, shaking hands, playing touch football on a beach in a town called Hyannis Port. The images were strange, surreal, as if every object—every person, every vehicle, every shadow—were gliding across the screen, slowly but gracefully. Or was it my family, stuck in a languorous state of denial, which was operating in slow motion?

"In Dallas, Texas, three shots were fired at President Kennedy's motorcade in downtown Dallas," CBS anchorman Walter Cronkite told the nation earlier that day. "The first reports say that President Kennedy has been seriously wounded by this shooting."

But no, he was not wounded. He was dead, his wife transformed into a widow within seconds. The gunshots sounded harmless, as benign as the pop-pop-pops in a popcorn machine. But those shots killed a president and shattered a nation, and there we were, in the living room, stunned by what we saw on the television screen.

"But I thought he was dead," I told my parents, focusing on the footage of the president when he was young and vibrant and alive.

My mother looked down at me, a strange smile forming on a face convulsed in grief.

"Ay, Bobby . . . " she said, crying, unable to finish the sentence as a heartbroken smile froze on her features.

In El Paso, the people did not just love Kennedy; they adopted Kennedy. Alita called him El Kenny—a sweet, if fractured, sign of affection. And from barrio to barrio, residents would hang prints of two icons on their walls—Pope John and President Kennedy. One neighborhood family placed a print of the president above the stove, and whenever the mom cooked *fideo*, noodles, the steam would bathe him in a heavenly glow, as if El Kenny were drifting among the clouds.

The president visited El Paso in 1962, and my parents took me to see him. My father swung me onto his shoulders, and I grabbed his shirt, turning his collar into a pommel as I scanned the crowd for a sign of the great man. When he finally appeared, stepping up to a podium at the downtown *plazita*, a banner unfurled from the façade of a department store, named after the home where our chief executives reside: "The President of the White House welcomes the President of the White House." The crowd—there were thousands of us—erupted into a celebration worthy of ten Cinco de Mayo festivals.

I tightened the grip on my makeshift pommel, afraid that the thunderous roar would knock me off my perch.

"You'll remember this moment for the rest of your life," my father, who usually hated crowds, told me afterwards.

A year later, the president was dead, and we were sitting in the living room, our eyes glued to tragedy. Alita remained on the front porch, reciting the rosary. My mother wailed, *"Por qué, por qué, por qué lo mataron?* Why, why, why did they kill him?" My father sat there passively, arms folded across his chest, inhaling and exhaling, inhaling and exhaling, as if trying to expel a dark burden in his soul.

"He started that war, but I'm sure he would have gotten us out," he said quietly, looking down at me. "He was a good man. We have to start praying for our country, Beto."

Now here we were, in Bakersfield. 1964. A year after the assassination. With the campaign between Johnson and Goldwater heating up, I thought about what the old man had told me that night in El Paso. Was our country a lost cause? Is that what my father meant when he told me to start praying? Did our nation need help? Did it need St. Jude? I felt ashamed of my reaction to the present Alita sent me.

The statue reminded me of what happened in 1963. But it was not the incident that I remembered. It was the trauma, the trauma that afflicted an entire family, an entire nation. The pain was distant but immediate, sharp but haunting, and it would not let me go.

Whenever I thought about the assassination, I forgot about Randy Reed. But the pain I escaped was not worth the pain I remembered my parents and my grandmother enduring. And the more I thought about the murder—and what it did to our country—the more shame I felt over what I had done to the statue. Then one night, unable to bear the guilt any longer, I accepted the saint on my dresser. My mother had turned him around weeks before, but he was not facing me anymore. I was facing him. I was facing the dark turn my story had taken.

"Thank you, Alita," I whispered as I finished my prayers in bed.

19

# The Holidays

Christmas was approaching.

I yearned for a present I was unlikely to receive: the disappearance—from my world, if not the world—of Randy Reed. But how do you gift wrap an impossible dream? How do you stick it underneath the Christmas tree?

During the winter, Mrs. Chaney wore a navy-blue beret. It made her look like a French officer—stern, deliberate, and unforgiving. I knew all about French officers from a movie I saw on TV with the old man—*Paths of Glory*, starring Kirk Douglas. I sat through the whole thing, even though there were only a few battle scenes, because the old man liked it so much. It was based on an antiwar novel by Humphrey Cobb, but I would not discover that until years later. That must have been why the old man let me watch a movie with violence in it—the antiwar theme.

Mrs. Chaney jammed the beret onto her head, and it made her hair, fanning out on both sides of her massive skull, look like the wings of a giant, prehistoric bird. I snickered one morning, and she glared at me. She asked me if somebody had said something amusing, and I said "no," and she told me to save my laughter for the next Mark Twain or Ambrose Bierce reading in class. I said, "Yes, ma'am."

One morning, about a week before the Christmas holidays, Mrs. Chaney strolled up and down the rows of desks, handing a square of paper to each kid—pieces of index cards she had clipped with the scissors on her desk. She told us to write our names on the squares. Then she walked up and down the rows again, telling us to drop our cards into her beret. She did all this without one word of explanation. Then, getting more exercise than she had all year, she retraced her steps, up one row and down another. And, as she passed by this time, she told each kid to draw a card from the beret.

"Okay, children," she told us, returning to the head of the class with her empty beret. "Look at the name on the card in your hand."

Mine was Ellen Simpson.

"You will be responsible for getting that classmate a Christmas present," she said. "And make it no more than one dollar. Is that understood?"

"Yes, Mrs. Chaney," we answered in unison.

If I had drawn the Rachel Olsen card, I would have asked the old man to get her something grand, something like the car Buzz and Todd drove in *Route 66*. The cool Corvette. But I picked Ellen Simpson, a freckled, red-haired girl who was almost as shy as I was. I bought her Silly Putty, that weird, gum-like substance that came in a plastic egg.

We deposited the presents under the artificial Christmas tree in a corner of the classroom, and on Monday, the last day before the holidays, Mrs. Chaney passed them out. She was wearing a Santa cap, a colorful, pointy version of her beret, which she jammed onto her huge head. I resisted the temptation to snicker.

"All right, children, you may open your presents!"

The students obliged with a flurry of activity, displaying an energy we could never maintain during class assignments. My present was from Randy Reed. Why did he have to draw my name? And what could he have bought me? It was shaped like a can. I shook it, but the movement provided no clue. Maybe it was a can of Play-Doh, the clay you could form into all kinds of strange figures. There was a small card attached—"Merry Christmas, Randy." It seemed benign, but . . . I opened it, and I shrank into my seat. It was a can of refried beans.

The rental home—I thought of it as the home, not our home—

remained as stark and bland as ever, with no decorations to reflect the joy of the season. Not even a tree. When it came to the yuletide, the old man was a minimalist. And my mom, well, she never embraced Bakersfield, so why should she embrace Christmas in Bakersfield?

Beyond the rental home, life was different. Christmas was different. The streets were magical, with strands of golden light streaming across the downtown intersections. Telephone poles, stop signs, street lights—everything was wrapped in red and white paper, each strip arranged diagonally, to resemble a candy cane. Crews of industrious elves—were there any other kind?—toiled in window displays, beckoning the kids, and their parents, to shop in the department stores. Yes, they were mechanical, but to some kids, fake elves were more magical than the real thing.

Christmas was in the air, an atmosphere so pure and translucent that nobody could spoil it. Not even Randy Reed. I forgot about the gift he gave me and the other gift, the impossible gift, that I had secretly coveted—the disappearance of Randy Reed.

One day, my mother took me to Brock's Department Store, a squat, rust-colored building at 20th Street and Chester Avenue (I was sure they named the street after the old man). This was an "outing," so she abandoned her house dress in favor of a navy-blue suit—skirt, jacket, and white collar so long and floppy that it made her look like a sailor. We took the bus. I could have ridden my bike and arrived there faster, but my mother was a bus person. She never learned how to drive, never even wanted to learn, so she relied on the bus or the old man, and the old man was on one of his freight-train trips that week.

When we arrived at the store, my mother headed to the cosmetics section, leaving me in front of the department store Santa. He sat on a red throne, fat and sluggish, exhausted from the only physical activity he seemed likely to undertake—smiling at the needy children on his lap. I looked at him, frowning. Dozens of kids lined up to sit on his ample lap, but I already knew what I wanted, and it had nothing to do with Randy Reed, not really. I wanted Christmas in El Paso, Christmas with my beloved Alita. So I just stood there, loitering, until my mother returned with her perfume.

"Did you talk to Santa?" she asked.

"Yes," I lied.

The old man returned from his freight train trip the next day, tired and dirty and happy. He was not in the Christmas spirit—not really. Never one to revel in the materialism of the season, the old man said he already received what he wanted: a Lyndon B. Johnson victory in the presidential election on November 3. We had waited for the returns that night, and I will never forget Howard K. Smith, the ABC anchorman, describing the triumph as a "landslide." I pictured Johnson, the gruff old Texan, riding a chunk of dirt as it broke off one of the hills in Los Angeles. *Ay, cabrón.*

"Not that kind of landslide," my father said, smiling.

If the old man got what he wanted, I would soon get what I wanted, wanted more than anything—a trip back to El Paso. My mother and I were going to spend Christmas in my hometown, and when she told me about her plans, I looked at her, too excited to express my emotions outwardly. The good feelings bubbled inside, content to stay where they were—in my heart and soul.

"Be sure to give Alita my love," the old man told me the day before my mother and I headed to El Paso. "And when you hug her, hug her so tight that her warmth and spirit enter your body."

He smiled.

"I will," I said. "I will."

The old man would remain in Bakersfield during the holidays, two weeks of self-imposed isolation that he did not mind. It would give him a chance to work on his short stories, free of the interruptions that family life usually hurled at him—vacuum cleaners, clanging pots, profane spouses. He needed a break. But what was a mere recess for him was a reprieve for me—a chance to exchange misery for joy, however temporarily. The old man could have his hobos; I had my friends and my Alita.

We left on Wednesday morning, two days before Christmas. The old man parked the Rambler in the alley next to our rental home, across from the Texaco Station where the workers fixed the flats on my bike for fifty cents. It was about 6:30 a.m. when we hopped into the car. The old man always liked to leave early, as if trying to beat a deadline imposed by a higher force—an editor in the sky. I did not mind; the sooner we jumped into the car, I thought, the sooner we would get to El Paso.

The old man was driving us to Los Angeles, where he would drop us off at the train depot. I sat in the back. It was a quiet morning, solemn and decorous, and as we pulled out of the alley, all the shops seemed artificial, as if they were tiny models in a toy exhibit. Darkness seems to shrink everything, I thought. Everything except your imagination. My mother handed me a thermos of hot chocolate, and, as we hit Interstate 5, I thought about El Paso, about my friends and my grandmother. I asked the old man when we would get there.

"In about two hours," he said.

"Two hours?" I said, smiling. "We'll be in El Paso in two hours?"

"No," he said, laughing. "We'll be in LA in two hours."

Still groggy from lack of sleep—I had tossed and turned all night, anticipating the trip to El Paso—I stared out the window, my head pressed so close to the glass that I could see my reflection in the darkness. My eyes were agate marbles, and my nose was a cretaceous landscape, with pores as deep as craters. The reflection gave me a headache.

"When are we going to get there?" I asked the old man.

"Didn't you just ask that?"

As we drove along the freeway, the road stretched into forever, a long gash illuminated by tiny automobile lights. The old man drove so slowly that the Rambler looked like an elephant in a caravan of circus animals. We would never get there, regardless of whether *there* was Los Angeles or El Paso.

"Why is Los Angeles so far away?" I asked the old man.

"Well," the old man answered, "if Los Angeles were closer to Bakersfield, then it would be that much farther from El Paso. Which would you prefer? Closer to Bakersfield? Or farther from El Paso?"

"Huh?" I answered.

The old man laughed, and as his laughter faded, I could see the green highway sign—LOS ANGELES.

"Dad, is that it?" I asked. "Are we almost there?"

"Yup."

We arrived at Union Station about 10:00 a.m., slowed down by the inevitable rush hour traffic in Los Angeles. It was a crisp, sunny morning. The depot looked like a mission, with high, arching doorways that opened into a cavernous waiting room. People scurried in and out, many of them with their children in tow, lugging trunks and packages. Were the boxes filled with Christmas presents? I wondered. I did not have time to answer my own question. I ran to the bathroom, my bladder brimming with all that hot chocolate. There was a sign above the toilet in the stall:

WINOS, DON'T LEAVE YOUR BOTTLES IN HERE.

When I pulled down my zipper, I noticed three empty bottles on the floor, behind the toilet. The acrid odor was almost unbearable, as if the bottles had been full of urine, not wine. I remembered what my grandmother used to say about my friends, that they smelled like *baños publicos.* She was wrong; my friends smelled like peach blossoms compared to the restroom at Union Station. *Hijole.*

"What took you so long?" the old man asked.

"I really had to go," I said sheepishly.

I peered through the window, once again turning the glass into a microscope aimed back at me, but this time the window was on the train. I stared at my face, and my face stared at me, my features enlarged by my proximity to the glass. It was 2:30 p.m., almost four hours after we arrived at Union Station, and the train was pulling out of the depot. It was a pleasant day, cool and fresh, but the sun was blinding, creating long flashes of light that radiated like the points on a crown. The sky was on fire. As I looked up, leaning forward with my forearms resting on the window rail, I felt another headache coming on, so I plopped back onto my seat.

"Ay, Bobby, will you relax?" my mother said, putting down the *Good Housekeeping* magazine she was reading. "Don't make this trip any longer than it has to be."

"All right," I said.

A husky man, dressed in white, pushed a cart down the aisle. He was playing a weird instrument as he strolled down the narrow corridor between the seats. It was a xylophone, my mother told me, and it complemented his lyrical voice.

"Lunch," he called out. "Hamburgers, sandwiches, hamburgers . . ."

He was dark, darker than me. I had not seen many people like him, whether in Bakersfield or El Paso, but I remembered a story the old man had told me about Bill Willis and Marion Motley, the great Cleveland Browns players who broke the "color line" in the National Football League. I kept staring at the husky man in the white suit. He smiled at me.

"I'm hungry," I told my mother.

"*Ay Dios mio*," she said, handing me a bean burrito wrapped in tin foil. "*Toma!* Here!"

She smiled and tousled my hair.

The train rumbled into the night. We were in Arizona. "Yuma," the sign said. The saguaros looked like phantom watchmen, their thorny branches pointing to the diamond sky. I stared out the window, this time from a distance that would fail to induce a headache. The moon played hide-and-seek with the train, visible one second, AWOL the next, depending on the curve of the tracks. My mother sat next to me, jammed so tightly into her seat that her head seemed to be receding into her neck. In the dim light, she looked like a troll, a creature scrunched into herself, benign but misshapen. I started laughing.

"*De que te ríes, menso?* What are you laughing at, dummy?"

"De nada," I said, trying to stifle my laughter.

When we arrived in El Paso, it was cool and crisp, just as it had been in Los Angeles. But the cool seemed cooler, the crisp seemed crisper, and the sun seemed sunnier—radiant in its crystalline majesty. El Paso. We were in El Paso.

"*Como estas, mi'jo?*" Alita greeted me. "How are you, my child?"

She was staying with one of my aunts, Tía Maria, and she was waiting on the sidewalk when my mother and I arrived by taxi, each of us holding a suitcase.

"*Bien, Alita, estoy bien*," I said. "Fine, I am fine."

Alita was wearing a brown dress and a purple sweater, with a black shawl draped across her frail shoulders. I smiled, and when she smiled back, I noticed a feature I had never detected before. Her eyes were brown, a dull brown, but they seemed bright, liquidy, and they sparkled despite the flat color. *Mira no mas*. Just look at that. I hugged her; she was so thin that my hands formed a bridge at the small of her back, as if I were hugging myself.

It struck me that, of all the nicknames she hung on my friends, at least one could apply to her—*La Flaca*. Skinny. But those eyes. Those eyes made my grandmother seem stronger—and younger—than she was.

"*Estoy bien*," I repeated.

I kept hugging her, trying to see if her spirit would enter my body, as the old man had told me it would.

"*Y el* Randy?" she said.

"*Cual* Randy? Randy who?" I asked, pretending I did not know why she had sent me the statue of St. Jude.

"*El cabrón que te sono*. The jerk who hit you."

"Randy?" I said tentatively.

"*Ese mero*. That's the one," she said excitedly.

"*Como supiste de* Randy? How do you know about Randy?" I asked.

"*Tu mama me escribio*. Your mother wrote me," she said. "*Me dijo todo*. She told me everything."

I looked down.

"*Sabes que*, Bobby, *no le hagas caso*. You know what, Bobby? Don't pay attention to him."

"Okay," I said, smiling. "Bueno."

Alita told me to hurry into the house, a red-brick, two-story home in the same neighborhood where we had lived before moving to Bakersfield. The house had a balcony, supported by two wooden pillars that reminded me of the columns in a Roman temple. It looked gladiatorial, appropriate considering how combative my aunt could be, but it was an upgrade over the duplex where my grandmother used to live with us—a big upgrade, even though it was only about two blocks from our old place.

"*Ándale, tengo frio*. Hurry up, I'm cold," Alita told me.

I climbed the monkey bars, the steel rungs cold and gray. It was overcast. The clouds rolled across the sky, dark and amorphous, an odd occurrence in El Paso, a town known as Sun City. The sun was up there, somewhere, but I could not see it, its daily appearance delayed by those stubborn clouds. I kept climbing, rung by rung, toward the invisible sun. And as I climbed, I felt a pull on my left leg, my lag leg. Bah! I said to myself. I struggled to keep climbing, but before I knew it, I was on the ground, my butt digging into the soft soil of the playground. Randy Reed! But when I got to my feet, there was nobody there. . . . And then I woke up, trying to rub the horrible dream from my eyes.

It was Christmas morning. Alita summoned me to her bedroom. She dragged her folding chair to the closet, telling me to grab the box on the top shelf.

Still in my pajamas, I jumped on the chair, stretching until I reached the box. I handed it to her, and she handed it back to me. I could smell the rich, nutty odor of history.

"*Abralo*, Open it," she said.

It was her Christmas present to me. The box, wrapped in a white shawl, was full of *reliquias* that included rosaries, missals, and leaflets featuring radiant images of the saints. She told me to ignore everything except the two photos on top. Maybe they were pictures of *El Padre Panfilo,* the pastor of her old church in Chihuahua, *La Iglesia de la Virgen de Guadalupe*. But why would I want them?

"*Ándale!*" she said, hurrying me.

Still standing on the chair, I handled the photographs gingerly, as if newborn twins were swaddled in the shawl. They were framed, both of them, with ornate curlicues carved into the rich, auburn wood. I had never seen pictures so fancy, with frames and everything.

As a family, some of our pictures ended up in albums, especially images of the old man my mother saved to chronicle what she called "*La Vida del Reportero*," "The Life of the Reporter." But most of the photographs were tossed into old shoeboxes, discarded like unwanted bills. *Pero estos*? But these? I looked at Alita.

"*Estos son . . . especial*," Alita said, beaming.

I smiled.

"*Ándale!*" she said, pointing to the photos. "*Pronto!*"

Inspecting the photographs, I let the shawl tumble to the ground. Alita tried to catch it, but she was too slow, grabbing a handful of air as she swiped at the garment. "*Cabrón*," she cried in frustration. I started to apologize, but her anger was directed at herself, not at me.

"*Ándale!*" she said, hurrying me.

Dull and grainy, the photos showed a boy who was about my age, maybe a little older. He was wearing a sailor suit in one photo, a coat and tie in the other. His blond hair was parted in the middle, his curls flowing into waves on either side. He was smiling in both photos, but it was not the photo smile, goofy and awkward, that kids flash when a photographer says "cheese." There was a hint of a smirk in those curved lips. And the smile radiated from his eyes, not his mouth. Who was this kid? He seemed natural, confident, mature. How could a kid that age boast such self-possession, especially when he was wearing a stupid sailor suit in one of the pictures?

Holding a photo in each hand, I stared at the boy. Then I stared at Alita. Why was she showing me these strange pictures? I looked at her, my eyes forming the question before my mouth had a chance to.

"*Ay, tontito, es tu papa!* Oh, little dummy, it's your father!" she said. "*Cuando tenia pelo*. When he had hair."

Alita laughed.

"*Y cuando era gringo*. And when he was a gringo."

*Cuando era gringo?* But the old man was still a gringo, right? I asked my grandmother. *Que no*? Is that not true?

"*Pues*, . . .Well, . . ." she said hesitating.

I waited for an answer.

"*Que no*?" I repeated.

She finally walked out of the room, my cue to follow her, but when I remained in her room, confused by her reticence, she snapped her fingers.

"*Ándale*," she said impatiently.

I followed her. She walked outside, and as she settled into one of the folding chairs on the porch, I backed up to the front of the house, sliding until I was forced to squat, my butt thumping onto the cement. Alita rolled her eyes. I waited for her to speak. She stared toward the gully, half a block from our house, as if searching for something beyond the horizon.

"*Ay, Robertito*," she said.

She always called me Robertito when she was exasperated with me, but what she was feeling was not exasperation. Not this time. It was something worse; it was resignation.

"*Mira ese gato*," she said finally, pointing to a cat lounging on the sidewalk. "*Ese gato no puede cambiar. Siempre va ser gato. Siempre. Un pinche gato. Entiendes?*"

I said yes. A cat is a cat. And it will always be a cat.

"*Pero un hombre . . . un hombre puede cambiar. Un hombre, un verdadero hombre, escucha a su Corazon*. But a man, a man can change. A man, a real man, listens to his heart," she said. "*No importe donde nacio o donde se creo. Nadien lo manda. Puede hacer lo que le da su chingada gana*. It makes no difference where he was born, or where he was raised. Nobody rules him. He can do what he damned well pleases."

I laughed. *Chingar* was the funniest word in the world. Chingar and all its derivatives – *chingada, chingazo, chingele, chingon, chingao* (a border bastardization of *chingado*). Chingar was the Spanish term for the F-word. But the way my grandmother used *chingado* and *chin-*

*gele*, the words meant damn or dammit. And they could be uttered in anger or awe.

*"Es verdad.* It's true," Alita said sternly. *"Tu papa nunca hiso nada a medios chiles.* Your papa never did anything half-assed."

Alita laughed. And then, just as abruptly as she started laughing, she stopped. It was eerie.

*"Te quiero decir halgo.* I want to tell you something," she said. *"Tu papa nacio gringo, pero va murir Mexicano. Tu eres Mexicano porque tu mama es Mexicana. Tu papa es Mexicano porque quiere ser Mexicano. Entiendes?* Your father was born gringo, but he's going to die a Mexican. You are Mexican because your mother is Mexican. Your father is Mexican because he wants to be a Mexican. Understand?"

I thought I understood. When I asked the old man why I was Mexican, I was asking the wrong question. It was not about me; it was about him. Why was *he* Mexican? Defying geography and bloodlines, the old man became Mexican.

The old man was not Mexican-American, a subtle blend of two cultures. He was Mexican and American, two distinct individuals in one body. One man was born in Cleveland, the other in a place where men pursue their dreams and desires. Is that what Alita was telling me?

Could he really become a Mexican just because he wanted to? It seemed preposterous. And yet I knew Alita would never lie to me. But how could he turn into a Mexican? Did Alita mean that the old man respected, valued, and, yes, loved Mexicans so much that their spirit melded into his spirit?

When did the moment arrive? The epiphany when he decided he wanted to become a Mexican? Was it the night he met my mother? Or was it the morning he ate those enchiladas and eggs in Chihuahua?

Whenever it came, it was the moment Chester Seltzer became a Mexican, blood and geography be damned. It was the moment he became Amado Muro. But all I knew—all I knew for sure—was that the old man loved Mexicans, and if the old man loved Mexicans, who was Randy Reed to tell me that Mexicans were not worthy of love? *Cabrón*.

We stayed in El Paso for almost two weeks, but whatever else transpired during that period has fallen into the abyss of lost memories. The Cleveland Browns played the Baltimore Colts on December 27. It was for the NFL title. They won, 27-0. Frank Ryan threw three touchdown passes, all of them to Gary Collins, and Jim Brown—the great Jim Brown—rushed for more than 100 yards, his speed and power softening the defense for the quarterback and his receivers. The experts called it an upset.

I loved the Browns because the old man loved the Browns, so I asked Alita to watch the game with me. We saw it on the little Magnavox in her bedroom. She called the Browns "*los Cafes de Cleveland.*" But I remember nothing else, not a single rush or pass or tackle. What should have been a glorious memory was overshadowed by a simple present and a simple *consejo*—a simple piece of advice: *No le hagas caso*. Don't pay attention to him.

Alita's gift to me: a photo of my father, age ten.

# 20

## Syncopation

When we returned to the *friega*, the torment, in Bakersfield, I tried to forget about Randy Reed, the boy who created the friega.

"Beto, I wish you looked better," the old man told me.

I accepted his criticism.

"I know, Dad," I said. "I wish I looked better, too. I wish I looked like Napoleon Solo."

Napoleon Solo—played by the handsome star Robert Vaughn—was the lead character in *The Man from U.N.C.L.E*, a violent television series Alita used to let me watch when the old man was out of town.

"No, I mean I wish you looked happier," the old man said. "You're too young to be sad."

The old man was right, but what could I do? He said misery did not discriminate. Discriminate? He defined it without forcing me to consult the dictionary. Misery, he said, afflicts everyone—young, old, black, white, Mexican, American and sometimes, as with me, Mexican and American.

"Bury yourself in the things you love," he told me. "Music, books, riding your bike . . . okay?"

"Okay, Dad."

I decided to bury myself in what the old man loved. Words. He loved their sounds, their rhythms, their meanings, and when he maneuvered through that world, he helped me forget mine.

One day, I asked the old man a question. Hoping to lose myself in one of his informal lectures, I was prepared—and eager—for a long explanation. The old man did not disappoint me.

"Dad, what does syncopation mean?" I asked the old man after the trip to El Paso.

The old man sat on the couch, relaxing, his legs propped on his makeshift ottoman, the coffee table.

"Syncopation?" he asked.

"Yeah, syncopation."

I pronounced it with a long *i*, as in "wily," so it came out sounding like two words—sign and copation.

"Where did you hear that word?"

"I saw it on a poster at the record shop downtown. It was for, uh, a jazz singer . . . or, uh, a jazz group, Dizzy something, I think."

Walking up and down the aisles, flipping through the albums, I would take a stack of records to the listening booth, where I savored rave-ups by the Kinks, the Animals, and the Beatles. The songs exploded with emotion—so much emotion that, most of the time, I did not even buy the albums. I just listened to the songs that transported me to another world: "Under My Thumb," "You Can't Do That," "You Really Got Me," "The Story of Bo Diddley."

"Dizzy, huh?" he asked, pausing. "I see."

"Well . . . ?" I responded.

"Could it have been Dizzy Gillespie?" he asked.

"Yes, Gillespie!" I said. "Dizzy Gillespie!"

"Look it up," he said. "Look up the word."

Look it up. My memory bank must have been defective. I forgot that, whenever I asked the old man what a word meant, he always told me to look it up. It was his way of encouraging me to explore the world of words, a world he loved and admired—and wanted me to love and admire, too.

Instead of looking up the word, I looked up at the ceiling, frustrated with myself for failing to hear those three simple words—look it up—in my inner ear. The old man smiled. I walked over to the short, squat bookcase in the living room, a bookcase filled with the novels and short-story collections my father loved. There were books by writers with strange names—Tolstoy and Dostoevsky, Chekhov and Gogol, Flaubert and Sartre, Hemingway and Steinbeck. The pages—hundreds of them—were dog-eared, turned down to mark the passages that enchanted the old man, passages like this one from *The Pearl* by Steinbeck:

> High in the gray stone mountains, under a frowning peak, a little spring bubbled out of a rupture in the stone. It was fed by shade-preserved snow in the summer, and now and then it died completely, and bare rocks and dry algae were on its bottom. But nearly always it gushed out, cold and clean and lovely.

The dictionary sat on top of the bookcase, an exalted spot worthy of the Bible. It was the book of books, the volume with all the words his favorite writers used. The writers arranged them, but the words were here, all of them, in this dictionary, the building blocks they assembled to construct their sentences, their paragraphs, their chapters.

The old man read the dictionary as though it were a real book, a book with a story. He discovered words he had never seen or heard before, and when he found one that pleased him, you could see his mouth crease with a slight but exquisite smile. It was the only book in the house without dog-eared pages, because he could start it wherever he wanted and end it wherever he wanted, always leaving it open to the page with the last word he had read.

"Dad, I can't find the word," I pleaded.

"Are you looking for a word that starts with *s* and *i*?" he asked.

"Yes," I answered.

"Try *s* and *y*," he said gently.

"Okay."

**syn-co-pa-tion** (s ng k -p sh n, s n -) *n.* 1. Music A shift of accent in a passage or composition that occurs when a normally weak beat is stressed.

I read the definition, mouthing the words as I tried to decipher them. Dictionaries were supposed to help you, not aggravate you, but the more I read the definition, the less I understood it. I turned to the old man.

"What's wrong?" he asked

"I need a definition for the definition," I said.

The old man laughed.

"Okay," he said, smiling. "It's a little complicated, but I'll give it a try . . . I hope I get it right."

Then he asked me to do him a favor.

"Bring me a Beatles album."

I dashed over to my room, returning with *The Early Beatles*. I handed it to him. He looked at the cover, inspecting it as though he were a detective studying a piece of evidence.

"Okay," he said, handing it back to me. "Now take it over to the record player and play me your favorite song."

Flipping the record to the *B side*, I fit the hole in the vinyl into the spindle. I watched it drop onto the rotating turntable. Then I waited for the first song to explode in our ears. It was "Please Please Me."

After listening for about a minute he said, "Is that your favorite song on the album?"

"Yes," I said, sheepishly, afraid that, like "(I Can't Get No) Satisfaction," it was not the type of tune an eleven-year-old should love. I had turned eleven during the school year, but I felt no more mature than I did before.

"That's all right," he said, detecting my anxiety. "It's a great song. Do you notice how one word can have two different meanings—please and please? An entreaty and an action?"

I looked at him, dumbfounded, wondering what he meant.

"Huh?"

"That's okay," he said, smiling. "We can talk about that another time. Right now, we're discussing syncopation, right?"

"Uhhh, yes," I said.

"Okay, syncopation . . ." he said, pronouncing the word the way I had—sign-copation. "So play the song one more time."

Picking up the needle, I let it drop onto the groove before "Please

Please Me."

"One more time," the old man said when the song ended.

I played it again, wondering where the old man was heading.

"Do you remember the chorus—come on, come on, come on, come on?" he asked when I lifted the needle off the vinyl.

"Yes," I said.

"A tough come on is followed by an easy come on—tough, easy, tough, easy—all the way through, right?"

"Right," I said.

"Well, that's sign-copation."

"That was easy," I said. "Why didn't the dictionary just say that?"

"Well, it did, sort of. But, sometimes, dictionaries create little mysteries for us, and it's our job to solve them."

I smiled, sliding the record out of the spindle.

"And don't forget," the old man said. "Always look it up first, before you ask me, okay?"

"Okay."

I headed back to my room, holding the album to my chest.

"And one more thing . . ." the old man said.

He was going to ask me about school. About Randy Reed. I knew it.

"If you break one of God's commandments, what is it called?" he asked.

"Huh?"

"What is it called?"

"A sin?"

"Right. A sin . . . now say sin-copation."

"Sin-copation."

"Good."

Taking a few steps back to my room, I quickly turned around.

"Thanks, Dad."

The old man loved words, loved their texture and substance. Where other men saw objects, he saw the words that stood for those objects. He did not see a mountain; he saw the word mountain. He did not see the ocean; he saw the word ocean. He did not see the sky; he saw the word sky.

The world was a novel, and he read it voraciously, its rhythm and cadence so seductive that his inner ear heard words that were never spoken, speeches that were never delivered. If I had possessed the same talent, I would have looked at him, and I would not have seen a man. I would have seen the word *writer*, bold and clear and dramatic:

> **(writ-er)** Pronunciation: /rît.r/ a person who writes books, stories, or articles as a job or regular occupation

The old man developed his love for words early. His father—the old man of the old man—was Louis B. Seltzer, the editor of the *Cleveland Press*, himself an accomplished writer. He joked that his son emerged from the womb reading a book. I believed it. And the book must have been as big as the baby himself. Something by Tolstoy. Maybe *War and Peace*. Or *Anna Karenina*.

Picture books held no interest for him. If he wanted images, all he had to do was open his eyes. The world was full of images, a kaleidoscope of scenes and portraits so vivid that they looked like works of art. He did not need a picture book to capture what the universe already provided; he needed words.

One evening, years before Young Chess started making his journeys to the library, his father left a book on the coffee table, face down, open to the last page he had scanned. He was not reading the book, for he had read it long ago. He was skimming it, trying to find the sections that had captivated him as a kid. The next morning, he saw the book, and it was closed, its cover staring at him, bold and defiant—*The Adventures of Tom Sawyer*. The old man of the old man scratched his head, folded his arms. He looked at Young Chess, who sat on the sofa, his legs dangling four inches from the floor.

"Injun Joe was scary," the boy said.

"What?"

"Injun Joe was scary."

"You read the book . . . in one night?"

"Yes."

My grandmother holds my father, age about three, on her lap.

"But . . . but . . . "

Five years old, a year removed from his first English class in school, Young Chess was already exploring a world closed to most kids his age—the world of literature. His father was so impressed that he gave the boy a present when he came home from work that evening. It was a wooden desk, simple and basic, with a bookshelf rising from the end—three narrow tiers that could hold about sixty books, twenty per row, a universe of words. The surface was old and scarred, pitted with the holes gouged by a fountain pen that had dug into page after page on the desktop. It was another boy who had wielded that fountain pen, another boy from another time, and whenever he finished a book, he would scribble his thoughts on a piece of paper, holding the pen so tightly that it sometimes ripped through the paper. The boy, now a man, almost forgot the pleasure he had derived from the written word. No, he *had* forgotten. But when he heard his son utter those two words—*Injun Joe*—the joy returned, unbidden but not unwanted. And so he gave his son the same desk his father had given him.

"Well, my father was a writer," Louis B. Seltzer told his son. "I'm a writer. And now it looks like you're going to be a writer, too. What a chain of misfits, huh?"

Sitting at the desk in his room, Young Chess read . . . and read . . . and read. At an age when other boys were reading comic books, fueled only by their thirst for adventure, Young Chess read books to learn how to write, as if each novel or short story collection were a manual on the art of storytelling. His earliest books were by Mark Twain, Lewis Carroll, and Robert Louis Stevenson. He talked about the characters—Tom Sawyer, Huckleberry Finn, the Mad Hatter—as if they were childhood companions. His favorite was the pirate, Long John Silver, because his kind demeanor masked a scary side. How could the old man like a character so evil? Long John Silver was—what word did the old man use?—complicated? Yes, complicated. Like his creator, I was a Robert Louis, and one day, I asked the old man if I was named after the great Scottish writer. He laughed.

"No," he said. "We named you after your grand-uncle and grandfather. Uncle Bob and my dad, Louis."

He pronounced it Louie.

"Oh," I said, disappointed.

Later, as a teenager, Young Chess started reading detective novels, especially those by the British writer Herman Cyril McNeile, who went by the weird pseudonym, Sapper. The hero was Hugh Drummond, Bulldog Drummond, a retired policeman who freelanced as a private detective in London. He was suave but ugly, a man whose elegant language collided with his harsh countenance. That was how the old man described it. Harsh countenance. What did it mean? I never asked. The old man would have told me to look it up, and, then, after I looked it up, I would have been no more enlightened than I was before.

"A harsh countenance, that's what Bulldog Drummond had," the old man said.

I nodded knowingly.

"Do you know what that means?"

"Yes," I said, lying.

"What does it mean?"

"Well, uh, it means that he looks, uh, he looks . . . mean?" I said, framing the answer in the form of a question.

"Very good," he said, delighted.

Young Chess loved his books—*Don Quixote, Sister Carrie, Crime and Punishment, A Tale of Two Cities.* They nourished his soul, fed his imagination. It was almost as if he could crawl into the novels—see the same sights, smell the same smells, experience the same experiences, as the characters themselves. The books were so engrossing, so enchanting, that he was not even aware of this phenomenon, this ability to transport himself to another world, until one rainy afternoon.

He was sitting at the desk in his room, a book nestled in his lap, as he peered through a window pebbled with raindrops. The street was a war zone. Bombs dropped, soldiers fell, screams pierced the air. Young Chess witnessed the destruction from his bedroom, his hands trembling until they released the book on his lap. It dropped violently, a thud that jarred him from his reverie. He looked down at the thin volume. It was *All Quiet on the Western Front,* the classic novel about World War I.

"You never knew that I was Tom Sawyer, did you?" the old man asked me one evening.

"No," I said, intrigued, wondering if the old man had played Tom Sawyer in a high school production.

"Well, I was," he said. "I was Jim Hawkins, too, the boy in *Treasure Island*. And Robinson Crusoe, who knew a little something about islands himself. And Päul Baumer. You don't know about Päul Baumer, not yet, but you will when you read *All Quiet on the Western Front*."

"Okay," I said, waiting for him to finish listing his roles.

"I was all of those, all of those, and a lot more," he said. "A lot more."

"Dad," I said, "you never told me you were an actor."

"An actor? What makes you think I was an actor?"

"Well, you played all those characters."

"Play them? I didn't play them. I was them. I was them when I was reading the books. The beautiful books."

"So you could become anyone you wanted?" I asked. "Anyone?"

"That's right," he said. "But I had to want to. I had to like the character, admire him."

If the old man assumed the identities of his favorite literary characters, could he step into other shoes as well? Could he become another person, real but imagined, who had nothing to do with books or movies? A person with a different heritage, culture, and language from his own? And if he did, would it last until a book dropped from his lap, shattering his reverie? Or would it last longer, becoming a part of his soul, his being?

"Dad?"

"Yes."

"Dad, do you think I can be anyone, too?"

"Of course, you can."

"Dad, you remember when I told you I fell off the monkey bars?"

"I remember," he said.

"I . . . uuuhhh . . . I'm glad you knew I was lying," I said.

And then he smiled.

## 21

# The Night the Old Man Lost Tolstoy

It was nighttime.

I was in bed, banished to my room long before I was ready for sleep. I could hear the hum of the television set in the living room, a painful reminder that I was barred from a cool, fascinating world. The world of late-night adventure on the small screen.

As I raised my head from the pillow, I heard another hum, just as soft and gentle. It was my parents. They were talking. I got out of bed. The floorboard creaked, my heart pounded, and I thought the old man would hear the hammering in my chest.

I stood behind the door in my bedroom, the creaking beneath my feet growing louder—a long, scary groan that thundered in my ears. *Ay Dios mio.* It was 10:00 p.m., two hours past my bedtime. I closed my eyes and held my breath, as if shutting out the outside world would shut out all the noise it produced—including mine.

I cracked the door open, my heart racing like a hot rod. They were watching *Gunsmoke* or *Maverick* or *The Untouchables* or . . . I could not tell what they were watching. I was focused on their conversation. The old man was telling my mother a story. . . .

It was dusk, the clouds glowing with silver flashes of fading light.

Chess loved the twilight, that magical seam between night and day, when the earth seemed to stand still, on the precipice of forever. But that mystical quality belonged to another world, another time. The sky held no magic for Chess. Not tonight. He was on a bus, heading toward prison.

The sun was sinking over Ohio. Or maybe Indiana. It was too far to tell. Chess was in Central Pennsylvania, about 260 miles east of Cleveland. He was twenty-nine.

Throughout the bus trip, Chess wondered how it would feel when he saw the prison for the first time, and now, there it was, staring at him from the rolling hills of Lewisburg, Pennsylvania . . . Lewisburg, Pennsylvania, so close to Cleveland, yet so far away, so damned far away. . . . The bus rumbled up the final hill, through the prison gates, ready to drop off the new inmates.

It was 1944. When Chess hopped off the bus, he felt detached, aloof, a man who had stepped outside his own skin. The air was cool and crisp, with a hint of rain on the horizon. He felt the wind on his cheeks, and he heard a murmur in the distance, a cooing that was soft and sweet, as if the trees were whispering to each other. Will it start raining before they haul me into the prison, Chess wondered. "I hope not," he said to himself, smiling. Then he inhaled. "Damn."

Lighting his final cigarette in the outside world, Chess dropped his duffel bag on the ground in front of the bus. He was one of six men who stepped off the vehicle, loitering in front of the great prison that represented their future for longer than they cared to contemplate—much longer. They shuffled their feet, cleared their throats, cussed under their breath. The men were all the same, and all different—similar in their anxiety, different in their reasons for being there, the crimes ranging from assault to robbery.

Chess took a puff, and he stared at the prison, and he wondered why he was so calm—so strangely, eerily calm. The other inmates—inmates-to-be—seemed nervous. Not Chess. Chess shrugged, flicking the ashes of his cigarette into the cold air.

As he studied the prison, struck by its unique architecture, Chess forgot about the duffel bag, forgot about it until he entered the prison, and by then it was too late. No matter. It was just a duffel bag; it held nothing of consequence. Not really. Just newspapers and magazines and books . . . well, one book, a copy of essays by Leo Tolstoy.

Except for an occasional shit or fart or damn, he rarely cussed. But fuck. The newspapers and magazines meant nothing to Chess, but he cherished the book, a collection of essays on civil disobedience and nonviolence. And he would never see it again. Never. Not in that incarnation, anyway—a slim paperback with an ink portrait of the great writer himself. His favorite. Leo Tolstoy.

Chess loved the book, loved it the way a preacher loves a hymn—a hymn that nourishes both mind and soul. He would carry it with him wherever he went, caressing its cover every time he opened it, whether he was in a bus, a library or a coffee shop. And now? It was gone, gone forever. Fuck.

Well, he thought in the days and weeks ahead, here I am, out in the wilderness, Nowhere, USA. Maybe a wolf got the book. Or a bear. Or, hell, even a squirrel, which, being a vegetarian, would have to digest it in tiny portions. And maybe, just maybe, Chess said to himself, the book would change that wolf or bear or squirrel for the better, although squirrels were already pacifists by nature, right? Damn.

Rising from the hills of Buffalo Valley, a rural community in Central Pennsylvania, the prison evoked none of the menace he expected. It looked like an Italian monastery, bold but inviting, with three towers spearing the sky—a tall one in the middle, two shorter ones on each flank. The strangest features of the facility—the features that struck him immediately—were the Gothic windows. There were eight of them, stark but majestic. They lined the front of the facility, each one about twenty feet high, and although it was hard to tell in the dark, Chess could make out—thought he could make out—the stained glass on those windows.

In the enveloping darkness, Chess could not distinguish the portraits—the magnificent, inspiring portraits—etched on those windows. Why he thought a federal prison would feature something as sublime as stained-glass windows, he could not say. But no matter. They were there. He knew it. And morning would confirm his hope—no, his belief—that they were there, for in the morning, the sun would execute a triumphant swipe of its paint brush, and it would reveal the artistic glory that was there all along, the glory painted by a higher hand, concealed during the night, exposed during the day. Damn.

Chess had spent two years in work camps throughout the country—Colorado, Illinois, Connecticut—before he was transferred to the prison in the summer of 1944. He had spent a week in Cleveland after leaving the work camp in Norwich, Connecticut. And he felt nothing upon his arrival in Lewisburg—no fear, no dread, no anxiety. Maybe it was the stained-glass windows that soothed him. Maybe it was the sweet scent of coming rain. Maybe it was the Pennsylvania countryside, the gentle hills dotted with barns and tractors and hay—bales of hay so enormous that they looked like the building blocks for the Great Pyramid of Giza. Or maybe, just maybe, it was the prison itself, its design so benign, so reassuring. Whatever it was, Chess accepted it, and when he stepped off the bus, dropping the duffel bag at his feet, he stared at the prison, transfixed by the facility that would be his home for the next year.

"So this is where they put Capone," he said, referring to Al Capone, the infamous crime lord who was sent to prison for tax evasion. "Damn. He got off easy."

As he contemplated the Chicago mob boss, lightning whipsawed across the western sky, and rain fell in thick, gray curtains. Wielding their flashlights as if they were batons, the prison guards herded the inmates into the facility. Lewisburg Penitentiary would be Lewisburg Sanctuary—if only for one wet, dreary night. Damn.

It was not painful or torturous, but Chess thought that first night would never end. Those were his words—not "my first night in prison," but "the first night," period, as if the phrase required no context, no explanation. When Chess marched into the facility, he noticed the silence—a silence that seemed deep but fragile, ready to be broken by a thousand screams. It overwhelmed him, expelled its cold breath on him, and he sensed the paradox that had struck him since he was a snot-nosed kid posing for photographs in his sailor suit: The quiet that seemed the most invincible was the quiet that the slightest sound—the weakest footfall, the most delicate quiver of breath—could shatter. The stronger the silence—the more impenetrable it seemed—the easier it was to break. Chess was no longer posing for photographs in his sailor suit; he was a prisoner of the United

States. But the quiet he felt that night was the quiet he had recognized since his childhood—only worse. It was dark and ominous and eternal. . . . Fuck.

When the guards left, their flashlights fading into pinpricks in the enormous void, Chess watched them disappear. Where am I, he said to himself. The prison seemed impenetrable—not physically but emotionally. The outside world was, well, outside—remote, inaccessible.

Chess was on the second floor. There were four floors in the prison, each with two rows of cells, one on the west end, one on the east. About forty yards apart, the rows were separated by open air, a vast pit of nothing, from the ground to the ceiling. It was like a hotel with an atrium in the middle. A hotel. Chess laughed at the thought. When the prisoners stepped out of their cells on the upper floors, the walkways were so narrow that, if not for the short, iron barriers at the ledge, the poor inmates would have tumbled to their deaths. Splat. Some hotel. Ha! Chess laughed again.

"When is checkout time?" he imagined himself asking a guard.

"One year," the guard answered.

"One year? You mean I cannot leave this damned hotel until 1945?"

The bed was a slat—hard, flat, and narrow. So narrow that his arms and legs dangled over the edge. He struggled to fall asleep, and as he tossed and turned, he reached for the Tolstoy book on his nightstand, but Tolstoy was not there, and neither was the nightstand, and as he flailed for the book, he realized that something else was gone—his future. And then he thought about Tolstoy, poor Tolstoy, lost in the woods forever, as hopelessly marooned as any of the inmates in Lewisburg Penitentiary. The great Russian writer, the genius, reduced to the harshest servitude, a prisoner with the worst sentence imaginable—eternity. Eternity in the woods of Lewisburg, Pennsylvania. Fuck.

When Chess woke up the next morning, his initial thought struck him as silly. No. Worse than silly. It was shameful. I cannot wear what I want to wear, he thought to himself. I cannot wear my favorite khaki pants or my favorite wool socks or my favorite beige shirt, open at the collar. The thought assaulted him like a thousand left hooks from his favorite fighter, Jack Dempsey. And then, for a fleeting moment, his initial thought did not seem so silly, so inane. It seemed real, and it seemed hard, and it seemed . . . inescapable. Chess realized he could not do all the simple, stupid things he had taken for granted in the outside world.

In the morning, Chess saw the rest of the facility, the facility he could not see in the darkness the night before. He was amazed, dumbstruck. The prison was beautiful; at least its entrance was—so warm and humane, its bowels as benign as its façade. There was nothing menacing about the entryway, nothing disquieting. Where am I? the old man thought to himself.

Chess saw the great hall for the first time; it was cavernous, as majestic as any cathedral. And as the guards shuffled the inmates through the giant room, Chess paused, stumbling as he looked at the ceiling. My God. It was this room that featured the Gothic windows he had noticed the night before, but when he saw those windows in the morning light, he felt an overwhelming sense of loss.

He had been wrong about the windows, wrong about what the sun would reveal in the light of day. The sun revealed nothing. The windows were just windows—sheets of naked, empty glass. There were no pictures on those windows, no portraits of Jesus and his Apostles. Nothing to inspire the prisoners—or anyone else—in Lewisburg Penitentiary. Chess was crushed. Whatever made him think Jesus was there in the first place?

They processed the inmates in an office near the great hall, a cold, dingy room where the men stood under a pendant light. The old man was the first to go. It was 8:00 a.m. The doctor bumped his head against the light, and as the old man stifled a smirk, he noticed the shadows on the wall, fading and reemerging as the light swung back and forth. He was stripped to his shorts, as naked as Tolstoy in the forest. The doctor pressed the stethoscope to his chest. Asked him a few questions. That was it.

The next day, in the same room, another doctor asked him some more questions. This doctor was a psychologist. The session was brief, as perfunctory as the examination by the physician the day before. He asked the old man a few questions, and he marked a pad on the desk, and that was it. The notations he made were simple:

Chester Seltzer
29 years old—white.
Father is head of *Cleveland Press*—is said to earn $600 a week.
His family background is excellent.
No psychosis.

So Chester Seltzer was not crazy.

In the days and weeks ahead, Chess started thinking, and thinking, he discovered, can be a dangerous thing. If thinking does not lead to action . . . if the ideas, positive or negative, remain lodged in the person who thought them . . . if they cannot escape through words or deeds—or through dreams fulfilled—those thoughts can be bad. No, they can be worse than bad. They can be paralyzing.

The prison entombed Chess. But it did just not shut out the other world, the real world. It made his world—the world he was inhabiting now—seem smaller. And it was this sense of claustrophobia that made the great hall so striking. It was an open space within a crowded cage. Were the prison officials toying with the inmates? Were they rubbing their incarceration in their faces? Were they?

Chess did not realize that a man could feel isolated despite his proximity to dozens—no, hundreds—just like him. But prison taught him a lot of things, and a lot of those things were bad or worse than bad. A lot of those things were ugly, destructive.

When he entered the prison, Chess did not think about the year he would be confined behind its walls. He thought about the first night, and the second night, and the third night . . . and . . . It was when he went beyond those first few nights that the thought of prison—not prison itself, but the thought of prison—started to smother him.

Chess finally realized the evil of incarceration. Any man could take being locked up, he thought. Why any child, banished to his room for a few hours, could take it. Right? But to think of punishment without end—that was the problem. Chess would be in for a year, which may not seem like an eternity, but when you are inside those walls, wondering what the world is like on the outside, Monday becomes no different from Tuesday, Tuesday no different from Wednesday, Wednesday no different from. . . . And when time stops, life itself might as well stop. The walls keep the outside world from coming in, but they also keep hopes and dreams from coming in. Fuck.

22

# The Conscientious Objector

Someone turned on the hall light. It was the old man. I dived into bed, scrambling to wrap myself under the blankets.

"Betty, are you asleep?" he asked.

"Betty" was his variation of Beto.

"Betty?" he repeated

I moaned, turning on my side.

"Huh?" I groaned.

"Okay," he said. "Never mind. Good night."

The next morning, the old man was reading the newspaper in the living room, and I told him about the story I had heard the night before.

"Dad," I asked the old man. "Did you . . . kill someone?"

"What?" he responded.

"Did you . . . kill . . . someone?"

I felt stupid, the words jamming in my throat, unable to exit smoothly and coherently.

"Did . . . you . . . kill someone?" I repeated, afraid of what the answer would be.

He scrunched his face, his features accordioned into a wrinkled mess.

"No," he said, quietly.

"Then why did they put you in prison?"

"For refusing to kill anybody," he said.

"What?"

My first heroes were killers. Matt Dillon, the marshal of Dodge City, would shoot a bad guy on *Gunsmoke*, and before the blood started to spurt from his wound, a Lucky Strike or Quaker Oats or Alka-Seltzer commercial would interrupt the chaos. There was no time to consider the consequences on TV. Death was cool—a quick resolution to a thorny problem. Men died, died quickly and horribly, but you cheered the hero and scorned the villain. And, besides, who cared about the guys who died? They deserved their fates. *Cabrónes.*

The old man let me watch *Gilligan's Island* and *The Munsters* and *The Adam's Family* on TV. They were harmless programs—innocuous fun. Better to corrupt the kid with stupidity than with evil. Was that his thinking? Maybe. I was too young to decipher his reasoning, too young to care. Whatever his reasons, *Gunsmoke* was out. *Gunsmoke* and *The Untouchables* and *The Man From U.N.C.L.E.* Out—all out.

I watched them, anyway. I watched them during his freight train journeys, because my mother felt sorry for me, and because she thought I was too young to follow his "crazy" moral code. El Gringo could follow his strict adherences—that was his business. But, *chingado*, Bobby was going to watch what the other boys watched, if only when the old man was out of town.

"You watch what you want to watch," my mother told me. "You watch what you want to watch."

Right—but only when the old man is on a freight train heading to God knows where.

The old man told me he was a conscientious objector. He always used big words, but . . . conscientious objector? Conscientious—a term that boasted more syllables than any word I had ever heard, except when Alita turned cabrón into an elastic noun, stretching it until it seemed longer than the road back to Chihuahua. Or any road anywhere. And objector—a word that seemed almost as long as conscientious. And together? Together, they represented a verbal marathon, too long for me to negotiate—or understand. So I asked the old man a question—a question so hard to ask that the words, coming out of my mouth, burned my throat.

It was the first time the old man had ever scared me. Not that he tried to frighten me. It was just the length of the words, conscientious and objector. Their length . . . and the weight of their meaning. Whatever the term meant, I knew it was heavy. Not heavy in the way that kids in the late 1960s would use it—a term for depth and profundity. But heavy as in . . . menacing.

"What do they mean?" I asked. "Those two words? Con-con-sci . . ."

I stared at the floor, and I felt the tears welling. I closed my eyes, but the river kept threatening to burst through those two flimsy dams—my eyelids. If I cried, I said to myself, the old man would think I was a sissy, and his contempt would flow like vomit, and the bile would come out in words, and he would tell me, "Bob Olson was twice as tough as Randy Reed, and look what I did to him. I hope Randy Reed kicks your ass. Maybe it will make a man out of you."

"What do they mean?" he repeated. "Conscientious objector? What do those words mean? Is that what you're asking?"

He pointed to the dictionary on the squat, little bookshelf in the living room.

"Dad," I said, pleading. "I don't even know how to spell those words. How can I look them up?"

"I know," he said, smiling. "I know. . . . I'll tell you what they mean."

And so he did. He told me that sometimes—not all the time, but sometimes—people tell you to do things that are wrong. And the people who tell you to do these things, these wrong things, are sometimes—not all the time, but sometimes—people in positions of authority, priests or teachers or coaches, and their status carries so much weight that you think to yourself, well, if they are telling me to do this thing, this wrong thing, can it really be that wrong? And, instead of focusing on the thing they are telling you to do, you focus on the people who are telling you to do it, and you breathe a sigh of relief, and you say to yourself, well, if this priest or teacher or coach is telling me to do this thing, then it must be okay. It must be. But no. Sometimes, you know more than any priest or teacher or coach, and sometimes you must obey the voice within you, the voice you trust. And when you do that, the old man said, when you do the right thing while those around you are telling you to do the wrong thing, you are a conscientious objector.

"Does that make sense?" the old man asked, finishing his definition.

"I think so," I said softly. "I think it does."

Afraid that I would cry, I shut my eyes again, shut them so hard that I could feel my forehead twitching, and when I reopened them, the old man was smiling at me.

"It does, Dad," I repeated. "It . . . does."

There was a long pause, and I stared at the dictionary on the bookshelf.

"So . . . " I said, hesitating. "They put you in prison for . . . "

"For refusing to kill anybody," he said.

"*Chingele,*" I said softly.

I felt like crying again.

"Dad," I asked, "how come you never told me you were in prison?"

"I did," he said softly.

"You never told me," I said, challenging the old man. "Never."

He stared at me, his cold, hazel eyes disputing my claim.

"But you didn't," I said, weakening. "You didn't . . . "

He refused to debate me.

"You did?" I asked, stammering. "But when?"

"Remember that day you asked me to tell you why you were a Mexican?" he asked. "It was after Randy Reed tore your surfboards. You never told me he had ripped them apart, but your mother did, thank God, and so I knew. . . . Remember that day?"

"I remember," I said, ashamed.

"Well, that's the day I told you I was in prison," he said gently.

"You did?"

"Yes."

That was the dark turn in his story, the detour into the menacing alley I had missed the first time around.

"But why?" I asked. "Why did you tell me on that day?"

"Because I could tell you were feeling bad, and I wanted you to know that I understood," he said. "Randy Reed assaulted . . ."

"Huh?"

"Oh, assaulted," he said. "You don't know what that means. . . . "

He pointed at the dictionary, but I kept looking at the old man, for once undaunted by his gesture.

"Assault is when someone hits you, when someone forces himself on you," he said, finally. "Randy Reed assaulted you, he struck you. You never told me that's what happened, but I knew somebody had mistreated you. Oh, he did not attack you physically, at least not on that particular day, but he attacked you emotionally. He made you feel bad about yourself.

"You don't know remember what I told you that day, because Randy Reed made you feel bad. That's what evil people do to you. They make you feel bad, and they make you feel so bad that you can't think about anything but the hurt you're feeling inside. It wasn't your fault you didn't hear me. You wanted to escape, and you did. You escaped into the story I was telling you."

I stared at the floor.

"I wanted to let you know that everyone has a Randy Reed," he said softly. "Everyone."

He was sitting on the sofa, and I was standing in front of him, and he looked at the newspaper on his lap. I stared at him. And I closed my eyes—again.

"When I refused to fight, an FBI agent asked me how I got this strange idea—this idea that killing was a sin," he said, resuming his story. "I was working in San Antonio back then, and he came to talk to me in my apartment."

The old man told the FBI agent he had gotten the idea from Tolstoy, and the FBI agent asked him where he could get a hold of "this Tolstoy guy."

"That might be kind of hard," the old man told him.

"Why?"

"Because Tolstoy's dead," the old man said.

When I stood by the door the night before, eavesdropping on my parents, I pictured *The Untouchables,* the television series about the Chicago mob, some of whose members were hauled off to prison for crimes that included murder. Their leader was Al Capone, a devil in a pin-striped suit. Al Capone, the crime lord who served time in the same prison where they locked up the old man. I heard him say it. I heard him. Capone and the old man—my old man—in the same prison. How did it happen?

And then the next day, when the old man was discussing his prison experiences with me, I stopped listening, just as I had stopped listening all those months before, when the dark turn emerged in the story about how he met my mother. I felt the same sensation I had experienced before, a kaleidoscope of images swirling in my mind—images of the old man as a young man, too young to be encaged. I saw the bus. I saw the hills. And I saw the old man standing in the prison yard, under the Gothic windows that loomed over the entrance of the facility. There was no Jesus in those windows, no heavenly Father to guide him through life in the hellhole.

The old man was sitting on the sofa, his head bowed. He was pondering his next comment, and as he thought, I scanned our surroundings, our crummy rental. The squat bookshelf, the naked walls, the typewriter on the dining room table, the . . . I hated the house, hated it, and yet the old man lived in a prison, and who was I, a *chavalo cagado*, a crappy kid, to complain about where I was living?

I started listening again. The old man did not mean to scare me, but he did scare me. I was too young to understand what happened to him in prison, but I knew it was horrible—or could have been horrible if he had allowed it to be. Not knowing what to think, I did not think at all. Not really. I took it all in—every word, every gesture—but I was like a diner who consumes his meal without digesting it.

There was one thing I did know. I knew the prison officials tried to break him, strip him of his heart and character, the two things that made the old man the old man. And I knew they failed.

Whatever happened to him inside the penitentiary, he was the same man outside the penitentiary, his soul and spirit intact. They could not destroy the man, and they could not destroy the man he wanted to become. But who did he want to become? Did he want to become Amado Muro, a man who could describe his experiences from a fresh perspective? The first Amado Muro stories were years away, but decades later, I would wonder if the tales—and the man who produced them—were born in that dark cage.

Could you be your own man by stepping into the shoes of another man? Could Chester Seltzer find himself by becoming Amado Muro? Or was he already Amado Muro, with or without the pseudonym? Was he already a man who embraced others, feeling what they felt, dreaming what they dreamed?

Whatever path he would take beyond Lewisburg, something happened to him in the penitentiary. Something bad. Something life-altering. Maybe the shift from Young Chess to Chess to—what?—would have happened, anyway, over the natural progression of years, the passage of time leading him from a determined young man to a determined older man, his passion rendered more intense, more desperate, by the years he lived in that damned cage.

Somewhere along the way, Young Chess became Chess and Chess became . . . what? Chess became the old man, and the old man became Amado Muro, his humor tempered by desperation, a sense that whatever he had to do, he better do it right away, before they robbed him of more time on this earth.

Alita tried to help me understand why Chester Seltzer morphed into Amado Muro, but she did not go far enough. It was not her fault. His motives were too vague, too complex, and she did not know the full story. The old man was a lifelong outsider, and as an outsider, he hid behind walls that were difficult, if not impossible, to storm. But the reason for his transformation, his identity switch, lay in those very walls. The barriers protected him, but they also isolated him, and the isolation became stultifying.

For all my confusion, I began to recognize a paradox that was impossible to ignore. The old man fit in—or at least started to fit in—for the very reason that I did not: because he was Mexican (if only in his heart). The walls were still there, but now they were different walls, walls of his own choosing, and they allowed him to live the life he wanted to live, identifying with the people he loved and respected.

As with all outsiders, the problem was not the old man; the problem was the insiders, the people who failed to understand him, viewing his noble spirit as eccentric or, worse, demented. It started early, when he began reading Tolstoy, Dostoevsky, and Chekhov—a devotion that revealed the chasm between Young Chess and his friends, who thought Tolstoy, Dostoevsky, and Chekhov were college football players. It continued with the waitress trick in the diner, the ploy that sickened him and delighted his friend. And it peaked with his decision to become a conscientious objector, refusing to fight a war that was, in the eyes of millions, justified.

I remembered a story my grandfather told me. It was a frigid night in December, a few weeks before Christmas. Chess was seventeen. He came home without his shirt and jacket, so cold that his lips spluttered as he struggled to get the words out: "Puh, puh, puh, puh, puh." The words lodged in his throat.

"My God, Chess, what happened?" his father yelled.

The boy, a lean but powerful athlete, seemed fragile, skinny, as if his body were cannibalizing itself. He bent over, and his father threw a quilt around him. His mother made him some hot chocolate.

"What happened, Chess?" his father repeated.

The boy finally responded. It was getting dark, he told his father, and he saw a man standing on the sidewalk near Shaker Square. He was thin and gaunt, a ragged silhouette in the fading light, too weak to ask for money. Dozens of people passed him by. It was so cold that icicles had formed on his gray beard. Chess stopped, and the man looked at him, shivering. He was wearing a long-sleeved shirt, but it was so big that it fit him like a shawl. The boy noticed his eyes, narrow and bloodshot, with sockets so deep that he seemed to be peering out of tiny caves.

"Here," the boy said, reaching into his pocket for a dollar. It was all the money he had.

"Thank you," the man said, so cold that he could barely get the words out.

The boy nodded. He started to walk away, taking a few steps before stopping. He took off his jacket, and his shirt, and he gave these to the man, too.

"What?" the man said, unable to grasp the compassion the boy showed him.

"Please take them," the boy said.

The man took them, and Chess walked away, bare-chested, picking up the pace as the cold pierced his bones.

"My God, Chess," his father said as the boy finished his story.

They were sitting in the living room, which was filled with Victorian furniture, including a piano that nobody played.

"My God," his father repeated.

And then the boy repeated a line from an essay he had just read by Leo Tolstoy. "My privilege disgusts me."

Young Chess—an outsider in his own family. When Alita gave me the *retratos* for Christmas, I started grappling with his dual identity. I thought I understood, but after he told me about Lewisburg Penitentiary, I realized that my notions were too romantic, too quaint. Amado Muro wrote the short stories, but Chester Seltzer lived them. The old man had a history, a back story, and it was this back story that informed every word he wrote. It was a story of alienation and a desire to rise above it, on his terms. He did it by becoming Amado Muro, finding refuge among another group of outsiders, Mexicans, who were marginalized by the larger society. They helped the outsider become an insider. The old man would never admit it, but he wanted to belong, and now he did. His soul was plundered by one group and restored by another. The result was remarkable. He did what all great artists do—he internalized the voices of others.

Did I understand this at the time? No. But I understood that the old man created Amado Muro just as surely as Amado Muro created his characters, and it was this creation, this identity switch, that made him whole.

"I had a Randy Reed," the old man told me, finishing his story about his incarceration. "But my Randy Reed was bigger than yours, a lot bigger. But the size of your enemy doesn't matter, does it? Do you know who my Randy Reed was?"

"No," I answered.

He looked down at the newspaper again, now crumpled in his lap.

"My Randy Reed was the US gover. . . ." I interrupted the old man.

"Dad," I said. "I do know who he was, I mean, what it was. I do know."

And I did. I felt ashamed. My Randy Reed was a stupid kid. But he had his own Randy Reed. And it was not Bobo. . . .

# 23

## The Old Man Teaches Me the Meaning of Naïveté

It was three o'clock in the afternoon, a cool, breezy Saturday in October—autumn in Cleveland. Young Chess spotted a tree in the middle of a park, its long roots clawing the soft soil. The tree was tall and sturdy, an oak; it looked like a column in a Greek temple. The boy smiled.

He had been strolling through the park for about ten minutes, looking for a spot where he could relax and view the world, the passing parade. And, when he found it, he quickened his pace. He jogged up to the tree, and then he turned abruptly, resting his back against the trunk. The boy paused to savor the world around him—the grass, the trees, the shafts of sunshine lancing the clouds.

Young Chess looked at the sky, its brilliance flashing and fading as the clouds drifted past the sun. Autumn. There was no better time of year, and no better city in which to experience it. He pressed his back against the tree, sliding down the trunk until his legs curved into a sitting position. The smile broadened. And then, whomp, his butt hit the ground, and he was sitting on the soil.

The boy pictured Tom Sawyer fishing by the river, a blade of grass twirling between his teeth. Lake Erie was his Mississippi River. He wished he were Tom Sawyer, bold and reckless and alive.

Young Chess loved Lakewood Park, a park so big that it looked like a town unto itself. The park hugged Lake Erie, but from his spot under the tree, the water was about one hundred yards away, behind a row of trees, so he could not see it. But he could smell it. The scent, sweet but pungent, rode a wave of air that swept into his nostrils. He looked to the north, toward the lake, and then he looked around him, inhaling and exhaling, marveling at the trees, their leaves laced with the bold but translucent colors of autumn. He saw a shadow flicker to his left, but when he turned around, the shadow sprouted four legs, one head, and one tail. Damn. The collie loped across the park, loose and languid—graceful in its gangliness. He followed the dog across the grass, chasing it with his eyes, but the boy could not keep up. The dog was too fast, his eyes too slow. He redirected his gaze to the world in front of him, the world he loved, Cleveland in autumn.

The boy closed his eyes, and the sunspots drifted in front of him, tiny, crazy swirls that resembled amoebas. He saw the spots clearly, despite his shuttered eyes, and he wondered if his eyelids were movie screens—tiny white sheets that served as the backdrops for these kaleidoscopic images. Damn.

He kept staring at the spots, and he wondered how he could feel so dizzy, so spectacularly dizzy, while sitting still. And then he opened his eyes, and the spots disappeared, and he marveled at how he could see objects when his eyes were closed but fail to see them when they were open.

The clouds dispersed, and the sky turned a bluish gold, like the flames on a stove. Young Chess folded his arms across his chest, drowsy with peace and contentment. He tried to capture in words the beauty around him. Under the tree, with no pen or paper, he closed his eyes, and he composed sentence after sentence, each one true and fresh and pure . . . and then . . . and then he woke up.

The dream came to him every night, and it was always the same, tinged with a sense of joy and dread. He was fifteen, always fifteen, a boy with a goal—to become a writer. But not just any writer. A writer who could describe the world as clearly as he saw it. But dammit, his desire was greater than his ability to fulfill it. Maybe he wanted it too badly, too desperately.

A great writer. Uttering those three words intimidated him. A great writer. If only he could write with his eyes; if only he could look at the world, savor its beauty and purity, and filter those images into words. . . . If only . . .

It was a quiet fantasy, but beyond the sunshine, there was a shadow that crept into his soul. Was it the cloud cover in the sky—the cloud cover he saw in his dreams—with the sun flashing in and out, providing him with glimpses, only glimpses, of the golden opportunities beyond? The old man never answered the question. He never had to. The answer assaulted him every time he woke up.

If the dreams hinted at sadness, their aftermath exploded with it. Every time his dreams ended, he woke up to the same thing, the same realization: life in a cage. Dreams were about possibilities; prison was about stifling them. Fuck. He was dreaming those dreams in prison.

The old man never settled into a routine in prison. The routine settled on him, imposed itself on him. He slept; he woke. He slept; he woke. And, in between the sleeping and the waking, he thought about the sleeping and the waking. The old man crawled through life.

Time was not a smooth, easy march. It was a bitter slog. And the more time passed, the more it seemed to stand still. Three years. He had spent two years in work camps, and he had one more to go, in this cage. How would he survive it? And then, one day, the old man rebelled.

The old man was wrong about prison. It did not keep the world out; it let the world in. But what flowed into the penitentiary was the sewage of the outside world, the flaws that represented a stain on humanity. And inside, where goodness was so scarce, those flaws seemed magnified. It sickened the old man.

What was the old man expecting? His naïveté staggered him. That was the word he used. Naïveté. I interrupted his story.

"Dad?"

"What?"

"I don't know what naïveté means," I said, pronouncing the word slowly.

He looked at me, a smile shining through the glower he tried to flash me.

"Okay, I'll look it up," I said, my shoulders drooping.

Trudging to the bookshelf, I sensed his eyes on my back. The old man was always studying me—when I was eating, when I was reading, when I was walking to the bookshelf. It was as if he were watching a movie or reading a book, his eyes glowing with expectation.

"Dad, I can't find it."

"How are you spelling it?" he asked.

"N-I-E-V-E-T-A-Y," I said, uncertainly.

His mouth curved into a warm but devilish smile.

"Actually, it's N-A-I-V-E-T-E," he said, repeating each letter slowly.

"Okay," I said, flipping through the dictionary again.

"That's alright," he said. "I'll tell you. Naïveté means being, uhm, younger and less mature than you think you are. It means you are not the intelligent and brilliant individual you may pride yourself on being."

I looked at him quizzically, unable to fathom how anyone could think the old man was less intelligent than he was.

"Anyway," the old man said.

The real world swept into the penitentiary, he said, past its locked gates, its giant towers, its barred cells. And then, once the evil entered, it stayed; like the prisoners, it stayed. Every man lost his freedom in Lewisburg, but some prisoners had less to lose. It was wrong, the old man said, but freedom was not a birthright. It was granted to you, or not granted to you, by the government.

The lighter your skin, the more freedoms you enjoyed. Whites enjoyed more liberties than Mexicans, who enjoyed more liberties than blacks, who enjoyed more liberties . . . well, the old man said . . . blacks enjoyed more liberties than animals.

"Why, Dad?" I asked. "Why do people treat them like that?"

"Why do you think Randy Reed hates . . . dislikes . . . you?" he asked.

"Because he's mean?"

"Well, that's one answer."

"Because he's dumb?"

"That's another answer, although I prefer the word ignorant," the old man said.

"Because he's . . ." I could not think of a third reason.

"There are a lot of answers," the old man said. "A lot more. It's complicated. If people, some people, don't like something about themselves, it makes them feel good when they look down on somebody else. . . ."

One day in prison, the old man met a new inmate, and it was like looking in the mirror. It was not just that the two men looked alike, although they did—same brown hair, same piercing eyes, same glow when they discussed their ideals. And it was not just that they were both conscientious objectors. No, it was more than that.

The old man was from Cleveland, the son of a prominent newspaper editor. The other man, Dave Dellinger, was from Wakefield, Massachusetts, the son of a lawyer. There was one difference between the two, though. The old man was a quiet rebel, but Dellinger went on to fame as one of the Chicago Seven, the group of protesters assaulted by police for demonstrating outside the Democratic National Convention in 1968. But that was years later, more than twenty years later.

Both men could have chosen easier paths, exploiting their circumstances to escape the harsh realities of life. But—how did the old man put it? They pissed on privilege, both of them. That was a new one for me, a new cuss word—piss. And the old man apologized for using it.

"What I mean, Beto, is that when you believe something, you can't always worry about how your decisions might hurt you," he said, pausing. "If you don't act on your beliefs, it might hurt you even more. . . . Do you understand?"

I said yes, I understood. Yes, yes, I stammered. The old man looked at me. His lips quivered into a smile, but it was a weak smile, and I thought he wanted to cry.

"Did the other prisoner—Mr. Dellinger—feel the same way, Dad?" I asked.

The old man looked at me, shocked, as if he had forgotten his train of thought.

"Yes . . . yes, he did," he said, finally. "He felt the same way."

When he regained his composure, the old man told me about the hunger strike, an act of rebellion he might not have undertaken without the inspiration of his fellow prisoner, Dave Dellinger. The prison was no hotel, he said, but it was worse for the black prisoners. They were treated as if they were—different—less valuable. The old man looked at me, trying to make certain I knew what the word valuable meant. I did, but not because I had heard it or seen it in the dictionary. I just knew. The old man stroked his chin, and as he told the story, his memories washed over both of us, a flood of anger and outrage. It was then that I realized he was talking about the black prisoners as human beings, that they were valuable *because* they were human beings.

The old man said the black prisoners were segregated from the other inmates, but he stumbled over the word segregated, and then he replaced it with the word separated. But, again, I knew what he meant. I am not sure how, but I knew. He said the prisoners were separated, black from white, human from . . . animal? They did everything separately. They slept separately; they ate separately; they worked in the yard separately.

"Why?" I asked the old man.

"Remember, I told you that some people are ignorant and, because of that ignorance, they look down on people for no reason, other than their religion or skin color?"

"Yes, sir," I said.

"Well, the prison officials were ignorant."

So the white prisoners, including the old man and Dave Dellinger, coordinated a hunger strike to protest the racial discrimination in the prison.

Hunger strike? The guards scoffed. Just wait, they told the inmates, your bellies will overrule your hearts, and when that happens, a trough will not hold all the food you want to stuff into your pathetic little mouths. The guards were wrong. The men never collapsed.

News of the strike spread through the surrounding community. Townspeople were appalled. The *Daily Item*, a local Pennsylvania newspaper, condemned the strikers:

> It is news for the reason that the 'strikers' are conscientious objectors to military service—not on religious grounds—but for 'philosophical' reasons, which is another way of varnishing plain draft dodging, but it is nonetheless disgusting.
>
> That a group of able-bodied young men, unwilling to discharge their obligations to their country in a time of acute peril should languish in prison while others sacrifice their all is bad enough, particularly when it is remembered that sentences were passed either for ignoring the selective service law entirely, or for refusing to report for work camps provided for objectors, but the added spectacle of such a crew objecting commensurate prison discipline is absolutely repugnant.

The inmates persevered. It was the prison officials who caved, ordering the guards to force-feed the men with rubber hoses they jammed down their throats. The hoses pumped slop into their bellies, and with that, the hunger strike ended. Three weeks. The strike lasted three weeks, a period during which the inmates consumed nothing more substantial than fruit juice. They looked like orphans in a Dickens novel, skinny and haggard, their ribs as prominent as the slats on a fence. It was the first time I had heard the term force-feed.

"Why would you have to force a person to eat?" I asked my dad.

The old man laughed. Then he told me that one of the guards, trying to shove the hose down his throat, cut his nostrils. Cut them so bad that the blood dripped onto the hose. The old man grimaced, and when he looked up, he noticed that the kid—my father said the guard must have been in his early twenties—had a strange look on his face, a look of compassion, even regret. It was so temporary—little more than a facial tic—that the old man wondered if he had been hallucinating. No matter. That look, however fleeting or illusory it may have been, haunted the old man for years. And he would always feel sorry for the kid.

The old man never told me if the hunger strike worked, if the inmates forced the prison officials to treat the black prisoners like human beings. And I never asked him. I was afraid to. I was afraid to find out that all the hunger, all the suffering, resulted in nothing more than empty bellies.

Why would you punish someone for not killing another human being? The old man told me about the draft, about the war that society regarded as a "virtuous struggle." He was working as a reporter in San Antonio, and as they hauled him before the judge, they told him it was the state that would be doing the killing, not him, but he admired Gandhi, and he read Tolstoy, and he figured that if he hurled some poor Germans or Japanese into eternity, they would have a right to blame him, not his government. So he said "no," and they locked him up for three years, first in work camps, then in the prison.

"Son, don't you understand you're not going to be responsible for the killing," the judge in San Antonio told him.

"If you believe that," my father replied, "you need help more than I do."

I did not understand his stance—or the commitment that produced it—but there was one thing I did understand. World War II was a popular war, unlike the conflict that gripped the nation in the 1960s, and what was conscientious objection for some was cowardly opportunism for others. The old man could have run to Mexico or Canada, but he remained in the United States, the country he loved but refused to obey. He was no coward.

The old man told me about Ernest Hemingway. He called him a "great American writer." Hemingway sounded like an older version of the old man, a man whose commitment to the written word was all-abiding. Hemingway hated war, too, my father said.

"A defensive war, which must necessarily turn to aggressive at the earliest moment, is the necessary great counter-crime," the old man quoted Hemingway. "But never think that war, no matter how necessary, nor how justified, is not a crime. Ask the infantry and the dead."

The old man recited the quote, word for word, as if it were a poem assigned by Mrs. Chaney. He did not ask me if I understood it. But I did.

I never considered the old man a criminal, an ex-con. Other family members were not so lenient. He came from a conservative background, and some of his relatives excoriated him. One of his beloved uncles refused to talk to him, carrying his silence to the grave, but the one Seltzer whose opinion he treasured—his father, the great newspaperman Louis B. Seltzer—supported him. LBS, as he was known throughout Cleveland, could not comprehend his position, could not fathom it. But, while he did not support the decision, he supported the man who made it, and that was all that mattered to the old man.

"Our children were taught by us to think for themselves," his father wrote. "Our son, consistent with this, made a decision. I believed at the time he made it and believe now it was a wrong decision—tragically wrong. It was, nevertheless, his decision, one which he, as a grown man, had the right to make."

The column—signed L. B. S.—appeared in the *Cleveland Press* on May 31, 1944.

> All of his life, he has abhorred killing in any form. He does not believe force has really settled anything for long in the world. Again I think he is wrong, but I respect the courage and determination he has shown supporting his convictions. He has chosen a hard and lonely way, and he has neither asked for nor received any favors.
>
> I envy fathers whose sons are fighting. I wish my own son, as brave and honorable a boy as I have ever known, were fighting, too.

Despite his position on the war, my father was modest, seeking neither approval nor publicity. The old man followed his conscience, but he nourished it quietly, through his readings of Tolstoy and Jesus.

He did not need intellectuals, whether friends or acquaintances, to stoke his ego—or validate his worldview. The old man went to the work camps and the federal prison because of a moral stance, but his sentence transcended symbolism; they were the roughest years of his life, and there were moments when the calendar seemed like his cruelest enemy, each day reminding him of the freedom he had lost.

When he got out of prison, the old man returned to Cleveland, and his father offered him a job at the *Cleveland Press*, where he was the editor. The old man turned him down. It was another act of quiet rebellion—not against his father or his family, but against the comfortable lifestyle the job represented. If his father had forged a successful career through hard work, that was one thing, but the old man did not want to benefit from something he had no part in acquiring. It would have made him feel guilty, unclean, just as he had all those years before, when he and his friend perpetrated that horrible trick on the young waitress.

"Please, Chess," his father told him. "You're such a fine writer. You'd be a great employee. It has nothing to do with your being my son."

"I'm sorry, Dad," he said. "I just can't."

"I understand," his father said wearily.

After resting a few months in Cleveland, the old man took off again, heading back to the Southwest, this time to El Paso, where he met the woman he would marry—my mother. He took her heart, and while she took his name, he took hers as well, adapting Amada Muro as the pseudonym for his short stories. The quiet rebellion continued, although I was not sure why he changed his name—not really.

To me, the old man was just the old man, regardless of what he called himself. But when Chester Seltzer became Amado Muro, it was another declaration of independence, for he ensured that whatever success he attained would be on his own terms, not because of his family name. It was an irony he acknowledged but never discussed: His most ingenious fictional character was not Cecilia Rosas or Maria Tepache or Tio Pascual. It was Amado Muro, the man who created those characters. The ruse was gentle but effective, designed to allow him greater intimacy with his subjects while distancing himself from the family whose name and wealth could have helped pave the way to literary success. I was too young to recognize it at the time, but the pseudonym was one part literary device, one part family therapy.

After his three-year sentence, he was a changed man, stripped of any materialism he may have taken into that dark cell with him. He cared about his family, and he cared about his short stories, and that was it. The old man could be funny, but frivolity was a luxury in which he rarely indulged. He never let me play with toy guns, afraid, perhaps, that the hostility I feigned on the playground might become all too real on the battleground. My mother bought me a cap pistol one day, but she told me to play with it away from the house, where the old man could not see or hear the offending firearm. Whenever I was through playing cops and robbers, she hid the pistol in an empty shoe box in the closet. I always felt guilty and scared afterward, scared that he was aware of our deception, but if he was, he never mentioned it.

"Remember, Beto, it's just a book," he told me after encouraging me to read *Treasure Island* by Robert Louis Stevenson. "Hurting people—killing them—isn't the way we settle arguments."

"But you like boxing, and boxers hurt people," I said.

"That's different," he said. "Referees control the violence, and . . . and . . . boxing is an art. Two men poised to fight each other, their only weapons their fists. And sometimes, well, you just have to stand up for yourself."

"Hmmm," I said.

Was he talking about Randy Reed?

"Okay, Dad," I said.

24

# El Enojon

When Alita called my father an *enojon*, an angry man, she was not kidding.

The old man had a temper, usually triggered when somebody interrupted his work, and because he worked constantly—at home, on his short stories—the possibilities for provoking him were endless. I escaped his tirades through discretion. If I saw him on the sofa, knitting his brow as he struggled for the right word, I would blend into the background, becoming another pebble in the domestic mosaic. Sanctuary in the midst of chaos. It was a talent I acquired early.

My mother was not so delicate. She loved the idea of being married to a writer, someone gifted in the language of her adopted country, but she appreciated the literature more than she did the craft that went into producing it. *El escritor,* the writer, she would call him. But when he sat on the sofa in his boxer shorts, the old man looked like a *flojo,* an *inutil,* someone who shirked his real duties by claiming he was working. *Que es eso?* What is that all about?

The consequences? They were ugly. My mother was volatile, but the old man expressed his anger in waves, first as irritation, then as hostility. Gently rubbing his face—as if to indicate his control over the situation—he soon lost that control. When my mother cleaned the house, the vacuum cleaner throbbed with an annoying insistence, stifling the only sound that mattered to him when he was writing—his inner voice. Goddamn it! The machine muted the writer inside him.

"Amada," he growled. "What the hell is wrong with you? Can't you see I'm writing?"

"Why don't you go to the library to write?" she yelled. "Why don't you act like everybody else once in a while? Why don't you act normal?"

Everybody else? Normal? The words must have jolted the old man. He could no more act normal than a schizophrenic could act well-adjusted. Not that he was crazy. But, *chingado,* my mother fumed in frustration. Here he was, a man who prided himself on his tolerance, but if he were so goddamned tolerant, so goddamned accepting, why was he so inflexible when it came to his writing?

*"Tu y tus pinches historias!* You and your damned stories!" she screamed, pointing to the Underwood typewriter in the middle of the kitchen table.

So flustered that his outer voice joined his inner voice in silence—if only momentarily—the old man would storm off, his huge vocabulary reduced to the only words he could think of:

"Goddamn it!"

When he settled down, which he always did, he would tell me how much he loved my mother. He was headstrong, and she was headstrong, and sometimes their two strong heads collided. That was all, he said. I wanted to ask him if they were going to get a divorce, but I never did; I was afraid of what the answer would be.

"I know," I said whenever he told me that he and my mother loved each other. "I know."

The old man married my mother in 1950. And now, for the first time, I realized he was on the rebound—not from a lost love, but from a lost period in his life: He had walked out of Lewisburg Penitentiary a few years earlier, his view of the world no longer obstructed by clanging bars. He was still young, in his midthirties, but the experience hardened him, made him realize that whatever he wanted out of life—friends, family, time to write his stories—could vanish in a maelstrom of dashed hopes.

Now that I knew about his prison sentence, I understood—or thought I understood—why he had a temper . . . and why he pursued his craft with such single-minded devotion. His family and his short stories. Sometimes, his two loves clashed, and to a boy who wanted his father home every day, it seemed as if the short stories always won. It was worse that year in Bakersfield, because every time I wanted to talk to him, the old man was off on another trip, riding the rails to write about men who were drawn by the "lonesome dreary moan of a drag whistling the highball."

Deep down, I wanted him to be like other dads. We never went on summer vacations, and he never "treated" me, unless it was Christmas or my birthday. Except for one afternoon, when he brought me a Hershey Bar. . . . a Hershey Bar . . . *Chingele* . . . It was during the summer, with neither Christmas nor my birthday in sight. We were living in El Paso, and I accepted the candy with the glee of a starving orphan. I thanked him, and he told me he had bought it to get change for a parking meter in front of the El Paso Public Library. The gift no longer seemed like a gift, and I tossed it onto the kitchen table. Alita devoured it later that afternoon.

After I found out about his prison sentence, I stopped judging him so harshly. My mother was not so lenient. She hated the freight trains and the places they took him—the flophouses, rescue missions, and hobo jungles. When we moved to Bakersfield, he hit on a solution, driving us to Fresno or Los Angeles, where I could play with my cousins while he visited skid row during the weekend.

I loved my cousins in Pico Rivera, a suburb of Los Angeles. Alma was my age, as charming as she was mischievous, with eyes that sparkled every time she giggled—and she always giggled. She would have been at home in the hobo jungle. Alma could simulate the sound that Fifi, the Coltrane of crepitation, made the afternoon we visited Big Bill. She would cup her hand under her armpit, then flap her arm up and down, as if it were a bellows. It was an art I never mastered.

Her brother Frank—we called him Kiko—was a high school sophomore. He liked to perform his wrestling holds on me—evil, sinister moves that Johnny Valentine, Kinji Shibuya and "Bearcat" Wright—his favorite professional wrestlers—executed on TV every

Saturday afternoon. Kiko asked me, during one visit, if he could "lay a figure four" on me, promising not to hurt me in the process. I said "Okay," unaware of the pain it might cause. Twisting me like a piece of taffy, he rearranged my limbs until I resembled the number four. I screamed, and he released me, my arms and legs springing to their original positions like a Slinky, the coiled spring that was one of the most popular toys of the early 1960s.

"*Chingado*, Kiko," I said, trying to straighten my back.

He walked away, satisfied that he could perform the move his wrestling idols carried out on television.

"Where's your Dad?" Alma asked me during one of our visits.

"He's on skid row," I said.

"Skid row? What's that?"

I did not have the heart to tell her, and when my father picked us up on Sunday afternoon, my mother yelled at him in the car.

"Who do you think you are, dumping us off like that, and then picking us up whenever you want?" she said. "Don't you know your son is being mistreated at school? Don't you know he needs you?"

I waited for the old man to respond, but he never did. I could see him staring at me through the rearview mirror, his eyes betraying neither anger nor contrition. He seemed to be thinking. The old man was always thinking.

25

# The Chihuahua

The old man worked at the daily newspaper, the *Bakersfield Californian,* and I loved to visit him on Saturday afternoons, a time when frenzy yielded to languor. The news did not always go on strike during the weekends. It just seemed that way.

When he was working at the office, he always had time for me on Saturdays—always. I once found him asleep at his desk, his head slumped onto his chest, as the typewriters clacked away at other workstations. No one seemed to notice—or care. The old man was probably crafting sentences in his subconscious, the cadence of the words lulling him into dreamland.

I always visited him after *American Bandstand,* a program I watched in spurts, rushing to my room during the commercials to see if the disc jockey was playing the Beatles on the radio. It never failed; week after week, at some point during the hour-long *American Bandstand*, the Beatles would perform on both radio and TV. Simultaneously. My solution? I stood in the hallway, halfway between the radio and the television, listening to "She Loves You" with one ear and "She's a Woman" with the other. What a delicious tug-of-war, rock-and-roll style, each ear straining and each ear winning.

One Saturday afternoon, after another tug-of-war, I jumped on my bicycle to visit the old man at the office. I took the same route every time, a simple but perilous path, with the main stretch on Oleandar Street. I loved Oleander. It was a broad street, cool and majestic, with tall oaks that created a latticework of shadows on the asphalt below. What a neat phenomenon, especially for a kid from the desert. The shadows seemed organic, swaying and rippling with the wind, their shapes shifting as I glided above them on my bike.

How could such a street be perilous? It was the Chihuahua. Every time I rode past the green, two-story house on the third block, the Chihuahua shot out of the bushes, barking with the screeching monotony of an alarm clock. "*Pinche perro.* Damned dog," Alita would have yelled. I pedaled harder, but the Chihuahua refused to yield, staying so close that it looked like a sidecar on a Harley—a tiny sidecar, shrill and annoying. The dog nipped at my tires, forcing me to zig and zag through a street that suddenly lost its majesty. *Pinche perro.* Pedaling with one leg, I tried to kick the dog with the other, a maneuver that made me look like a clown spinning around on a unicycle. Come see Robert Seltzer and his Barking Chihuahua at the Oleander Circus. The Chihuahua was so persistent that he followed me for blocks, his bark finally receding into a distant but irritating *yip.*

Whatever agony I endured to get there, the destination was worth it. The *Bakersfield Californian.* I parked at the bicycle rack, near a cement fountain, using one of those locks that twisted the spokes if you tried to ride away without removing the damned thing. Why would a thief want a broken bicycle? A "deterrent," the old man called it.

My father worked in a huge office, the desks arranged like dominos, one cluttered mess after another. It looked like a white-collar factory, decades away from the clinical environment newsrooms began to adopt in the 1980s, with workers honeycombed in their own private cubicles. Progress.

When I visited the old man on weekdays, I could sense the tension, the electricity, as if the reporters were greyhounds chasing a mechanical rabbit. The rabbit was the news, but there was no joy in victory, for as soon as you caught one rabbit, another would emerge . . . and another . . . and another, each one faster than the one before. It was a thrill—except on Saturdays. The reporters needed a break, and the calendar obliged.

During his twenty-five years in journalism, my dad covered everything, from title fights in Miami to traffic accidents in Bakersfield. The old man exuded history, and I wanted to breathe the same air he breathed—the dank but exhilarating air of boxing gyms and jail cells and city halls. He must have been born with a notebook in his back pocket.

"I saw Lou Ambers fight in Miami," he told me, referring to the old lightweight champion. "He was skinny, kind of like you are. Thin arms. Concave chest."

"Concave?"

"You know the Roman centurions in the movies?"

"Yeah."

"They wore those breastplates that made them look like Hercules, right? Imagine if a gladiator took a hammer to one of those plates, leaving a big dip in it, like a bowl. Well, that's concave. And that was Lou Ambers. Skinny arms. Concave chest. But he was a great defensive fighter, one of the best I ever saw, maybe better than Ali."

Cassius Clay, who defeated Sonny Liston for the heavyweight championship a few months before, had changed his name to Muhammad Ali.

"You couldn't hit Ali with hand grenades," my father said. "Ambers was the same way."

The old man was passionate about books, boxing, and work (despite the occasional nap at his desk). It was a treat to see him in the office, the sphere for one of his passions. My mother traced his career in photo albums, and he looked the same in every picture—intense but happy, with an elegance that never veered into self-consciousness. The photos were black and white, all of them, and the images seemed soft, blurred, as if the photographers had selected the wrong setting for every shot. It made the pictures more evocative, more romantic, somehow.

He wore baggy suits in every frame, suits he did not wear so much as inhabit, they were so loose—but they looked good on him. The styles changed, and the old man changed with them, but he would never look as cool again. Not as he did in the forties and fifties. The new suits were more confining, and they always seemed at least one size too small for him, with the collars as tight as nooses. I felt sorry for him, but only because he seemed so uncomfortable. There was something about the new look, something I liked. The coolness was gone, but who cared? Not me. Elegant in one era, rumpled in another. I preferred the rumpled version.

In Bakersfield, he covered all kinds of stories—traffic accidents, murder trials, city elections. He even convinced the editors to let him write a weekly column in Spanish. It was titled "*Algo de la gente de habla espanol.* Something about the people who speak Spanish." It ran without an editor's note to explain why the paper would publish an article in a foreign language. The byline said "por Chester Seltzer" (by Chester Seltzer).

> Timoteo Garay, 67, hace su vida en las calles de Ciudad Juárez gracias a su arpa y los santos.
>
> Su arpa y los santos han sido sus mejores amigos desde hace 52 anos; su arpa porque la gente que lo eschuchan dicen que toca muy bien, y los santos porque hay tantos.
>
> Timoteo, hombre modesto y bondadoso que tiene amigos en las cienes, toca su arpa desde antes del medio dia hasta que se metio el sol.

> Timoteo Garay, 67, makes his living on the streets of Ciudad Juaréz, thanks to his harp and the saints.
>
> His harp and the saints have been his best friends for almost fifty-two years; his harp because the people who hear him say he plays very well; the saints because there are so many of them.
>
> Timoteo, a modest and generous man whose friends number in the hundreds, plays his harp from noon till sunset.

He worked in a short, squat building—drab but solid, with more substance and character than the other downtown structures. I loved it. The staff was polite and friendly, especially the women at the front counter, who made me feel important whenever I visited my dad.

"Chester's at his desk, young man," they would tell me.

The old man was writing editorials that year. One of them was about farm workers north of Bakersfield. They were being organized by Cesar Chavez, an activist who was forming unions to help the laborers negotiate with the landowners. The old man picked peas on one of the farms, and the resulting editorial was headlined "These Men Are Americans, Too."

He loved writing the editorials, but the assignment ended when he let integrity trump self-preservation. He wrote an antiwar editorial—an antiwar editorial—in 1964, before the Vietnam War turned the country into one huge battleground, with doves on one side, hawks on the other. What was the old man thinking?

In about three years, the enemy would be everywhere—American versus American, engaged in a civil war that was no less passionate for being undeclared. But we were not there, not yet. This was 1964. Before sit-ins and love-ins and all-the-other-ins. Before protests and demonstrations and moratoriums. Before "Ohio" and "Fortunate Son" and "Give Peace a Chance." Before Jane Fonda and Abbie Hoffman and Eldridge Cleaver and . . . Dave Dellinger, his friend from Lewisburg Penitentiary. . . .

What was the old man thinking? Was he thinking of his own prison stretch? Was he thinking of his favorite authors, men who sparked his hatred of war: Leo Tolstoy, Humphrey Cobb, William March, Erich Maria Remarque? Or was he thinking of that waitress in the diner, the young woman whose destiny he may have altered through a childish antic?

Whatever motivated my father to write the editorial, it proved to be his last for the *Bakersfield Californian*. The old man was speaking for himself, not the newspaper, when he crafted the editorial, but the piece fell through the cracks, drifting past the discerning eyes of his editors. Was he sabotaging the newspaper? Hardly. There was nothing disingenuous about the old man; he could not fool a naïve child, much less a staff of hardened newsmen.

Why, then, did he do it? The answer was simple: Guided by passion and idealism, he forgot he was a mouthpiece for the newspaper, not a spokesman for his heart. The editorial ran the next day, and when the editors discovered that their support for the war had waned without their knowledge, the old man was back in the newsroom, writing news stories and feature stories.

"Chester's at his desk, young man," one of the women at the front counter told me.

I walked across the broad corridor, my shoes clicking on the bright tile.

"You're sweating," my dad said.

"The Chihuahua."

"I see," he said, smiling. "Are you hungry?"

"Not really," I said.

I was, but not for a sandwich or a hamburger.

"Do you want to go to Dewar's?"

Dewar's was an ice cream shop, the kind where Ricky Nelson and Beaver Cleaver slurped their malted milks on television. I remembered the Hershey Bar. Did he need more change?

"Yes," I said, smiling hesitantly.

We sat at a table across from the long L-shaped counter where the girls prepared the malts and shakes in steel mixers. I craned my neck, fascinated, to view the ceiling—fans whirred above us, oscillating back and forth, back and forth, like little mechanical sentries. My milkshake arrived—chocolate, my favorite.

"Enjoy your milkshake," my father said, smiling.

Smiles are supposed to travel, from your mouth to your eyes, lighting you up from within. This was not that kind of smile. This smile was different. It began and ended at his curved lips. There was no joy in it. No sadness, either. Not a deep sadness, anyway. Just a vague melancholy.

"Enjoy your life," my father told me, his half-smile fading into a non-smile.

"Okay, Dad."

26

# The Movie Reel in my Head

Randy Reed was my biggest enemy; the clock was a close second.

Old enough to wake up early, I was too young to stay up late, so I missed out on the TV shows I yearned to watch—*Gunsmoke, Have Gun Will Travel, Wanted: Dead or Alive*. They tamed the Wild West without me. . . . *Pinche* clock. I hated it.

The old man would not have let me watch those shows, anyway. They were too violent. The TV gave me a window into the world, into its rich, vibrant past, but the old man drew a curtain on it, depriving me of all the mayhem and gunfire I longed to view. My father understood my youthful fascination with televised violence, but as a man who frowned on toy pistols, he was adamant about the curfew.

I lurked in the hallway one night, quietly watching *Maverick* as the hero drew his six-gun during a poker game. The old man spotted me during a commercial, and when he arose from the couch, walking toward me slowly and deliberately, he assumed a Maverick-like pose—stern and menacing, with just a hint of satirical irony. The irony was not enough to save me. He banished me to my room, where there were no horses, no saloons, no six-guns.

There was one source of solace, one bright note in the dark symphony of my strict upbringing (at least I thought it was strict). My parents could put me to bed, but it was harder to tuck in my spirit, my restless yearning. And so, when they doused the lights, they ignited my imagination, which took me on journeys a travel agent could barely imagine: Mars, Olympus, even Heaven—and yes, it was full of clouds and men in white robes.

Then, one night, the old man let me break the curfew. It was a school night. We got into the Rambler, and he dropped me off at El Tejon Theater. He gave me a dollar—fifty cents for the movie, another fifty cents for snacks.

"Thanks, Dad," I said, stepping out of the Rambler in front of the theater.

Get lost in the things you love, the old man had told me. It will help you forget your problems at school. He was right; for the next two hours, Randy Reed was the last thing on my mind.

The lady at the candy counter—she was a girl, but female teenagers looked like ladies to me—was tall and cute, with a face full of pimples that looked like cherry blossoms. She asked me what I wanted. I hesitated.

"Uh, uh, uh."

"Yes?"

I gulped.

"Uhm, I'll take some FUCKS," I said.

"What?!?"

"Some FUCKS," I repeated, gulping again.

She looked at me, dumbfounded, turning to the candies on the display case behind her.

"Oh, I see," she said, finally.

The lady handed me a box of candies. They were marked FLICKS, but the *L* and the *I* were so intimate that I turned them into a single letter, a *U*. I did not realize my gaffe until the box was in my hand, and by then it was too late. Alita would have summed up my predicament in three words, and they were not "*Chingele, chingele, chingele.*" They were "*Ay Dios mio.*"

"Thank you," I said sheepishly, handing the lady the money.

"You're welcome," she said, smiling.

I found a seat about three rows from the screen. Should I get closer? I wondered. Or should I move back? I stayed put. Waiting for the movie to start, I felt young and happy—happy in my innocence and self-absorption. I thought I would stay young and happy forever. Oh, time would rush by—I knew that—but I would remain immune to its irresistible force, making me a child for eternity. Or so I thought—if only for one shimmering moment.

Sitting in the dark, my box of FUCKS, uh, FLICKS nestled in my lap, I waited for the thick, red curtains to part—theaters had curtains back then. I gripped the armrests, my body tightening with a nervous joy. Hurry, please, hurry. I wanted time to speed up.

"I'll remember this night for the rest of my life," I told myself.

Then the curtains opened, and the screen ignited with the joy and exuberance of four young musicians—an explosion of sounds and images that startled me. I dropped my FLICKS. *Chingele.* Shifting in my seat, I looked down, surveying all the gum wrappers and paper cups and popcorn boxes, but my search was futile, and as the music exploded above me, I decided to leave the FLICKS wherever they landed, booty for some lucky usher.

When I looked back up, the Beatles were sprinting down a narrow street, laughing and stumbling to one of the most famous opening chords in rock 'n' roll history. Maybe the most famous. The song—the movie—was *A Hard Day's Night.*

For weeks—or was it months?—afterward, I relived every scene in the film, each golden image flashing from the movie reel in my head. I saw John smirking, Paul smiling, Ringo fretting, George stroking his face, trying to determine if his scornfulness had twisted his features (as Ringo claimed it would). I saw it all, savored it all. But the best part—the part I would treasure forever—was the music, the Beatles in concert, coaxing those amazing sounds out of their instruments, from rave-ups like "Can't Buy Me Love" to ballads like "And I Love Her."

The movie was funny and irreverent, but there was one tender scene: As the Beatles launched into "And I Love Her," George stopped strumming his guitar, embracing the instrument as though it were a long-lost lover. You could almost hear him sighing.

"I'll remember this night for the rest of my life," I repeated at the end of the movie, still flush with the joy of watching these four young geniuses on the screen.

My father picked me up in front of the theater, and as I hopped into the Rambler, I wondered if I would ever see the movie again, maybe on *Saturday Night at the Movies*, the NBC program that aired old films. This was before DVDs and DVRs. If I did see it again, I wondered, would I repeat my comment?

"I'll remember this night for the rest of my life."

Imagine. If I repeated the comment, would I be an old man when I repeated it? I could not get the thought out of my head. What if I said it again? What if I said the same thing in my old age—in my twenties, thirties or forties—that I had said as I child? It was eerie. As an old man, the rest of my life would be much shorter than I had envisioned it as a kid. . . . It made me shudder. . . . But this night—the night I saw the movie—was not a night to dwell on mortality; it was a night to swim in the vast, joyous pool of youth.

I wondered if I would regale my kids with tales of the night I saw the movie. And I wondered if they would react with the same lack of enthusiasm I showed when the old man rhapsodized about Russ Columbo, a pop singer of the 1930s. The old man broke into the chorus of "Prisoner of Love" one day, his voice quavering when he hit the high notes, and I tried to stifle my laughter.

One evening, before dinner, the old man sang another tune, "*Ay, Jalisco, No Te Rajes*"—a song popularized by his favorite Mexican artist, Jorge Negrete—with the same comical result.

Would my kids react the same way if I tried to sing "Tell Me Why" or "I'm Happy Just to Dance With You"? What if they did? I would try to be like the old man, cherishing my memories while allowing my kids to forge their own.

27

# The Confession

The Rolling Stones—nobody called them the Stones back then—were playing "Get Off of My Cloud." It roused me, drained the sleep from my eyes. I raised the volume, and the radio popped, the nightstand trembling under the ominous drum roll by the great Charlie Watts.

As Mick Jagger launched into his bitter put-down, another noise muted the snarl in his voice. It was my mother. She was yelling at the old man.

"*Ay Dios mio*," she said. "You didn't even tell me you were leaving."

"I thought I did," he responded.

"You think," she said. "You think. You always think. 'I thought this, I thought that.' *Chingado*."

The door slammed, and the screaming stopped. I could hear Jagger again. He was "sick and tired, fed up with this." The bitterness faded to boredom, but the snarl remained in his voice, as thick as spit.

I trudged to the bathroom in my bare feet, wondering why Jagger always seemed bored or angry, as if his fans were there to entertain him, not vice versa. I washed my face and brushed my teeth. The scrubbing finished what Charlie Watts started; it woke me up. I put on my school uniform, a pair of khakis and a blue shirt, and I headed to the living room. My mother was slumped on the sofa, watching

*The Today Show* with Hugh Downs.

"Mom . . ." I started to ask.

"What?" she yelled.

"Where's Dad?"

"Where do you think he is?" she asked, as if she expected me to answer.

I thought about heading to school without saying another word, but my mother answered her own question.

"He's on another pinche trip to God knows where, on one of his pinche freight trains. That's where he is," she said finally.

"Oh."

My lunch sack was on the coffee table. It contained my lunch and breakfast. I usually ate my breakfast on my way to school, riding my bicycle with one hand while eating my meal with the other, usually a sandwich or burrito.

"Mom?"

"What?" she yelled.

I was going to ask her what she made me for breakfast and lunch.

"Nothing," I said.

As I walked out the door without saying good-bye, I checked the lunch sack. There was a sandwich and burrito inside, just as I thought. The burrito was bean and picadillo; the sandwich was bacon and egg.

Whenever I ate a burrito for lunch, I ate it furtively, holding it with two hands while it was still in the sack. I lifted the bag to my mouth, my head bowed conspiratorially, so I could eat it without letting anyone see what it was. "The chili's eating his burrito," they would say. I was like a wino, hiding the bottle in a sack.

When I saw the bacon-and-egg sandwich, I decided to save it for lunch, even though my mother had intended it as my breakfast. I jumped on my bike, and I set the lunch sack onto the basket hooked to the handlebar. Then, as I started to pedal, I fished inside for the burrito, eating it with one hand while holding the handlebar with the other—a skill I had perfected throughout my childhood.

It was Wednesday, the day reserved for confession and mass. The

St. Francis administrators thought we could remain free of sin from Wednesday to Sunday, when they expected us to receive Holy Communion. We would attend Sunday Mass, bright and eager, our souls untarnished by sin, or so they thought. The administrators were optimists or, as Alita would have said, *pendejos*.

We skipped recess to attend mass on Wednesdays. It was like swapping a birthday party for a firing squad. The church was five blocks away, and we walked it single file, a chain gang of kids with teachers walking along at about fifteen-yard intervals. It usually took us about twenty minutes.

Mrs. Chaney wore one of her matador outfits that day, an ensemble so tight that her rotund body bulged into rolls of fat. The outfit was bright yellow, the skirt, the blouse, the vest, everything—bright yellow. If her aim had been to pick a color rivaling the blinding flash of the sun, she had succeeded. You could almost feel the heat radiating toward you in languid waves. *Vieja loca.* Crazy woman. There was only one hint of delicacy on the outfit—a plastic rose she had pinned to her left sleeve.

"All right, ladies and gentlemen," she said, standing at the door. "File outside and turn left. I don't want any nonsense from you this morning."

Turning left onto Palm Street, we walked under a canopy of oak trees, their branches locked in a leafy embrace. The trees, and the tattered quilt of shadows they cast, usually fascinated me. But not today. I did not give a damn about the trees or the latticework of shadows they threw onto the sidewalk. I was thinking about the old man and his freight train trip.

"Don't dawdle, Robert," Mrs. Chaney said, walking alongside me. "And stay in line."

I was no saint, but most of my sins were acts of mischief I had left thousands of miles behind—in El Paso. I had no friends in Bakersfield, no coconspirators for my transgressions. So, every time we marched to the church in Bakersfield, I took an inventory of my soul, and I usually came up empty—empty of sin. I never stole. I never missed mass on Sunday. And I never disobeyed my parents, except when my mother let me watch the violent television shows my father scorned. Or when I lied to the old man. I was one of those kids who made the St. Francis administrators confident in their assumption that we could remain free of sin for four crummy days.

So what could I tell the priest? I could not invoke a temporary vow of silence, kneeling in the confession booth until the priest banished me from the church. I had to say something. So I usually lied, listing sins I had not committed, sins I had not even contemplated. The last sin was the only one I considered genuine—lying. Lying to the very priest who was absolving me with his penance.

I was tired of lying, tired of a game only I knew I was playing. But what to tell the priest? I thought of the old man and his freight train trip. Was it a sin to abandon your son when he needed you? Was it a sin to choose hobos over your own family? And if it was, what would the priest tell me? Would he give me the penance and tell me to relay it to the old man?

We crossed the final street to St. Francis Church, H Street, and I noticed that Randy Reed was walking in front of me. I had not noticed him before. He paused to scratch his back, and as his hand scraped his spine, he made a fist and raised his middle finger—the gesture that we termed *chinga tu madre* in El Paso.

"Randy, get a move-on," Mrs. Chaney said, not realizing he had made the gesture.

It was a new church, built that year. There were no steeples, no grand foyer. Just a white concrete block. You entered through heavy black doors, each one embossed with a cross. The interior boasted none of the rich, nutty odor I associated with the saints. Mustiness equaled holiness in my eyes, and this church was not holy—not yet.

Inside the church, I stood under the Stations of the Cross, waiting for my turn at confession. Jesus was staring at me, his cheeks bloody, his body ravaged, his eyes forlorn—scenes depicted on the stained-glass windows. The scenes were there, etched by an artist long ago, but the sun brought them to life, giving light to darkness. And it made Jesus seem so . . . alone. Did he know I was free of sin? Did he know my only sin, lying, would be committed in the confessional? And if He did, would He forgive me?

As I pondered those questions, I decided not to lie. I would finger the old man instead. The old man was the sinner, not me. I would confess his sins.

Rachel Olsen stepped out of the confessional. It was my turn. I entered the booth. I closed the curtain. I kneeled. I could see the priest behind the screen, stroking his chin as he awaited my litany of transgressions. I sighed.

"Bless me, Father, for I have sinned," I said finally. "My last confession was one week ago. . . . I have missed mass on Sunday, and I have used the Lord's name in vain, and I have disobeyed my parents, and . . . "

"Is that all?" he asked.

I considered the question, wondering why I decided to spare the old man the wrath of God. Was it because he had suffered enough? In prison? I felt ashamed, more ashamed than I had ever felt in the confessional.

"I said, is that all?" he repeated.

"Yes, Father, yes . . . that's all."

"Okay. . . . I want you to say four 'Our Fathers' and three 'Hail Marys.'"

"Yes, Father."

"And son . . ."

"Yes, Father?"

"Next time, don't dawdle. . . . Surely, you know what sins you've committed before you enter the booth, right?"

"Yes, Father."

I recited the "Act of Contrition":

Oh, my Lord, I am heartily sorry for having offended Thee
And I detest all my sins because of Thy just punishment
But, most of all, because Thou art good and deserving of all

my love
I firmly resolve, with the help of Thy grace, to sin no more
And to avoid the nearest occasion of sin
Amen.

And as I stepped out of the confessional, I noticed our Lord on one of the windows, his sad, vacant eyes ignited by the sun.

# Mala Torres

## *A Story by Amado Muro*

Now my old friend Memo Torres, once nicknamed La Malita, is different. He wears a black suit and a black hat and a Roman collar whenever he appears in El Paso. He comes to El Paso once a year, and that is the only time Salvador Zavala and I ever get to see him. He still calls Chava and me by our first names and jokes with us when we are on our lunch hour at the ice plant. But now we are always polite to him and wait until he has gone before we finish our stories about Mexico.

"Good afternoon, Padre Guillermo," I say to him.

Chava and I were in our Lady of the Thunderbolt Church in Parral, Chihuahua, the day Memo said his first mass and became different. The church was crowded with people, relatives and friends, but Memo did not make a mistake. Chava knew because he was once an altar boy. Memo and Chava used to serve Mass together when they went to Our Lady of the Thunderbolt School.

That was long ago—before Memo took the holy orders. He was like us, then. He lived in our neighborhood La Primavera, and his father worked in La Prieta mine like ours. We played La Viborita and the Burro and the Rayuela every day in the streets.

Memo Torres had big placid eyes and a round smooth face with freckles across his nose. He had a calm air, which underlined his deep, slow voice, and his black hair was always combed flat with every strand in place. Broad-shouldered and compact, with bulging biceps, he was stronger than any of us. When we went to the General Rodrigo Quevedo Gym, he bench-pressed more weight and punched the light bag faster than anyone. Skipping rope, shadow boxing, and working on the body bag, he looked so much like Carlos Malacara, the Chihuahua lightweight who once beat Champion Juan Zurita, that countrymen called him La Malita or Little Mala. "The boy moves like the great Mala himself," they enthused. "He's *muy Mexicanota*."

Memo was a year older, and we all tried to be like him. The boys in our neighborhood always let him be the leader. He had an air of importance which appealed to us in a way that more reasonable people had never done. We did everything he said. When he told Chava and me to play hooky with him, we carried out his order, though our mothers called us *vagos* for it. But Chava and I agreed a scolding was a small price to pay for a footloose day with Memo Torres.

Memo could think of more reasons for playing hooky than a country Mexican can for going to Chihuahua City. Memo and Chava and I lived within tobacco-spitting distance of school. But at least once a week we never got there. Memo led us down to the Street of the Crazy Women instead. Wandering up and down it was more fun than staying in a classroom.

"It's more educational, too," Memo always insisted, and we couldn't help but agree. What we saw and heard there we never forgot. The classroom was different; what we heard there we never remembered.

The street that enthralled Memo so wasn't much to look at. It was just another broken-down street in a mining town that had many like it. But to Memo and Chava and me, it was an exciting change from our own neighborhood with its poor homes on crooked streets that wound up hillsides.

Then, too, in those days the Street of the Crazy Women was a village in itself, northern as the nopal. One Viva Villa was worth four Viva Zapatas there, and its mariachis sang of Blondie López instead of Gabino Berrera. Chihuahuenses said this long, dusty street held more poor Mexicans than jails do. Its sights and sounds made them all feel at home. Mesquite wood smoke fogged it. Bawling vendors filled it. Misty vapors from steaming cornmeal drifted down it. There, women vendors scrubbed griddles with maguey fiber brushes, and countrymen scrubbed their teeth with their fingers in primitive Mexican village style.

Toward sidehills matted with chaparral, mesquite, and gobernadora, stood adobe homes with blessed palms hanging over their doors to keep evil spirits and lightning away. Stumpy cottonwoods, misted with gray veils woven by caterpillars, leaned before them. On clear days, the gossiping housewives, whose doings gave the street its name, sat on rush-plaited chairs under the heavy-leafed trees where, wrapped in thick mantas woven by High Sierra Indians, they patched Tenancingo rebozos and Santa Maria prayer shawls in the sunshine.

Their conversations were famous. They talked mostly about their husbands. Some said they wished they had gone into the convent instead of getting married. Others disagreed. "Ay Madre, it's better to undress one-horned drunkards than dress plaster saints," they insisted. Sometimes we listened until they drove us away.

We liked the street vendor's crowing cries, too. They merged into a boisterous tympany. It was like Memo said. There was always something to see, something to listen to on the Street of the Crazy Women.

At one end of the street, near Jesús Maria Alley, was a rabbit-warren cluster of rickety *puestos* that slumped and sagged like miniature Towers of Pisa. Robust women with nicknames like Maria la Bandida, La Trompitas, and La Chata Micaela operated these foodstands, popularly called *agachados* because they are so lowslung.

When we got hungry, we went to the Pearls of Coyame puesto run by Petra Porras, a buxom, smiling woman nicknamed Petra la Pozolera. In this little hut, made of rough boards so badly painted the wood's natural color showed through, we were always welcome.

Petra the Pozole Vendor, gray haired with a broad, pleasant face, greeted us with a wide smile that showed the glittering gold fillings of her teeth.

"*Mira no mas—pura raza,*" she said when she saw us. "*Ay, Jesus me valga.* What vagabond faces you have."

Sometimes we helped her scrub with shuck brooms and a bucket of hot water and lye. Then, too, we carried water on shoulder yokes, emptied ash buckets, and brought ice cubes for *tepache*.

"Now we'll eat with the big spoon," Doña Petra promised after all the chores were done.

The Pozole Vendor worked a la Mexicana, singing at the top of her lungs. While she cooked pozole in a big black *cazuela*, we listened to her sing *corridos* that exuded blood and gunpowder and watched Jesús Maria Alley's milling crowds.

Many of the men going past us trudged as if they were exhausted or sick, their bodies stooped as if bent by pain. Where they'd been and where they'd yet to go, we couldn't tell. But many hungry men, broken by suffering, came to the Pozolera's puesto. Some, so weary they spoke in a whisper, told her they lived on mesquites, *quelites*, and even *sabandijas*. She never turned them away.

"Money is only a means of capping hunger," she said when she served them. "Eat, and may San Francisco give you his most sacred blessing."

The Pozolera's dark eyes were steady with hope and courage, and to us she was beautiful as an angel of Puebla. Many times this kindly woman told us about the destitute men who came to her puesto.

"They are men for whom a day without work is a tragedy—Ay Madre, the wind blows colder on them," she said. "Most don't have enough flesh on them for an *albondiga*, and all have a hunger from here to Balleza. May Nuestro Señor give them all a good place in the sky *con todo y zapatos.*"

After lunch, we camped on a grassy bank near the Guanajuato Bridge, where the Parral River was brown and swift and deep with quicksands making little whirlpools on the surface. The riverbank was a nice place to be. The sound of the wind in the cottonwoods was like a gentle rain, and doves teetered nimbly on the branches and opened and closed their wings. Beyond the stone bridge, Parral looked like a mirage city with its low-built homes and broad, quiet squares colored by stone-bordered flower beds.

We built a chunk fire on a patch of beaten grassless earth, and then sat down on the ground with our backs against a big limestone rock. We talked of far-off places and read dog-eared copies of *El Ruedo* and *Box y Lucha* until the first stars appeared and were reflected in the quiet river.

When Memo was poring over boxing and bullfighting magazines, he read poems by Juan de Dios Peza and Manuel Plaza. Their poems inspired him to write poetry, too. One poem, about the San Jose Bakery, I remember especially. This was probably because Jacinto Turrieta, a spindly Southerner with a dark, scowling face, owned the bakery.

Don Chinto Turrieta came from Michoacan, and his high-pitched voice was pleasant with the slurred, lilting drawl of Mexico's big harp country. His way of speaking was like a song in our ears. But he was high-strung, and when he got mad his breath came with heavy, rasping gasps.

I remember the day Memo printed his poem on the San Jose Bakery's front window. It was pale and windy with the chilled tang of approaching winter, but Memo was bareheaded and the sleeves of his home-sewn shirt were rolled high on his biceps. With the incontrovertible assurance that characterized him, he stepped up to the window and wrote boldly and legibly. When he finished printing with yellow chalk, he stood back and studied the poem, which read:

*El que puso este letrero*
*No supo lo que ponia*
*San Jose fue carpintero*
*No tuvo panaderia.*

(The man who named this place didn't know what he was doing.

Saint Joseph was a carpenter. He didn't have a bakery.)

Chava and I waited to see what would happen. We did not have to wait long. Soon grinning paisanos gathered to read the verses. Their laughter filled Noche Triste Street like fresh notes on a musical scale, bringing Don Chinto out to see what the trouble was.

"Tengo monos?" he snapped petulantly when countrymen smiled at him.

Don Chinto wrinkled his brows together, and read the poem. Then anger made him double up his fists, and he glared darkly at Memo.

"Son of the bad sleep, I'll make tortillas out of your snout!" he shouted. "By the barricades of Guerrero I swear I'll carve a *Viva Mexico* in your face."

But Memo, resolute and composed, remained adamant.

"What I wrote is the truth as God lives," he maintained.

When Don Chinto's tantrum subsided, he rubbed out the poem and then was quiet again. But not long after that, he changed the bakery's name to El Suriano.

Now Memo is different. He has taken the holy orders. He wears a black suit, and we don't joke with him any more.

"Good morning, Padre," I say to him now.

28

## El Enano

"We're going to have a visitor from Cleveland."

Whenever my father uttered those words, I smiled. The visitor was my grandfather—the old man of the old man. I would never have called him "the old man," though. Never. He was tiny, almost impish, barely scraping five-foot-four, but he was proof that stature had nothing to do with feet and inches. About five inches shorter than the old man, my grandfather walked tall, taller than he was, with the sweeping, purposeful stride of a man who boasted long legs. Really long legs. And it was not a bantam rooster strut, either—the strut of a short man trying to appear tall. In my eyes, he was tall.

Tía Maria called him *El Enano*, the Dwarf, behind his back, but then, she called my father El Gringo behind his back, too. And neither epithet bothered me, not really. Why would it? Alita never disparaged my father for his heritage, and that was endorsement enough for me. If she had been a cartographer, Alita would have dropped Cleveland into Mexico, right in the middle of her beloved homeland, among the Jaliscos and Guadalajaras and Zacatecas—a map with boundaries created by a bond stronger than any river, gorge or mountain. *Ándale, tía. . . . mugrosa.* Take that, lousy aunt.

As for my grandfather? Well, whenever my aunt called him *El Enano*, I stewed quietly, but my anger dissipated as I recalled my favorite piece of advice—*No le hagas caso,* suitable for thousands of situations, whether at home or at school. *No le hagas caso*—thank you, Alita. And besides, in the eyes of his eleven-year-old grandson, my grandfather was tall, measurements—and judgmental aunts—be damned.

My grandfather visited us two or three times a year, pursuing my father wherever he landed—Dallas, Las Cruces, El Paso, and now, Bakersfield. They were a study in contrasts, these two men. My grandfather—Louis Benson Seltzer—retained the elegance my father had lost over the years. He wore a suit almost everywhere he went, whether it was an opera house or a hardware store, but he was so graceful—and unpretentious—that the attire seemed casual. He called my dad "Chess," and my dad called him "Dad."

They were different in other ways. My grandfather was conservative, my father liberal, and their debates were passionate but civilized, each man expressing his viewpoint with the air of a chess master—soberly, almost clinically. They talked about Johnson and Nixon, Goldwater and Humphrey, war and peace, animated discussions that I followed intently, even though the issues—some of them, anyway—were beyond my eleven-year-old grasp. Nobody ever won these intellectual conflicts, but my father ended each discussion with a concession that was remarkable for a man with such strong convictions: "Well, I see your point."

My grandfather became editor of the *Cleveland Press* in 1928, but it was the work that got him there—the long years in the trenches of journalism—that my father admired the most. But that was the thing. The long years were not really long; my grandfather just filled them with long days and long nights, cramming so much work into so little time that his rise seemed preordained. He was thirty-one when he became editor. And that determination, more than anything else, is what impressed the old man about his dad.

My grandfather launched his journalism career in 1910, a thirteen-year-old boy who dropped out of school after the sixth grade to help support his family. He was a cub reporter for the *Cleveland*

*News*. A cub reporter—at thirteen years old. He was only three years older than I was in 1964, and the most ambitious thing I had ever done was ask for a box of FUCKS from the lady at the candy counter in the movie house. It was a sobering juxtaposition. Had the gene pool failed me? Or had I failed the gene pool?

In Cleveland, everyone called him "Louie," perhaps a carryover from his early days with the *Cleveland News*, where he wrote a column called "Luee, the Offis Boy," complete with his own drawings. He was no Picasso, but the images were simple and charming, the perfect complement to his clear, unassuming and (deliberately) ungrammatical prose. He went from office boy to reporter to editor, and as an influential journalist in Northeastern Ohio, he had been invited to the White House by every president from Woodrow Wilson to Lyndon Johnson, the man who assumed the office following the assassination of John F. Kennedy.

Some people called him tough and cocky, and maybe he was. But as he moved from one paper to another—and from one promotion to another—he retained the key ingredients that made him such a great office boy: joy, passion, and a willingness to shoulder work that others might have considered beneath them. Take away his editorship, strip him of his status and connections, and my grandfather would have been a great journalist, anyway—the old man told me so.

"He was a little man—dapper, slight and balding with a soft voice you had to strain to hear," Dick Wooten wrote decades later in the *Cleveland Press*. "His public image was that of 'Mr. Cleveland.' He was the kingmaker who some say made more politicians than any other man in the country.

"Cleveland was his home town and he loved it. He criticized it, harassed it and encouraged it. He knew the town and the town knew him. Everywhere you went you ran into people who bragged, 'I'm a friend of Louie Seltzer.'"

While my grandfather escaped hard times, my father embraced them, at least artistically. Motivated by compassion—and literary integrity—the old man experienced poverty throughout the Southwest, riding the rails, evading the cops, eating meals so sparse that he would utter "miss-meal" sighs thirty minutes later, gestures of resignation in the face of relentless hunger. He was not a voyeur in another world; he was a participant in another world. And these rich experiences, so far removed from the lives of most dads, underwent a rich transformation in the journey from his soul to his typewriter. He wrote dozens of stories about the poor who inhabit the dark underbelly of society, most of them published in literary quarterlies—"Hobo Jungle," "Hungry Men," "Helping Hands," "Night Train to Fort Worth."

"*Ay Dios mio, mira no mas,* Oh my God, look at that," my mother would say whenever another homeless man came to visit my father at our duplex in El Paso. "*Otro.* Another one."

My father met them everywhere—Pecos, Sweetwater, Big Spring, San Antonio. One of them, a grizzled old man called "Salt," saved him during one of his rides through West Texas. My father was sleeping in the boxcar; the door was open, and as the train rattled over a bridge near Big Spring, it started to tilt. My father, clutching the empty bottle of Clorox he used as a pillow, began to slide out the door. Salt grabbed him.

For the old man, the words and the experiences were inextricably linked. He wanted to write what he experienced, and since he did not live a life of poverty, he had to steep himself in it, if only for days or weeks at a time. So when the mood descended on him, which was often, he hit the rails—and the hobo jungles. The Great Depression was over, but the suffering it sparked, in towns like Bakersfield and El Paso and Fort Worth, remained, turning the old man into a latter-day Tom Kromer, Horace McCoy, Edward Anderson, or John Steinbeck, some of his favorite writers, although he never would have placed himself in their league. Never.

By the early 1960s, however, the old man was beginning to acquire a reputation he neither sought nor wanted. It was not the kind of celebrity that Kromer, McCoy, Anderson, or Steinbeck achieved. But it was celebrity nonetheless. And the old man hated it. Why? It was part of his makeup, this strange duality—the desire for success, the aversion to its by-product, fame. My grandfather understood, perhaps because it was part of his makeup as well. "Ambition and modesty are rare but wonderful partners," my grandfather told me once, "and they reside in your father's heart."

It was modesty that emerged as the dominant partner one strange evening in El Paso, about a year before we moved to Bakersfield. A man visited our duplex. He was an agent of some sort, the old man told me later, and he had come across some of the literary quarterlies that published the stories my father wrote. My mother served them coffee in the living room; Alita and I stood in the hallway behind the kitchen, trying to listen in on the conversation. Alita could not speak English, but she listened anyway, as if she had an interpreter, tiny but diligent, whispering in her ear. She did have an interpreter—me—but I was straining to hear too hard to translate for her. The man, it turned out, loved "Cecilia Rosas," a story he had read in one of the quarterlies.

"Mr. Muro, we think this is a brilliant story," the man said.

We? I heard only one man. Where was the rest of this mysterious group? As soon as I posed that question, however, I asked myself another: Why is he calling my father Mr. Muro? And then it hit me. I looked up at Alita, trying to stifle my laughter.

"*No sabe que se llama Seltzer.* He doesn't realize his name is Seltzer," I said, smiling.

Alita smiled back.

"We think it would make a fine film," the man said. "Of course, we would have to flesh it out a bit. After all, it's only a short story."

The story centered on a teenager who lived in Chihuahuita, one of the oldest neighborhoods in El Paso, its red-brick tenements so close to Mexico that you could almost hear the street vendors selling their wares on the other side of the river—"*Chicle, helados, orchata!* Gum, ice cream, orchata (a melon drink)!" Poor Amado—the name my father used for his first-person accounts—was in love. Hardly an earth-shattering story line, especially if you were thinking about adapting the story into a fine film.

Love is a mysterious and dangerous emotion, however, especially when the person stricken by it is a teenager. Poor Amado was no different. If not blinded by love, he was rendered myopic by it, for he saw things that were not there—and failed to see things that were. Worst of all, Cecilia was an older woman, in her twenties perhaps, and her age seemed to accentuate her exotic beauty—her obsidian eyes, her lustrous hair, her shapely figure. . . .

Cecilia liked the boy, and he could tell, but her affection was the kind a person might shower on a cute and adorable pet. There was nothing romantic about it, nothing that could blossom into an intimate relationship. . . . Besides, Cecilia had a boyfriend—and he was Anglo. Poor Amado, his devotion destroyed by his ethnic makeup—the dark skin, the black hair, the angular features that he felt were common among the indigenous people across the border. Everything—the skin, the hair, all of it—screamed Mexicano.

The plot was based on a true story, a crushing incident my father experienced in Cleveland. He changed the name of the boy from Chester to Amado, and he added the ethnic context so crucial to the tale. But everything else was the same. It looked like a ruse, a case of literary double identity, but Chester Seltzer and Amado Muro were one and the same, their characters forged by a man who saw kinship where others saw boundaries.

"We think this story is made for the silver screen," the man said.

My father said, "No." The story was for readers, not viewers, he said—afraid, perhaps, that Hollywood would corrupt his tale of ethnic pride and identity. Would they get Charlton Heston—a great actor who did such a miserable job playing a Mexican cop in that Orson Welles movie *Touch of Evil*—to portray one of the characters? The agent stood up, stammering, his composure undermined by this literary curve my father had thrown him.

"But . . . but . . . we think this would be a wonderful opportunity," he said.

"Thanks, just the same," my father said, and the man left.

My mother called my grandfather in Cleveland afterwards, upset by this missed opportunity.

"That's Chess," my grandfather told her simply.

A few years later, my father got a letter from a publisher who wanted to feature "Cecila Rosas" in a literary anthology, and the old man was a little more amenable. The publisher, a professor from Pan American University in Edinburgh, Texas, asked him what kind of fee he wanted for the story. The old man said publication of the story was payment enough:

> Dear Mr. Simmen,
> You are surely welcome to use the story Cecila Rosas in your anthology. I'm not a professional writer and don't make my living that way so there's certainly no fee.
> Thank you very much for your letter, and I wish you success with the anthology.
> Sincerely,
>
> Amado Muro
> 1232 Prospect
> El Paso, Texas 79902

If my father experienced poverty, my grandfather lived it. He was the oldest of five children, and his father—Charles Alden Seltzer—wanted to be a writer, wanted it so bad that he wrote his stories on sheets of white paper a neighborhood butcher had tossed out. He could not afford the store-bought paper that other writers used, but nobody, rich or poor, can purchase gumption at a store, and Charles Alden Seltzer had plenty of that. . . . He maintained other jobs, as a handyman, a brakeman, a floorwalker in a five-and-dime, but he kept writing the whole time, hoping his stories would find loyal readers beyond the Seltzer household.

Louie, his oldest child, was equally ambitious—maybe more so. He quit school in the sixth grade, leaving his classmates to launch what would be a brilliant journalism career. He wanted to be a writer, just like his dad, but his literature would be based on facts, and it would be written under the kind of deadline pressure a short-story writer could only imagine. A daunting challenge for a thirteen-year-old, but one he accepted gleefully. And no wonder. Louie was the happiest kind of kid you could imagine—a kid with a dream . . . and a kid who loved his hometown.

My father loved it, too, an affection built on a foundation established years earlier. My old man got it from his old man. Young Chess understood: It was part of his DNA, pumping from his heart and coursing through his veins. They shared so much—their love of books, their love of sports, their love of family—and the city seemed to be at the heart of it, a bustling town driven by the diversity of its people—Czech, Polish, Italian, Lithuanian—each group contributing to the vast stew of culture, language, religion, and literature in Northeastern Ohio. My mother and grandmother, the old man told me, would have called it a "melting pot"—*un revuelto de culturas* . . . .

As editor of the *Cleveland Press*, my grandfather let the readers know that the newspaper was there for them. It was not some monolithic giant producing a collection of words and photographs that landed on their doorsteps and newsstands every day. The reporters, editors, and photographers were Clevelanders, too, and their newspaper was as tough, vibrant, and emotional as the town itself. They cared about the town because they were part of the town. And it all started at the top, with my grandfather.

Like my father, my grandfather did not care about maps or boundaries. He cared about people. My grandfather had a global vision of Cleveland. If you lived in Cleveland, no matter where you came from, you were part of the town. You could have been from Poland, Lithuania, Czechoslovakia. It did not matter to my grandfather. Those nations may as well have been suburbs of Cleveland.

It was an attitude the old man called all-encompassing. All-encompassing. A term with so many syllables that I had trouble maneuvering through it.

"What does it mean," I asked my father one afternoon, repeating the word so slowly that it sounded like part of an incantation.

"Well," he said, smiling. "It means that your grandfather looked at things from a broad perspective."

I frowned.

"Okay," he said, starting over. "It means your grandfather saw

My grandfather, Louis B. Seltzer, hammers out one of the freelance columns he wrote after his retirement.

everything, considered everything. Look. If you were from Cleveland, he appreciated where you had come from, where your family had come from, and he knew how important your past was to you.

"Take your mom. She lives in Bakersfield now, right, with us? But she was born in Chihuahua, and your grandfather loves Chihuahua. Now he has never been there, to Chihuahua. Maybe he never even wants to go there. But because your mom was from there, the town means a lot to him. A lot."

And then he asked me if I knew what nostalgia meant.

"Nos-tal-gia?" I asked.

"Yes," he answered hopefully, as if he thought I knew the definition.

"No," I said.

"Oh," he said, smiling.

"Well," he said, "nostalgia was a precarious proposition." . . . *Ay Dios mio*. . . . I waited for him to ask me if I knew what a precarious proposition was, but he kept talking, his enthusiasm steamrolling his concern for my puny vocabulary. . . . Bah.

"Nostalgia," he continued, "turns beggars into kings and flophouses into luxury hotels. It makes you long for a time that never existed; it distorts your vision. So when I tell you about your grandfather and those old days in Cleveland, that's not nostalgia. That's the truth."

I smiled, somehow comprehending despite the absence of those verbal footnotes he usually supplied.

"So . . . his broad perspective . . . that was real?" I asked.

"Yes," he said, smiling. "That was real. Do you want me to give you an example of that broad perspective?" the old man asked me.

"Yes," I said, excited.

It was 1956, fourteen years after the war the old man refused to fight. The peace was fragile, my father said. The war was over, but the turmoil remained, scarring Central and Eastern European countries with violence and brutality.

Russia attacked Hungary, and because thousands of Hungarians had immigrated to Cleveland during the chaos, the press reports crossed the ocean and roiled the shores of Lake Erie. The news was horrible: The Russians gunned down student protesters, and the violence escalated, killing almost nine thousand. Bullets sliced the air. Tanks trampled the countryside. Shells cleaved the sky.

In Northeastern Ohio, isolated from the terror sweeping their homeland, the new Americans were safe and secure. But that security exacted a horrible price. It made them feel guilty and privileged, too privileged. And worse, the old man said, it made them feel impotent, for there was nothing they could do, nothing they could say, to help their loved ones so many miles away.

Safe from the bullets and bombs, these new Clevelanders were not safe from the tragedy inflicted by those bullets and bombs because whatever threatened their loved ones threatened them, too. No, the old man said, Cleveland was not a safe harbor for these new Americans. Not really. The violence entered a new war zone, this one closer to home—their hearts. They felt every bullet, every bayonet, every bomb. When a shell gouged the earth in Hungary, it gouged the earth in Cleveland. And so their world turned gray—the dull, ugly hue of destruction.

My grandfather knew the only way to help someone—and help yourself at the same time—was to act. So he acted, and he chose the perfect vehicle for that action, the newspaper. He organized an ambitious mercy mission, assembling a team of editors and reporters, along with community leaders, to collect food, clothes, and books for the dispossessed in Hungary.

Louis Clifford, the great city editor, flew to Austria, accompanied by members of the Red Cross and the United Hungarian Societies, a local organization. It was December. The team traveled to the Austria-Hungary border, where almost fifteen thousand Hungarians had fled, their souls deadened by war and winter. One woman was so grateful that she kissed the coat the Americans handed her. The city editor described the scene for readers back home:

> . . . as the seemingly never-ending stream of oppressed humanity flows through this dreary refugee center south of Vienna, flows on to the clear avenue of the Free World, there will be carried forever the symphony of gratitude that comes today from the people like Alada Szobonyai, Aranki Tihanyi and the others.

As the old man told the story, his voice grew softer and softer, muted by an emotion too powerful for words. He sighed—a sigh so forceful that his breath seemed to bisect the air. I waited for him to continue.

"Dad?" I said finally, uncertain of where I was going.

"Yes."

"Granddad is a lot like you, isn't he?"

The old man sighed again.

A few years before his trip to Bakersfield, my grandfather visited us in El Paso. The old man took us to eat at a downtown buffet, across the street from the public library, where the homeless men congregated. We walked out of the restaurant about an hour later, and my grandfather noticed a young man sitting on the curb, his shoulders hunched, his eyes sunk so deep that they seemed lost within their sockets. It was winter, and the wind was flinging invisible barbs into our faces, but the young man did not seem to care. He just sat there, quietly, staring at the ground.

As we walked past him, my grandfather paused. He sat on the curb, next to the young man, unconcerned about getting his suit and overcoat dirty. The old man and I kept walking toward the Rambler. We got into the car, and my father rearranged the rearview mirror so he could see the scene unfolding behind him. I sat in the back, staring at my father, more interested in the old man than in the images the old man was witnessing. We waited for about twenty minutes. I kept staring.

"You all right?" the old man asked my grandfather when he returned.

"I'm fine, Chess."

My father turned the key in the ignition, his lips trembling from emotion.

"How much did you give him?" the old man asked.

I could see a tear roll down his cheek.

"Fifty dollars."

Whenever my grandfather visited us, the old man let me stay home from school for at least one day.

"Chess, you shouldn't let the boy play hooky like that," he would tell my father, his stern expression finally exploding into a grin.

During his visits to El Paso, he loved to sit next to Alita, both of them perched in chairs by the living-room window.

"Thank you for being so nice to my son and grandson," he would tell her. "I appreciate it."

My grandfather would hold her hand, and Alita would bow her head, staring at the two sets of fingers in her lap—his perfectly manicured, hers gnarled and yellowed from all those Lucky Strikes. And then I would see something that I never thought possible: Already thin and frail, Alita would recede into herself, this tough, feisty nonagenarian reduced to an awkward, frightened lamb of a girl. If only Pito Peterson, the neighborhood ogre, could have seen her. It never lasted, though, this remarkable transformation. After a few seconds, she would look up again, beaming with pride.

"Thank you," my grandfather would repeat.

Alita could not speak English. My grandfather could not speak Spanish. It was confusing, for a kid my age, but their communication skills transcended language.

"We're going to have a visitor from Cleveland."

It was April, about a month before the end of school, and we were in Bakersfield now. When we went to greet him at the airport, the first thing I noticed was his long stride as he walked across the runway into the small waiting area.

"Hello, young man," he said, hugging me.

The old man let me stay up later than usual that night, and when I went to bed, I heard them talking about Randy Reed.

"Chess, who started the fight?" my grandfather asked.

"The Reed kid did," my father answered. "But it wasn't really a fight. The Reed kid hit him, hit him hard, and that was it. . . . I think the bell was ringing for the next class."

There was a pause.

"Chess, I've told you this story before," my grandfather said. "But I got into a horrible fight one day, and when I got home, my father said, 'Did you whip him?' I said no, and my father said, 'Go back out there, and don't come back until you do.'"

My father remained silent for several seconds. It must have been awkward for them, but it was unbearable for me. How long would it last? It was the old man who broke the silence. He started talking about Johnny Risko, the old-time heavyweight who loved hanging out with the kids in Cleveland. My grandfather said, "Ah, Johnny Risko," and they grew so rhapsodic that I thought they were talking about Muhammad Ali or Sonny Liston. That Risko, he was no dancer, they said, but he could move when he had to, and when he started flinging those left hooks, good Lord, they were brutal—as short and sweet as hatchet strokes.

I listened to their conversation, captivated by their journey to another time, another place. Johnny Risko. He must have been something. I felt as if I knew him, his toughness inside the ring matched by his tenderness outside. No wonder the neighborhood kids loved him. Was he like the Mexican fighter I met in that North Bakersfield gym, Cruz Ortega? I wondered. Then it hit me like a left hook to the liver. This conversation, far from pleasant, was . . . well . . . sinister. They—my father and grandfather—were trying to turn me into a modern-day Johnny Risko, someone who could pound the arrogance out of Randy Reed. I could see their point. I wanted to bust Randy Reed, too, but I was no Johnny Risko. I slept fitfully that night, and when I saw my grandfather the next morning, I dreaded to hear the first words out of his mouth.

"Good morning, young man," he said.

"Good morning, Granddad."

He stared at me.

"Your father told me about that boy . . . that Randy Reed," he said, pausing.

I waited for the Johnny Risko reference, the "don't-come-back-till-you've-whipped-him" speech. I waited and waited. But my grandfather just stared at me.

"You know what?" he said finally. "Don't pay any attention to him."

# 29

## The Baseball Game

When it came to screaming, only one person—only one person I knew—could rival Paul McCartney, whose yowl emerged from a deep, dark cavern in his soul. That person? My mother, the Paul McCartney of Bakersfield, by way of Chihuahua.

"Bobby, turn off the radio!" she yelled.

My mother was wearing one of her housedresses. It looked like a Japanese print with orange blossoms and pink birds. The colors, unlike her mood, were soft and serene.

"Your breakfast is getting cold, and you're going to be late for school!" she yelled.

The radio was blasting "Long Tall Sally," the scorcher by the Beatles, with Paul singing lead vocals.

"Just a minute, Mom," I yelled back. "I'm combing my hair."

I turned up the volume on the radio.

"Well, hurry up!"

Standing in front of the dresser, I stared at my image, and my image stared back, frowning. . . . I picked up my comb, the comb I had just put down, and I raked the hair I had already raked, determined to loiter in front of the mirror until the song was over. Two minutes. I stood there for two minutes, dragging the comb across my mop till the final ooh-ooh-ooh.

"Hi, Dad," I said. "I was combing my hair."

He was sitting at the breakfast table.

"Good morning, Betty."

I looked at the breakfast that was going to "get cold." It was a bowl of cornflakes. My mother was in the kitchen, but she was like Alita: No matter how far away, she was always within hearing distance.

"I think my breakfast got cold," I whispered to the old man.

He shrugged.

"I want to ask you a question," he said, sipping his coffee. "Are you still climbing the monkey bars?"

"Huh?"

"Are you still climbing the monkey bars?" he repeated, emphasizing every word.

The old man was always asking me questions that led to discussions—discussions I did not always like. This was one of those questions. I knew it.

"Well, sometimes," I said. "Most of the time, I just sit around by myself."

"You're always by yourself," he said. "Why don't you do something with the other kids? Play baseball with them. . . . It might prove to be analgesic."

"Anal-what?"

"Look it up," he said.

I told him I would, but I did not mean I would look up the word. I meant I would play baseball. But as I rode my bike to school, I started to regret my decision. I did not want to play baseball. I did not want to stand at home plate, waiting for a pitch I might not hit, with everyone staring at me, including Randy Reed. But it was one thing to lie to my mother about my hair; it was another to lie to the old man about baseball. I hated lying to the old man.

Our first class was English. I glanced outside, waiting for Mrs. Chaney to give us our instructions. It was overcast, but the darker it was outside, the brighter it seemed inside. The lights cast everything in a harsh, electric glow, a glow that seemed harsher—and more electric—on dark, rainy days. It was almost surreal—the perfect setting for the story Mrs. Chaney was about to assign us, "The Legend of

Sleepy Hollow." I loved those five words. They were meant to be together, united by the literary gods who gave birth to this beautiful quintuplet. "The Legend of Sleepy Hollow." Mrs. Chaney asked me to start reading:

> The dominant spirit . . . that haunts this enchanted region, and seems to be commander-in-chief of all the powers of the air, is the apparition of a figure on horseback without a head. It is said by some to be the ghost of a Hessian trooper, whose head had been carried away by a cannon-ball, in some nameless battle during the revolutionary war; and who is ever and anon seen by the country folk hurrying along in the gloom of night, as if on the wings of the wind. His haunts are not confined to the valley, but extend at times to the adjacent roads, and especially to the vicinity of a church at no great distance.

After English class, I lost my sense of wonder, too focused on my dilemma to glean any joy from my other classes. I wrestled with my problem all day, through prayers and readings and study halls, but as two o'clock approached—the time for PE—I was no closer to a decision. Would I play baseball? Or would I lie to the old man?

There were two moments each day when the tension grew unbearable for the kids at St. Francis Elementary. One was before lunch. The other was before PE. In both instances, the students stared at the clock for what seemed like hours, each tick bringing them closer to the most delicious feeling they could experience—the release from the shackles of their textbooks. The liberation was sublime; it was the wait, the getting there, which proved so tough to handle.

Mrs. Chaney could sense it, sense the anticipation building in our nerve endings, and she did nothing to relieve it. She was clock-gazing, too, and every day, five minutes before lunch or PE, she would tell us to close our books and—this was the challenging part—

shut our mouths. We were supposed to sit there quietly, as solemn as pall bearers, for three hundred seconds. The silence entombed us. We could hear our own heartbeats.

The wait was worse—agonizingly worse—on this day, because I was still deciding what to do. Should I play baseball, as the old man suggested? Or should I keep to myself, as I usually did?

In the midst of the mind-numbing silence, I walked up to Mrs. Chaney and asked her if she could spell "analgesic" for me. I pronounced it slowly. She arched her eyebrows, her thick glasses sliding down her nose, glaring at me as if I had crepitated in church.

"A-N-A-L-G-E-S-I-C," she said finally.

"Thank you, Mrs. Chaney."

As I walked away, her booming voice stopped me in mid-step.

"Robert, do you have a headache?" she asked. "Do you need to see the nurse?"

"No, ma'am," I said, wondering why she asked.

I kept walking to the wooden stand in the back of the classroom, a kind of lectern where the dictionary sat, as massive and imposing as a concrete block. I thumbed through the As—aerodynamic, amicable, antelope . . . Too far . . . Ah, there it was, analgesic:

(1) an agent that relieves pain.

Baseball was an agent that relieved pain. Aha! I smiled, and the bell rang.

We trooped outside, where we were greeted by our principal, Sister Francis Louise, a whistle draped across her neck. She was an all-purpose administrator, what the old man called a utility player in baseball. She was principal, coach, and umpire, and she performed all three roles with remarkable objectivity, never favoring one kid over another—or one team over the other.

Sister kept a bag of peppermints in her pocket, hidden deep within the folds of her long black robe. When she umpired a baseball game during PE, she indulged in her love of sweets, and it was a joy to watch. She would rummage through her pocket, a prospector mining for gold, and after what seemed like minutes, she would emerge with her treasure, a bag of peppermints. She would pop two—or three—into her mouth, smiling and working her jaw as if the candy were tobacco. Then she would stick her hand back into her pocket, depositing the plastic wrappers until she could find a trash can in the school building.

It was overcast. The clouds were low and brooding, streaked with silver where the sun tried to poke through their jagged edges. I loved clouds. The best thing about clouds—the very best thing about clouds—was that they had a dual presence, one in the sky, the other on the ground. If they sailed across the heavens, they sailed across the earth, too, casting giant shadows that flitted from object to object.

Preoccupied with the clouds—and the shadows they threw—I forgot about the baseball game. Then I heard Sister Francis Louise pick the two captains, Randy Reed and Wendell Wilson. "Choothe thides," she said. The peppermints made her lisp. The two boys chose their players, taking turns, first Randy, then Wendell, then Randy again . . . until each team had nine players. Wendell Wilson chose me.

Sister Francis Louise encouraged every child, regardless of which team he was on. It did not matter to her. Sister wanted everyone to play well, to succeed. She kept score, but the score seemed incidental, less important than how we played—and how much fun we had. There were no innings in playground rules. Gazing at the pocket watch she kept in the folds of her robe—next to her bag of peppermints—Sister determined the length of each game. She always let us know when the final at-bat was upon us.

We were down two to one, and I was up next. One boy was on base, on second. There was only one out, but it did not matter. Sister announced that I would be the last batter. I had not reached base the whole game, striking out the first time and popping up the second, and now here I was, responsible for whether we won or lost. Sister did not care, but I did, and so did all the other kids, including the girls who were watching us play. They stood under a tree about ten feet from the third base line.

Huge, ugly Randy Reed, whose delivery befuddled me, was their pitcher. When he tossed the ball, he lifted his arm slowly, casually, as if he were about to scratch his nose. You would wait for him to relieve his itch, and then, before you knew it, the ball was coming toward you, and there you were, unprepared, flailing at a pitch you never expected. . . . But not this time; this time I was ready for his crazy pitch. I crouched low, so low that my butt pointed toward the third baseman, as if I were trying to moon him. I was ready.

If I hit the ball just right, if I smack it dead center, I thought, I might be able to do to Randy Reed what he did to me. I could hit him . . . without hitting him. It would be my bat, not my fist, throwing the punch, because I would send the ball into flight, and the ball would hit him, striking him with a thud, a plunk, a blow so powerful that he would end up looking like the baseball, the seams gouged into his forehead, as deep as ruts. Is this how Mickey Mantle and Willie Mays and Rocky Colavito, the beloved Cleveland Indians outfielder, felt?

I stood at the plate, tense but unafraid. Randy Reed lifted his arm, that long, deliberate windup that seemed to last forever. I remained patient, and there it was, the softball emerging from his huge hand, a sphere that drifted toward me with the slow but graceful motion of a snowflake tumbling from the sky. I swung the bat, and the snowflake hurtled past the infield, a line drive that eluded the shortstop and screamed into the gap between centerfield and left field. *Chingao!* I hit it, I said to myself as I raced toward first base.

I heard a girl scream. Was it Rachel? I considered the possibility—the sublime possibility—for a half second, before I refocused on another sublime possibility, the possibility that I might win the game for my team. I rounded the bases, a surge of joy coursing through my body.

I knocked in the kid who was on second base, Larry Willems, the tying run, and as I rounded third, propelled by joy and adrenaline, I lost my footing—bah! I crashed to the ground, my face surfing the soft, dark soil of the playground, and I lay there for several seconds, wondering what happened—and how it could have happened. And when I got to my knees, spitting out the dirt I had just tasted, Randy Reed hovered above me, smiling.

Sister Francis Louise ran up to us, her robe flapping as she reached the spot where I had nose-dived. She helped me to my feet, patted the dirt off my shirt and pants. Then, after making sure I was all right, she turned to Randy Reed.

"Randy, my goth, did you twip Robert?" she asked.

"No, Sister!" he said, outraged. "I was covering the bases."

She glared at him, daring him to blame the stumble on me. He kept quiet. But, as she blew her whistle, directing us back to the classroom, Randy Reed stared at me, his lips curving into a satisfied smile.

"All wight," Sister yelled. "Everybody back to clath."

As we marched back to our barrack, Rachel Olsen walked beside me.

"Robert, why didn't you tell Sister what happened?"

I shrugged, too embarrassed to tell her I was afraid.

30

## *La Preciosa*

I had to admit it, if only to myself: there was something I admired about Mrs. Chaney.

Not that she was easy to admire—or like. But when you scratched beneath the surface, a project that took on the dimensions of a major archeological expedition, you found something unexpected, something rare and valuable. Mrs. Chaney loved poetry. And, if she loved poetry, she had to love what the poets loved—nature, honor, love itself. Right?

Yet, how to reconcile the poetry lover with the teacher who terrorized the kids? How could such a severe edifice house such a delicate sensibility? How? It seemed impossible. Mrs. Chaney was smarmy and hypocritical, with a built-in thermostat that allowed her to be cold one minute, warm the next, depending on her audience. Harsh with the kids, charming with their parents, she showed remarkable range, turning in bravura performances every open house.

The old man saw through her, but few of the other parents did, and if she refused to take a bow following these dramas, it was only because her acting ability was exceeded by her fierce desire to conceal it, which was further proof of her greatness as a thespian. The classroom was her stage. *Vieja hipócrita*, old hypocrite, Alita would have called her.

Alternately cold and hot, Mrs. Chaney was always cunning and manipulative—traits accompanied by the hubris that, time and time again, proved her downfall. She thought she could outwit the kids, but she was wrong. Poor Mrs. Chaney. Poor, benighted Mrs. Chaney, amateur sleuth. When she turned on the intercom in the main office, hoping to catch the students misbehaving in class, she heard a blast that would have shocked Patton—a blast that originated in the bowels of the tiniest, mousiest child in class: Wendell Wilson. The detonation was his Manhattan Project.

A great actress, Mrs. Chaney was no match for the comedy troupe in her fifth grade class. And yet . . . she loved poetry. I marveled at the dichotomy, the two faces of Mrs. Chaney, the strict disciplinarian warring with the sensitive soul. Mrs. Chaney never dissected the poetry, never discussed its content or meaning, but when she read out loud, you could see her parachuting into another world, a world brimming with kaleidoscopic possibilities. She lingered on some words, barreled over others, but she respected each one, knowing that different words demanded different rhythms, the individual units melding into an incandescent whole. Alita boasted the same quality with her everyday speech, stressing syllables to emphasize her point—*No le hagas caso a ese CA-brón*.

During most classes, I stared at the clock, discouraged by the slow, stultifying slog of time. It was a plod, a *pinche* plod, but time accelerated whenever Mrs. Chaney recited poetry; her voice, usually harsh and guttural, taking on a soft, liquid quality that helped transport you to the same world she was entering. *CHINgele*.

One morning, she passed out mimeographed sheets of a poem she called a "serenade." It was from a play by Henry Wadsworth Longfellow, *The Spanish Student*. The textbook featured dozens of poems by Longfellow, but this poem was not among them, so she copied it from another source. A serenade, she repeated delicately. She looked at the children, making sure they were quiet and attentive. And then she started reading the poem.

Stars of the summer night!
Far in yon azure deeps,

Hide, hide your golden light!
She sleeps!
My lady sleeps!
Sleeps!

Moon of the summer night!
Far down yon western steeps,
Sink, sink in silver light!
She sleeps!
My lady sleeps!
Sleeps!

Wind of the summer night!
Where yonder woodbine creeps,
Fold, fold thy pinions light!
She sleeps!
My lady sleeps!
Sleeps!

Dreams of the summer night!
Tell her, her lover keeps
Watch! while in slumbers light
She sleeps!
My lady sleeps!
Sleeps!

It was a short poem, but she read it with so much joy and energy that it seemed even shorter than it was. I looked up at the clock. It was time to resume the slog. But, no, she paused, holding the poem to her bosom, as if the mimeographed sheet were a cherished Bible. She took a few steps forward, slowly and deliberately, surveying the classroom with an almost haughty indifference. What was she doing? I wondered. Then her eyes—those dark, malignant orbs—settled on me.

"Robert, there's a character in the play, and she's known as *Preciosa*," Mrs. Chaney said.

She paused.

"Can you tell us what *Preciosa* means?"

I looked at the clock again, the clock above the blackboard. It was big and round, its white face edged with black trim. I could see the hands making their slow, painful journey through time. The slog resumed. I looked from wall to wall, noticing, for the first time, how silly and insipid the classroom décor was, how stupid. Trees and flowers plastered the windows, all the roses and oaks, all the daisies and elms made out of construction paper—the shabby equivalent of stained glass. It was pathetic. I looked at the ceiling; stars, moons, and planets dangled from strands of yarn, a faux firmament—another shabby, stupid attempt to recreate something finer, something grander: a sky, a planetarium, something. I looked at the bookshelves, each one topped with paper-maché ogres and fairies, their faces twisted in demonic smiles or foppish grins. And then, after my eyes swept the classroom, after I noted the walls and ceilings, the nooks and crannies, I looked at Mrs. Chaney, and I tried to remember what it was that I admired about her. I bowed my head.

"Well?" she said.

She waited.

"Surely, you, Robert, you, of all the children in this classroom, know what *Preciosa* means. . . . Do you or don't you?"

I looked at my desk, at all the dents and scratches, all the tiny letters that generations of students before me had carved into the wood—"rock 'n' roll, Go Dodgers, Ben [Heart] Donna."

"Well?"

I knew, but . . .

"I don't know," I said, my head still bowed.

"Oh . . . I thought . . . I just thought you . . . you, of all people . . . would know."

Mrs. Chaney stood in front of me, expecting me to respond.

"Well, children," she said, finally, "it means 'beautiful . . . beautiful lady.'"

When the bell rang to end the class, I remained in my seat for several seconds.

“Stupid chili,” Randy Reed said, standing over me. “You don’t even know your own fucking language.”

31

## The Dirty Pool

When a refuge stops being a refuge, it begins to symbolize all the woes and travails, all the ills and problems it once helped you escape. It becomes useless, a shrine with nothing to honor, a temple with nothing to commemorate. But, more than anything, it becomes a haunting reminder of its past glory, the comfort and protection it once provided gone, just like that, replaced by a sense of . . . what? . . . despair? vulnerability?

I still dangled from the monkey bars, still enjoyed the feeling of achievement I derived from performing a difficult but meaningless activity. That would never change. Never. I would hang from my arms and legs, bending myself into all kinds of weird shapes, most of them small and compact, as if I had been compressed by one of those machines at a junkyard, my body compacted into a bundle of bones, tendons, and nerve endings, with two mischievous eyes peeking out of the tiny bale I had become. . . . And then I would smile.

But the smiles never lasted. How could they? The bars were never about fun, not for me. They were about refuge, isolation, protection. And then, one day, Randy Reed stormed my fortress, hitting me in the mouth as I touched ground following one of my acrobatic leaps. It was a rough landing. Now the monkey bars were a collection of steel pipes, coated with the rust of generations. Just another toy in a playground filled with toys.

After the punch, I spent most of my time wandering the playground, watching the other kids play, and when I got tired of being a spectator, I sat by an oak tree, lost in reverie. They seemed like hours, the few minutes I spent there, sitting by the tree. And then, one day, I looked up at the sky, so clear and blue, its vastness fragmented by the trellis of branches above me. It was broad daylight, and yet there I was, staring at the sky with the intensity of a stargazer. . . . It felt cool. . . . It felt delicious. . . . The sky was hypnotizing me. . . . I started seeing sunspots, sunspots so blinding and piercing that I could detect them with my eyes closed—luminous dots, red, white, and yellow, colliding like atoms. It was like staring at those swinging medallions that real hypnotists used.

Gazing at the sky, mesmerized by the sunspots performing their impromptu ballet in the glazed heavens, I headed back to my hometown, retracing the steps that brought me here almost a year earlier. I started thinking about El Paso; I always thought about El Paso, but this was different. Now, I was in El Paso, reliving experiences from my past, one after another, each memory another slat in the bridge that connected me with my past. . . . I saw myself as a tiny kid. Was I three, maybe four? It was about six o'clock one evening, just after sundown, and the doorbell rang at our little duplex in Sunset Heights.

"*Contestalo, mi'jo.* Answer the door, my child," Alita said.

I opened the door, and a monster emerged from the darkness, his teeth gleaming with the blood of his latest victim. *Ay, cabrón.* Alita looked up from her perch at the window, startled, her Lucky Strike trembling in her fingers. I ran to the old man, wrapping my arms around his legs as he walked to the door, stiff-gaited from the four-year-old barnacle clinging to his legs. He was carrying a bag of candies. It was Halloween.

I saw myself at church with the old man. It was Sunday morning, the first service of the day, and we were late. We spotted an open area in the thick tangle of parishioners; as we headed to the pews, one of the nuns snatched the cap off my head, flinging it to the floor in back of me with a *harruummpphh.* The old man picked it up.

"Young man," the nun said, pointing her right index finger at me, "we do not wear caps in church."

"Sister," the old man said, picking up the cap. "I wonder if you could do me a favor. Could you point out the biblical passage—chapter and verse—in which the Lord hands down his righteous prohibition against young boys wearing caps at Mass? You see, I need to explain to my son the utter seriousness of his transgression."

The nun stared at the old man, slack-jawed.

"Thank you," my father said.

The old man placed the cap back on my head, gingerly, like a tailor outfitting a client.

"Sit down, son," he said as we settled into our seats.

I saw myself in late February, that hazy point in the calendar, not quite winter, not quite spring—a period of lovely expectation, even in the desert, where the vegetation followed the laconic schedule of the Southwest, reemerging slowly and deliberately after the chilly months of *invierno*. I saw myself in the backyard of our duplex, a backyard with a wooden fence that seemed superfluous, even dumb. There were no houses behind us, just acres and acres of desert, a carpet of dirt that stretched from Prospect to Hawthorne.

Alita asked me to throw out the garbage. It was about seven o'-clock, and I could smell every dinner from every home in the neighborhood—the scent of *rajas, frijoles,* and *tripas* (peppers, beans, and tripe) sailing through the cool evening air . . . Aaahhh. . . . Alita was in the kitchen, making *picadillo, aroz,* and *caldo* (ground beef, rice, and soup), her dinner menu far more exotic than her breakfast menu. I wondered if she would let me toss the trash without making me wash my hands afterward. *Nel,* I thought. No way.

The trashcan was next to the fence. I lifted the lid to dump the trash, and as I tilted the shopping bag full of garbage, I saw a tiny triceratops peering at me from the bottom of the can, its translucent, bloodshot eyes oozing malevolence. I froze. This was not some Halloween monster; this was the real thing.

"*Ay, cabrón!*" I screamed, dropping the lid onto the trashcan. "It's a dinosaur!"

My father rushed out of the house, slamming the screen door behind him.

"Your dinosaur," my father said, smiling as he peered into the can, "is a horned frog."

I lost my refuge, my monkey bars, but I retained my real sanctuary—my past. The past was there—it was always there—but it took a catalyst to bring it back, vibrant and unquenchable. The tree was not my catalyst. The sky was not my catalyst. The playground was not my catalyst. Randy Reed was my catalyst. And whatever pain he may have caused, whatever suffering and anguish he may have inflicted, I had to thank him for that. He turned me around; he made me look backward.

It was a jarring juxtaposition, this violent collision between my shabby present and my idyllic past, but I appreciated one as much as I dreaded the other, and I wondered when the real showdown would come—the final clash between the two of us, the Chili versus Randy Reed. And when it came, I wondered, would I fail, as I had failed the first time, frozen by shock—or fear—into taking whatever he handed me? Or would I respond like the pint-sized Johnny Risko that I knew my father and grandfather, deep down, wanted me to be?

Whenever the showdown came—and however I responded—I knew it would be on the playground. It had to be. When Randy Reed destroyed my fortress, he fortified his, and every time he called me a chili, he got bolder and bolder, his invincibility fueled by my vulnerability. He wanted to kick my ass, and this was where he wanted to do it, on the playground—the playground he ruled.

It was a big playground—big enough for a baseball field and a basketball court. The monkey bars were in the back, near a tall wooden fence that separated the school from the grandest home in the neighborhood. The home, a Spanish-style house with red tiles on the roof, had a swimming pool in the backyard; we could see it through the cracks in the fence, the blue water shimmering in the blinding sun—a mirage for the landlocked kids on the other side.

One day, after Randy Reed finished his lunch, he filled his empty sandwich bag with sand. It looked like a pouch full of gold dust. He twisted the top of the bag . . . twisted it with an almost disturbing delicacy . . . careful not to seal it completely. What was he doing? The kids stared at him, and he stared back, smirking. Then he lobbed the bag over the fence, using an awkward, sideways motion, as if the damned thing were a hand grenade. We scurried to the fence, watching the bag hit the water, a splat that sounded harsh but harmless. Randy Reed grinned.

The bag sat there, eerily motionless, like a basket of fruit on a patio table. Then it started to sink, and as it descended, slowly and mysteriously, the water grew murky, as if a shadow had descended on that side of the pool. Randy Reed grinned again, his teeth smeared with the peanut butter sandwich he had just eaten. He walked away, knowing that every kid was looking at him, awed and fascinated—a status he must have enjoyed because he repeated his performance every day for the next two weeks. Every day. The boys started calling him Sgt. Saunders, the hero of *Combat*, because of the way he lobbed the sand-filled bag as though it were a hand grenade.

"Hey, look at this," he yelled, pretending to pull a pin from the bag as he tossed it across the fence.

After two weeks, the pool started to look like a drainage ditch. The owners never complained. What was wrong with them? Did they enjoy swimming in muddy water, their bodies streaked with the dirt that fell from the sky? Then it dawned on us. The owners must have been on vacation, oblivious to the vandalism of the real-life Sgt. Saunders. But they would come back eventually, come back from Hollywood or San Francisco or San Juan Capistrano, and when they did, what then? Would we all be in trouble? Or would the trouble fall on one kid—and one kid only? Would Sgt. Saunders, a hero on television, become a loser in real life?

We found out the following week. Sister Francis Louise, the principal, addressed us on the intercom. Her voice was always authoritative, except when she was working on her mints, but this time it sounded harsher.

"I want it to stop—and I want it to stop now," she said.

She never mentioned what *it* was, but we knew.

"Did you hear that?"

There was a long pause.

"And, oh yes, I'll find out who did it."

She never did. The bag-throwing incidents stopped. But every time Randy Reed stood by the wooden fence, he grinned. And every time he grinned, I thought . . . what a *mamón*. Idiot.

32

# The Spelling Bee

As the school year drew to a close, Mrs. Chaney staged grammar and spelling contests, and I started reminiscing about my early forays into a strange land—the world of literature.

Literature—what a refined term for the dreck they served the first graders at Holy Family Elementary School in El Paso. I can see the textbooks now—flat, vapid pictures depicting flat, vapid adventures. And the characters. They were enervating, as dull and lifeless as their dog, through which they seemed to live vicariously.

"Run, Spot, run," they screamed, as if watching a dog run were grand entertainment.

Poor Dick and Jane, the main characters in these dreadful books. I guess they had no Alitas, no Apaches, no pomegranate trees in their lives. Just Spot, *pinche* Spot.

I longed for grand adventures, dramas wrapped in book covers, with characters who grew in stature as the generations passed—Ulysses, Huckleberry Finn, Long John Silver. Aaahhh. The old man rhapsodized about all these characters, especially Ulysses, whom he sometimes referred to as Odysseus. Where were they? Their absence confirmed a sad truth about the first graders at Holy Family: we were not ready for them. Our ambition exceeded our reading ability, so we were stuck with literary training wheels—short, clipped sentences that truncated our speech and, thus, our imaginations—"Run, Spot, run."

We sounded like Tarzan, reading one . . . word . . . at . . . a . . . time, slowly and woodenly.

Except on birthdays and Christmas, the old man was not a gift-giver, but he violated his unwritten rule one afternoon in El Paso, presenting me with a magnificent surprise. It was a book, and I knew it was magnificent before I even opened it. I could just tell. It was leather-bound, red with gold lettering, the title embossed on the cover, each bump and ridge a delicious reminder that books themselves—not just the words inside them—were works of art, as captivating as Rembrandts or Picassos. My father called it a "volume."

When I cracked the book open, there was a green ribbon inside, a kind of tassel, which I could use as a bookmark. I would need it. I had never seen a book so big, so monstrous; it was bigger than any of the encyclopedias in the school library. The old man had bought it, on the spur of the moment, during a giant book sale at the El Paso County Coliseum.

The book was *Ivanhoe* by Sir Walter Scott. My father said it was about knights and damsels, with more blood and violence than twenty episodes of *Gunsmoke*. This was magic, and I had not even started reading the book yet.

Then, a funny thing happened. I started reading the book . . . and nothing. The world inside the pages remained inside the pages, dull and moribund. Like all great literature, it was supposed to jump out at me, enthralling me with its rich drama, its colorful characters. But no. The writing was weird, too formal and stilted for my first-grade sensibility. What happened?

The harder I focused, the more the words eluded me, their meanings trapped in another century. This was in the days before my father would send me scurrying to the dictionary, forcing me to look up the words that confounded me. *Gracias a Dios!* Thank you, good-bye! I had no idea how to pronounce these words, much less spell them. I tried to read the words, tried and tried and tried, resting the book in my lap as I sat up in bed, my forehead furrowed in concentration. It was no use.

I sensed the silence in the room—silence so profound that I heard the dust dancing in the shafts of sunlight. I did, really. I know

I did. Shhh. Listen. Do you hear that? I asked myself. I soldiered on in the oppressive silence, and before I knew it, I had read forty-five pages—forty-five pages—but I could not remember a single word I had read. Not a thee, not a knave, not a wherefore. Nothing. How many jousts did I miss? How many beheadings? How many wars? And how many men fell in battle, I wondered, their swords and crossbows strewn across the hills like carburetors in a junkyard? How many? I would never know. Too dispirited to reread the pages I had just slogged through, I put the book down—for good.

"How do you like it?" my father asked, poking his head inside my room.

"I . . . I . . . I . . . I. . . . ."

"Not exactly *And to Think That I Saw It on Mulberry Street*, huh?" he asked.

No, not exactly. *And to Think That I Saw It on Mulberry Street* was my favorite Dr. Seuss book—my favorite book, period. It depicted a day in the life of a boy plagued by a horrible malady—boredom. Then, one day, he saw things that other people could not see, heard things that other people could not hear, and the world around him, once so flat and lifeless, became vibrant and exciting, a stunning alchemy he accepted with joyful appreciation. And why not? It was the boy—and his imagination—that caused the world to morph in the first place. And to think that he saw it all, savored it all, on a crummy street in a crummy town.

"No," I said. "It's not."

"Well, that's okay," he said. "One of these days, you'll love it."

"I know," I said, lying once again.

The old man downscaled his expectations—drastically but not condescendingly. He encouraged me to read comic books, and I embraced his strategy wholeheartedly, devouring all things Marvel—Thor, Daredevil, Spiderman, Captain America. Most of the heroes were reticent, quicker to act than to speak, but the villains, ah the villains, were grand speechifiers, their word bubbles overflowing with adverbs and adjectives, as if they could vanquish their opponents with verbosity. They were great English teachers.

Slowly graduating from the Dick and Jane books, I started bringing home one hundreds on my spelling tests. My mother bragged about me, but the old man asked her to be more "circumspect," afraid that my love of literature would be corrupted by an unhealthy pursuit of As.

The old man worried needlessly. The As were great, but what I really wanted to do was pontificate like a villain; I started sprinkling my speech with words I could barely understand—grandiose, omnipotent, cavalier. My friends got a kick out of it, especially Victor Serrano, who said, "*Mira el Seltzer. Se cre muy abogado.* Look at Seltzer. He must think he's a lawyer." None of them knew what I was talking about.

In the third grade at Holy Family, two years before we moved to Bakersfield, Sister Katherine Elizabeth staged a series of spelling bees, pitting the boys against the girls. I won all the contests, victories that made the boys proud, for we were considered dumber than the girls in almost every subject. Every subject except one—we viewed it as a triumph.

Siglinda Lucero was my main rival, a tall girl with long arms and spindly legs who looked like Little Iodine in the Sunday comics—a.k.a. *La Traviesa* in the Juárez newspapers. The first bee was the toughest. She and I were the last students standing, and with each word we pronounced correctly, I grew more nervous, knowing that all the boys were depending on me to defend their honor.

"Cool," Sister Katherine Elizabeth pronounced.

Cool? I thought to myself. This is getting silly. Why hurl such a simple word at us?

"Your turn, Siglinda," she said.

Siglinda cleared her throat. "Cool," she said. "K-O-O-L." Then she smiled.

"Wrong," Sister Katherine Elizabeth said. "Robert?"

"Cool," I repeated calmly. "C-O-O-L."

"Correct," Sister said.

The boys cheered, and Sister shushed them immediately. Then Siglinda, distressed by this strange turn of events, lodged her protest—passionate but futile. Sister heard her out.

"Sister, I know it's K-O-O-L," she said, pleading. "I know it is. My father smokes KOOL cigarettes, and it's right there on the box—K-O-O-L."

"Whom do you trust, Siglinda?"

Sister actually said whom.

"Whom do you trust? Me or the makers of the cigarettes?"

Sister waited for the answer.

"Well? Me or Madison Avenue?"

Siglinda bowed her head, and the debate, like the spelling bee that precipitated it, was over. "Thank you, Sister," Siglinda said, ignoring the boys who taunted her as she walked back to her desk, her hopes shattered but her dignity intact.

"C-c-c-c-c-ool," they stuttered, although it was hard to determine if they were trying to make the *C* sound or the *K* sound.

Two years later, I took my reputation as a good speller to St. Francis Elementary School in Bakersfield—an irony that chafed the kids who regarded me as a chili. I had trouble with words the old man threw at me, but I was an Oxford professor compared to some of the other students, who stumbled from sentence to sentence like modern-day Tarzans—Me Randy Reed, you Chili. And yet they considered me an interloper, someone who spoke English as a second language. I should have stuck to phrases like *buenos dias*, *hasta mañana*, and *gracias a Dios*, a phrase I mistranslated into "thank you, good-bye"—*gracias adios*—proving, perhaps, that I was culturally deficient, although not in the way that Randy Reed thought I was.

One afternoon, we were reading from our religion textbook, and Randy Reed was navigating his way through a slalom course of verbiage. He crashed into verbs, adverbs, adjectives and participles—although few of us knew what a participle was—and it was maddening to sit there, hearing him careen from word to word, as we waited for our turn to read. It was like watching a wreck on the Interstate.

"Om-ni . . . om-ni . . ."

Randy Reed was having trouble with the word "omnipotent"—a word common in the Thor comic books, because Odin, the father of the Thunder God, was always referred to as "the omnipotent Odin."

"Om-ni-po . . . om-ni-po . . . "

Mrs. Chaney, not known for her patience, waited silently.

"Om-ni-po . . . om-ni-po . . . om-ni-po-tent. . . ."

Randy Reed turned one word into four, pronouncing each one slowly and haltingly, and the third word—*po*—came out with a long O.

"Robert," Mrs. Chaney said, "could you help him, please?"

"Omnipotent," I said.

"Can you say that, Randy?" Mrs. Chaney asked.

"Om-ni . . . om-ni-po . . . om-ni-po-tent."

"Okay," Mrs. Chaney said, sighing. "Robert, continue with the next paragraph."

When the bell rang, I turned around, and there he was, staring at me with the malignant glare he had flashed that day on the playground. But the old man was right. I was starting to realize what Randy Reed was capable of. I stared back, more calmly than usual, and headed out to recess.

33

## The Alley of Doom

As summer approached, I waited for the pleasant longing to fill my chest, the ineffable joy of anticipation.

I felt it every year, felt it so acutely, so completely, that it almost validated something the old man had told me for years: Sometimes, wanting something is better than getting it. But not in this case; nothing was better than summer vacation. Nothing. Not even those lovely weeks before the last day of school, when time itself became your ally, turning the clock from cruel oppressor into noble liberator. Yes, those weeks were delicious. The slog, eight months and counting, would be coming to an end. Aaahhh. But nothing was better than the end itself. Not even the anticipation of the end.

The pleasant feeling never came that year. I waited, but it never came. It reminded me of the night I saw *A Hard Day's Night* at El Tejon Theater. I imagined myself in the movie house, waiting for the curtains to part, but once they parted, the screen remained empty, and I had known it would remain empty, had known it all along, so I just sat there, expecting nothing, anticipating nothing—no joy, no exuberance, no Beatles. *Que botas*. What the hell. Summer vacation was the last thing on my mind that year.

In El Paso, we lived in a neighborhood; in Bakersfield, we lived at an intersection, Brundage and Beech. It was like residing on a highway median, with a blur of whooshing metal on either side—so much for a front yard and a backyard. We lived next to a Texaco gas station, which was the only cool thing about our location. I liked the workers, and they liked me; one of them taught me how to fix a bicycle flat.

I headed to the gas station every morning, popping a wheelie over the rubber hose that crossed the pumping lane—the hose that rang like a doorbell every time a vehicle bumped over it. I loved the sound; it was a call to action. The old man scolded me, thinking the antic disturbed the workers, but none of them seemed to mind, especially Ralph Cotton, the manager.

Mr. Cotton—he kept telling me to call him Ralph, but I was too embarrassed to view him as a peer—was lean and wiry, his white hair trimmed so short that it looked like the fuzz on a tennis ball. He was about sixty, maybe sixty-five. But he looked young, younger than his years, except for the hair . . . the hair and the wrinkle that gouged his forehead, a rut so deep it must have puddled during downpours. It made him look severe, even when he was smiling. He waved every time I crossed the hose, *riiiinnng*, and I waved back, fishtailing as I hit the pebble-strewn alley between our rental home and the gas station. It was our way of saying "good morning." Then it was off to school.

Mr. Cotton waved to me that morning, flapping the red cloth he used to wipe the dipsticks under the hood. I waved back, and as I turned into the alley, the pebbles spluttered under my tires, spraying the trashcans that lined the alley like robotic sentries. *Ping, ping, ping.* Mr. Cotton smiled, a pleasant, good-natured grin—wrinkle or no wrinkle.

It was about 7:30 a.m., but the sun was already fierce, and as the sunlight streamed through the canopy of oaks, the leaves ignited, turning as bright and translucent as diamonds. I lowered my head, trying to shield my eyes from the sun. The world streaked by.

The more I thought of Randy Reed, the faster I flew. I hunched over the handlebars, my head jutting out like a hood ornament. The alley seemed to lengthen . . . and narrow, turning into a dark, lonely tunnel. I stared straight ahead, isolated and desperate, entombed by an overactive imagination—just me and my doubts. Just me and Randy Reed.

*No le hagas caso.* I kept hearing those words, laced with the wisdom and beauty of the woman who uttered them—my beloved Alita . . . *No le hagas caso.* Four lovely words. I recognized their value, their strength and legitimacy. But how could I ignore him? He was so sullen, so overbearing, so there. . . . That was it. He was so there, oppressive and inescapable, his hostility present even when his body was not.

The alley stretched from Brundage to Palm, a path broken by crossing streets every hundred yards. There were about five of them—five crossings—between home and school; once I reached the final street, I turned left for the last quarter-mile to school. It was the same route I took every morning, with only slight variations, the landmarks so familiar that I viewed them as road signs, mile markers on my journey to school: each house, each car, each cat lounging by a trash can telling me how much further I had to go. Who needed a map? I had my eyes.

My eyes. I did not need them that morning, and I did not need the mile markers, either. The alley was a tunnel now, a dark, lonely tunnel. I kept pedaling, faster and faster, conscious of nothing but my own breathing, rhythmic, concise, and constant—ah-uh, ah-huh, ah-huh. I crossed streets, going from alley to street, alley to street, without realizing it. *Pendejo.* Then I heard a sound besides my breathing—a car horn, a long blast that startled me from my self-absorption. I hit the brakes, skidding along the asphalt as I toppled to the ground, my bicycle landing on top of me. *Chingele.* The car, a white Chevrolet with a Goldwater bumper sticker, roared away, the blast growing fainter and fainter, like the shrill whistle of a freight train thundering into the night.

I lay there, pinned by my bike, my knee throbbing as I tried to slither out from under the wreckage. I surveyed the damage. The bike was fine, just dusty and scratched, the rear fender dented from the crash. I was fine, too, just a scraped elbow and an aching knee that my mother might not even notice when I got home from school;

my khaki pants did not rip, *gracias a Dios*, thank you, good-bye. My mother. If she did notice, it would be, "Chee whiz, Bobby, *pon mas cuidado en la calle*. Be more careful on the street," for about an hour.

The alley no longer a tunnel, I pedaled slowly the rest of the way, reaching school about ten minutes before the bell, my ego more bruised than my body. It was still hot, but it was a wet, gauzy heat, the kind that leads to thundershowers, and it gave the playground a soft, feathery quality. I looked up at the sky. Hmmm. A pall of clouds. I inhaled. Then I headed to the monkey bars. Ten minutes—enough time for a few daring routines. But no, once I got there, I settled in my perch on the top bars, my legs crossed under my butt Indian-style—like the chief on *Broken Arrow*, one of the Westerns my mother let me watch whenever the old man was on a freight train trip. I savored the view. Then the bell rang. Who speeded up the clock? Too tired—and shaken—for an acrobatic dismount, I settled for a more prosaic approach, descending like a roofer who had just finished his job, one step at a time.

Prosaic? Not prosaic enough. My foot missed one of the lower bars, and my hands, sweaty from the growing humidity, slipped from the top bar. I tumbled backwards, and as my foot got stuck on the lower bar, I spun in the air, my arms twisting one way, my legs another, an airborne pretzel. What luck. My second tumble in one day. I landed on my face, but in my disoriented state, it seemed as if the ground had ascended to meet me, rather than the other way around. I was minding my own business, and, all of a sudden, the ground elevated and smacked me in the face.

I landed hard, so hard that I remained on all fours for several seconds, dazed and confused, a stalactite of snot and blood dripping from my nose. Bloody *mocos*. I looked up, my vision blurred. I saw three kids standing above me, hazy and indistinct, their forms shimmering like heat waves. *Ay Dios*. I kept staring, my eyes narrowing in concentration and bewilderment. Then, as I regained focus, the three kids merged into one. It was Randy Reed.

"Ha!" Randy Reed shouted, cackling. "It's the chili. He's bleeding again. And, this time, I didn't even have to hit him. Ha!"

As I struggled to my feet, a girl rushed up to me.

"Robert, are you all right?"

It was Rachel Olsen.

"Yeah . . . I'm fine," I replied, desperately trying not to cry.

I was so embarrassed, so self-conscious, that I did not even see her solicitude as a sign that she might like or—could she possibly?—even love me.

"I'm fine," I repeated.

The second bell rang, the signal for the kids to get in line for the first class of the day. I reached into my pocket. My mother always made sure I had a fresh handkerchief every day, whether or not I had used one the previous day. God bless her. I swabbed my nose, and within seconds, the handkerchief looked like a sponge dipped in a tub of red ink. Mrs. Chaney would make a fuss, sending me to the nurse while the other kids scurried to class, and afterwards, Randy Reed would tell everyone that he did it again, pounded my face again, and they would believe him, because he had done it before, and every time you did something once, it became easier the second time . . . and the third time . . . and the . . .

But Mrs. Chaney never said a word. She stood by the door as we straggled into class, her demeanor the same as always—only slightly less severe and menacing than that of a drill sergeant. But nothing. Not a word. She let me enter, along with the other kids, glaring at us as we settled into our desks. We arranged our books and notebooks for another day of torture.

We stood up for the morning prayer, waiting for the homeroom teacher to start reciting the Our Father. Nothing. She stood there, hands on hips, her eyes bleeding the malignance that became her trademark that year. We waited. Still nothing. *Ay Dios mio.* I uttered a silent prayer—in lieu of our traditional class prayer—that she would notice my bloody nose, just to shatter the monotony. Still nothing. Just a dreary, oppressive silence.

Then we noticed the letters on the blackboard. Seven letters—two words—that grew sharper the longer you stared at them, just like the three Randy Reeds that coalesced into one.

FUCK YOU

The words were there, on the blackboard, as bold and distinct as our daily assignments.

FUCK YOU

An F-bomb. Splattered on the blackboard. Someone—one of us—left it there, big, bold, and dramatic. But who?

"Who did that?" Mrs. Chaney asked us. "Who wrote those . . . those . . . ugly words?"

No response. Not a peep. Not a chirp. Not a twitter worthy of a field mouse. Nothing. I looked at Rachel Olsen; Rachel Olsen looked at me. Our faces said what our mouths could not: Who would have written such a stupid thing? My first guess was Randy Reed, but even Randy Reed could not have been such a . . . *mamón* . . . could he?

As we sat there, dumbfounded, it started to rain. The sky darkened, and the thunder rattled the windows. We looked outside.

"Okay, children," Mrs. Chaney yelled. "Open your English books. Turn to page fifty-seven. . . ."

I could not keep my mind on the lesson. FUCK YOU. Who could have written it? Who could have been dumb enough to write it? I thought of all the *travesuras* (pranks) I committed in El Paso, most of them with my best friend, Victor Serrano. The scariest was the most memorable. Why does it always work that way? The two of us bicycled around Mundy Park one summer evening, our wire baskets, which were attached to the handlebars, loaded with water balloons. We surveyed the grassy hills for lovers locked in romantic wrestling matches. I spotted a couple, and I waved to Victor, and we hurled our water-filled bombs at the same instant. *Ándale!* The balloons hit the bull's-eye, between a pair of eager lips, and *chingele*, as soon as the balloons busted, the man—a teenager—sprang to his feet, his sense of urgency now directed toward a different consummation—our deaths. He sprinted after us, chasing us down Prospect, up Yandell, down Rio Grande, and by the time we gathered enough courage to stop and turn around, we were at the El Paso Public Library, about a mile from Mundy Park, our hearts transformed into percussion instruments, each beat a scary reminder of the hostile lover chasing us. Where was he? He was nowhere in sight. *Gracias adios*. We took a different route home.

I thought of the afternoon we went to see *From Russia With Love* at the Plaza Theater, Victor and I. It was a magnificent theater, ornate and baroque, with a lobby so vast that you had to stroll for a block before you reached the seats. The bathrooms were downstairs. We entered the door marked MEN, and we locked every stall from the inside, slipping underneath the doors to make sure they remained *trancadas*, locked. It was thrilling. As we left, we laughed so hard that we almost had to go back to pee.

When the movie ended, we returned to the bathroom, hoping to see a group of men banging at the doors, their faces red from having to go and not being able to. *Cagones*. Shitters. We were disappointed. The stall doors were wide open, and there was only one man in the bathroom, a man in a red sports coat—the head usher? Standing between the stalls and the sinks, he stared at us, his arms folded across his chest, his eyes exuding the cold, naked menace of razor blades. We headed to the urinals, unzipping our pants as we pretended to pee. How long does it take a person to pee if he does not have to pee? We stood there for about fifteen seconds. Then we walked out, quietly, meekly, without washing our hands.

I thought of the times we loitered on the first floor of the White House, the department store that exploited its connection with the home where President Kennedy lived in the capital. We lurked near the elevators, behind the perfume counters, waiting for someone to step inside; about a half-second after the doors closed, we pressed the DOWN button, and the elevator doors reopened, infuriating the customers who thought they were on their way up.

I thought of all those *traversuras*, all those blotches on my personal record, but they were harmless pranks, all of them, unless you were one of the victims. A FUCK YOU was different. A FUCK YOU was a *pendejada*. Idiocy. And on the blackboard, no less, in full view of everyone.

A FUCK YOU on the blackboard was worse than the CON SAFOS you saw scrawled here and there in El Paso—on fences, on walls, even on the sides of buses. CON SAFOS? Few of us even knew what it meant. But FUCK YOU was different. Its meaning was all too clear.

"Who did it?"

No response.

"Fine," Mrs. Chaney said.

That was it. As the day progressed, we moved on, the incident relegated to ancient news. We forgot about it. And then I went home.

"My God," the old man said that evening. "What happened?"

"Huh?" I responded.

"Your nose."

*Ay Dios mio*. My nose. I had forgotten about my accident.

"I fell from the monkey bars, Dad."

He stared at me, his eyes narrowing in a display of anger I rarely saw.

"Bobby . . ." he said. "Bobby, don't lie to me."

"Dad, please believe me. I'm not lying. . . . I swear."

The old man looked at me, a glare that pierced my soul. *Chingele*. Trying to break the awkward silence, I asked him if he was still planning to jump a freight train early the next morning, a trip he had planned for about a week. Was he heading to Barstow? Or Stockton? Or Fresno? I forgot the town; all I remembered was that he would be heading out, somewhere, again.

Focusing on his freight train journeys, I forgot about the inquisition, if only for a moment. I could see the old man, huddled in a boxcar, the floor shaking under his rump. The door was open, and the world flashed by, a blur of cows and crops and clouds. What attracted him to a world that others shunned? What did the hobos offer him that his own family could not? Why did he have to venture into that world, week after week, month after month? Why? They were questions I posed only to myself and only in my moments of deepest frustration. I knew the answers. The old man lived in two worlds, the domestic and the literary, and when he embraced one, he was not abandoning the other, not really. He was just . . . setting it aside. I understood his motivation. I did not like it—nobody likes to be set aside—but I understood it.

"Are you still going on your trip?" I asked.

"Yes," he responded. "I'm leaving tomorrow morning."

"What time?" I asked.

"Early," he said, annoyed at my questions.

"How early? Before I go to school?"

"Yes," he said.

He looked at me again, and I bowed my head, saddened that he would be gone on the final day of school, when I would have to face Randy Reed one more time.

"Bobby, school's almost over," the old man resumed. "You can't let him get away with it anymore. If you do, you'll regret it the whole summer."

"Okay, Dad."

"Look," he said, his tone softening. "Do you think Randy Reed is tough?"

"Yes."

"Why?"

"Because he just is. He's scary."

"Okay," the old man said. "Fine. He scares you. Does he scare anyone else?"

"Yes."

"Who?" the old man asked.

"Well, Wendell Wilson . . . and . . . "

"How big is Wendell Wilson?"

"He's small."

"How small?" the old man asked.

"He's the smallest kid in class."

"Who's the biggest kid in class?"

"Greg Bukowski."
"Does Randy Reed scare Greg Bukowski?"
"No," I replied.
"Why?"
"Well, he never tries to scare him."
"I see," the old man said.

# 34

## "Let's Do It"

"That's good advice," the old man said, trying to make himself heard above the roar of the song on the radio.

"Huh?" I responded.

"The Beatles song—'Slow Down.' You know, relax."

"Oh."

Then I realized what a remarkable exchange we had just experienced. The old man was not on a freight train, bound for God knows where, his notebook in one hand, his Clorox bottle in the other. He was home. The old man was home. I wanted to hug him.

"Dad, you're not . . ." I said, about to ask him why he had decided to forego his trip.

Did my mother lash out at him again? Or did he decide to stay on his own? I decided to drop it. *Chingado.* Who cared?

"You're home?"

"Yeah, I'm home. And, remember, slow down. Good advice."

When I woke up that morning, the alarm clock chased my dreams away, and I retrieved them the only way I knew how: I turned on the radio, just as I did every morning. The Beatles were blasting through "Slow Down," a rave-up built on a furious bass line. It was relentless, with a guitar riff so urgent and muscular that only one group—the Beatles themselves—could have maintained the pace vocally.

Slow down—it was a plea, and they screamed it. The song was an aural assault, the beat pushing toward a climax that proved elusive, as tantalizing as it was unattainable. Poor John, the lead singer. You could sense the desperation in his voice. "Owww!" he yowled between lyrics. The sexual frustration remained beyond my grasp, just as it had with "(I Can't Get No) Satisfaction," but I detected a delicious irony in the song, a recognition that filled me with pride and pleasure. The Beatles, pleading with their "pretty baby" to slow down, cranked it up musically, their sense of urgency driven by passion—a wonderful passion.

"Slow down, Beto," the old man was telling me. "Slow down. . . . Relax. . . . Don't worry. . . ." Relax? What was the old man talking about? And, yet somehow, I knew what he was saying. It was the message that counted, not the way it was expressed.

"Remember," the old man said. "You already know what he's capable of. You might think you're afraid of him, but he can't shock you, not anymore. Right?"

"Right," I said, repeating the word with a conviction that startled me.

"I don't mean you have to fight him," he said. "You just have to . . . stand up to him. Does that make sense?"

"Yes, sir."

For some reason, I thought the gravity of the situation required a "sir," a title I never used for the old man.

"Do you want a ride to school today?" the old man said.

It was the last day of school.

"No, thanks."

The old man hugged me.

"Good luck," he said.

My mother walked out of the kitchen.

"Bobby, don't you want some toast and *tosino* (bacon)?"

"Can I have the toast on the way?"

"*Ay Dios*, again?" she said, wrapping three pieces of buttered toast in aluminum foil. "Here. *Con cuidado*. Be careful."

"Thanks, Mom," I said, hugging her.

I opened the front door, and the air smelled clean and fresh, as if the angels had scrubbed the atmosphere during the night, wielding the celestial versions of mops and buckets. I took a big gulp of air, then let it out. Aaahhh. Hopping on my bicycle, I ran over the rubber hose at the gas station next door, *riiinnnng, riiinnnng*—one ring for each tire. Mr. Cotton emerged from the office, where he had been reading the newspaper, his feet resting on a box of Coca-Cola bottles by his steel desk. He flapped his red cloth at me.

"Good morning, young man."

"Good morning, Mr. Cotton."

"Call me Ralph."

"Yes, sir, Mr. Cotton . . . Ralph."

I headed toward the alley, just as I did every morning, but as I was about to hit the pebble-strewn surface, I turned around, producing another chorus of rings when I bumped over the rubber hoses. Mr. Cotton, halfway back to his office, turned around, frowning in mock indignation. Then he smiled.

"What is it, young man?"

"Mr. Cotton?"

"Ralph."

For the first time that year, I noticed a red patch on his white shirt. It was threaded with white stitching that spelled out "Ralph Cotton, Mgr." There was no "Mr." in front of his name.

"Yes, sir. . . . Well, uh, there's a boy at school who wants to kick my . . . ass," I said, embarrassed about using that word in front of an adult.

"Oh, there is, huh?" he said, resting his hands on his hips.

"Yes, sir."

"Ralph," he said.

I hesitated.

"Well, what are you going to do about it?" he asked.

"My Dad says I should relax."

"Relax?"

Mr. Cotton seemed surprised.

"Yes, sir."

Mr. Cotton scratched his head.

"Well, you know, son, that's good advice. Your father is a smart man, because if you're afraid, that boy will smell the fear on you, and it'll make him brave. Don't you make him brave."

"No, sir. I won't."

I turned around, twisting the handlebar as I crossed the rubber hose again, producing the final notes to the working class serenade—*riiinnnng*. The alley was an alley again, not a dark corridor of doom. I smiled.

As I shifted on the bicycle seat, the cool breeze stroking, my face, I thought about the long school year that was coming to an end. My mind drifted to that day, all those months ago, when Randy Reed shredded my surfboards. It was a week later when I asked the old man the question it was so hard for me to ask: Why am I a Mexican?

And I thought about Alita, about the *retratos* she gave me for Christmas. She made me realize I had asked the old man the wrong question. I was a Mexican because it was in my blood. My mother was a chili, and my father married her, and her blood flowed in my veins, as rich and thick as *champurrado*. I knew that, but Randy Reed assaulted my dignity, and it was the first time that I realized I had dignity that could be assaulted, and so I asked the old man a stupid question. Why am I a Mexican?

It was stupid not because I knew the answer, but because it was the wrong question. It was not about me; it was about the old man. I had no choice. My mother was born in Mexico. But the old man. . . . Why was he a Mexican? Born, nurtured, and educated in Cleveland, he rewrote his biography. He chose to be a Mexican.

I arrived at school later than usual—my conversation with Mr. Cotton slowed me down—and after I slipped my bike into the slot at the bicycle rack, I sprinted to class. Mrs. Chaney stood at the door, inspecting every student with the cold, appraising glare of a security guard. The last day of school meant nothing to Mrs. Chaney. Nothing. It may have been our last day, but release or no release, the prison warden was still a prison warden. *Chingele*. Oh, well. I smiled as I passed her, but she met my smile with a dismissive shrug, motioning me, along with the rest of the preadolescent cattle, into the classroom.

After we filed into the classroom, we stood by our seats, waiting for the last morning prayer of the year. Then we noticed the word, the F-word, still splattered on the blackboard, as shocking as it had been the day before. Mrs. Chaney never erased it.

She led us in the Our Father, reciting it so quickly that she sounded like John Lennon singing "Slow Down." Then she grabbed an eraser, and with the histrionic air she assumed on Parents Night, the homeroom teacher turned her back to the children, walking to the blackboard slowly and laboriously, each step as delicate as that of a tightrope walker.

What was she doing? Mrs. Chaney erased the word, removing the obscenity a day after its discovery. Why did she wait so long? She erased it so gently, barely feathering the blackboard, that the imprint of the letters remained on the surface, almost as distinct as the original words. We thought she would erase the obscenity, really erase it, scrub it, scour it, obliterate it, until each letter had been banished from her domain—our Lady Macbeth, with tight skirt and bulging eyes, washing away the transgression. But no, the word remained on the blackboard, as sharp as the chalk outline of a corpse in a back alley. Then, right above the ghostly outline of the FUCK YOU, Mrs. Chaney wrote our final lesson of the year:

> PRINT: "The Song of Hiawatha, Part I—The Peace Pipe" from your English textbook, P. 89. Please print in CAPITAL letters.

We began printing, a form of writing we thought we had outgrown years before. And on the last day of school. The classroom was silent—except for the turning of pages and the scratching of pens.

ON THE MOUNTAINS OF THE PRAIRIES . . .

FROM THE RED STONE OF THE QUARRY . . .
AND THEY STOOD THERE ON THE MEADOW . . .

On and on, an endless procession of subjects, verbs, and adverbs, stanza after stanza, that turned the classroom into a literary sweatshop, dull, harsh, and oppressive.

"Okay," Mrs. Chaney said, twenty-five minutes later. "Time's up."

"But, Mrs. Chaney, I'm not finished," Randy Reed said.

Mrs. Chaney glared at Randy Reed.

"Time's up," she repeated.

We passed up the papers, our names written in cursive at the top, and Mrs. Chaney tapped them on her desk, a tidy stack she started to peruse as she settled into her desk. "Randy, will you start reading the poem for us?" she said. "And please stand up . . . and please tuck in your shirt."

The students giggled.

"QUIET!" she yelled.

Randy Reed started reading.

"The . . . Song . . . of . . . Hi-a-wa-tha. . . . On . . . the . . . Mountains . . . of . . . the . . . Prai-rie . . ."

"Randy, sit down," Mrs. Chaney said. "Robert, will you read for us, please. I'm sure Mr. Longfellow would appreciate, from the remote recesses of the great beyond, someone who won't assault his beloved language—ENGLISH."

Frowning, she raised her right arm, palm out, as if telling me to wait.

"It just occurred to me, Randy," she said. "How ironic that your last name is Reed, when you seem to have so much trouble doing so. . . . Okay, Robert, go ahead. . . ."

I began reading, and by the time I reached the fourth stanza, I realized we were alone, unsupervised, a group of inmates without a warden. Mrs. Chaney had slipped out, quietly and discreetly, an act of stealth that seemed uncharacteristic. We were alone—alone with our depravity. I waited for Greg Bukowski and Wendell Wilson to spring from their seats, ready for a reprise of their youthful vaudeville act, as bold as it was combustible. Another explosion into the loud speaker. But no one stirred. No one. I kept reading, the words and emotions becoming part of me, as if Longfellow were using me as a medium.

"And the smoke rose slowly, slowly . . . "

As I approached the end, trying to savor each word as if it were the last bite of a candy bar, Mrs. Chaney walked into the classroom, followed by Sister Francis Louise, our principal.

"Thank you, Robert," Mrs. Chaney said. "You may sit down now."

I sank into my seat.

"Randy," Mrs. Chaney said. "Why don't you stand up now?"

Randy Reed stood up, his shoulders drooping.

"Randy, do you have something you want to say—to me, to the class, to Sister Francis Louise?" Mrs. Chaney asked.

"No."

"Are you sure?" she asked again. "Are you sure you don't want to apologize . . . about something?"

"Yes, I'm sure."

"I didn't want to do this, but you've forced my hand," she said. Holding the stack of Hiawathas printed by each student, she pulled one out. "Here, read this and pass it down," she told the girl at the head of the first row.

Silence. . . . And more silence. . . . And then the droning began, a hum that traveled up and down each row of desks. When the paper reached me, I saw the name at the top—Randy Reed. *Chingele.* Using a red pen, Mrs. Chaney had encircled every *F*, *U*, *C* and *K* in the poem—a bizarre, but effective, form of forensics. I looked up. Glancing from the paper to the blackboard—and back again—I came to an inescapable conclusion: The poem and the FUCK YOU were written by the same hand, one on loose-leaf paper, the other on the blackboard.

"Well," Mrs. Chaney said.

Randy Reed stared at her.

"It wasn't me," he yelled. "It wasn't me. . . . It was . . ."

Randy Reed pointed at me.

"Don't you dare blame Robert!" she screamed.

The bell rang for recess.

"Go on," Mrs. Chaney said. "Get out of here . . . all of you. . . . You, too, Mr. Reed."

As Randy Reed walked out the door, Sister Francis Louise stopped him.

"We'll be calling your parents," she told him.

Running toward the playground, wondering what would happen to the *pendejo*, I climbed the monkey bars, placing my foot on each bar with exaggerated caution, paranoid about repeating my mishap of the day before. No bloody *mocos* for me, not today. I wanted to sit at the top, safe in my perch, contemplating what a wild year it had been—for me and Randy Reed.

I never made it to the top. As I stepped on the first bar, I felt a tug from behind, a resistance, as if I were wearing a shoulder harness. The tug became stronger. I sprawled backwards, just as I had the day before, a silly spill that made me feel foolish, self-conscious. Did I look like Red Skelton, the comedian who made a career out of hilarious pratfalls? I wondered as I landed on my butt. I looked up, and there was Randy Reed, again, his body wired with hostility.

"This is it, Chili, goddamned, Chili," he screamed. "Let's do it."

I got up. The kids gathered around us, creating a wall of gawkers. I saw Wendell Wilson in front of the pack, so tiny that he looked like a lawn ornament, and I finally realized what the old man had been trying to tell me: Randy Reed was a bully, a kid who fed on fear and insecurity. I was too dumb to see it, too focused on the sinking ship to see the lifeboat in front of me, right in front of me, all along. The old man, Alita, Mr. Cotton—they were right, all of them. "Slow down." "*No le hagas caso.*" "Don't let him smell the fear on you." Every piece of advice, whether in English or Spanish, was the same: Relax. Let him know who you are.

I felt calm, tranquil, the same sensation my father and grandfather recognized—and cherished—in Johnny Risko, the old heavyweight contender. Aaahhh, Johnny Risko. There was no strut in the man, no swagger or pretense. He was just Johnny, as unassuming as the streets from which he sprang—cruel to his opponents, kind to his fans. I could hear them now, my father and grandfather, rhapsodizing about the great Johnny Risko.

Great? If Johnny Risko was a great fighter, it was not because of skill or technique or strength. No. He was a great fighter because he conquered the most crushing opponent of all: his mind. Every fighter was afraid—it was only natural—but Risko learned to live with his fear. He learned to walk the fine line that every fighter, every great fighter, must walk, the delicate balance between fury and serenity—the fury to punch, the serenity to know when not to. You cannot master your opponent until you master yourself. That was what my father and grandfather were talking about that night.

I did not grasp every nuance of their conversation, every shred of significance. And I did not know Zen from *huevos estrellados*. Sunny-side-up eggs. But I realized, there on the playground, with Randy Reed snorting in front of me, what my father and grandfather wanted me to do. Yes, they wanted me to be like Johnny Risko, but they did not want me to be a monster, an ass-kicker. They wanted me to hang in there. To relax.

Randy Reed threw the first punch. I slipped it nonchalantly, the way a batter moves away from a pitch on the inside corner. It felt great. He seemed surprised, but he punched again, more wildly this time, his arms spinning like rotary blades. I evaded each volley. The kids, pantomiming every wild punch, every evasive maneuver, started to giggle. All the kids except one. Wendell Wilson. He did not laugh; he guffawed, a roar that seemed too big for his tiny body.

With his hostility—and humiliation—enflaming him, Randy Reed tried again. He reared back, launching a punch with the wide, sweeping arc of a lumberjack, a motion so exaggerated it seemed comical. *Ay, cabrón.* I thought about the tall, lanky Mexican, Cruz Ortega, who "yardsticked" his sparring partner in that North Bakersfield gym all those months before. Randy Reed was no Cruz Ortega. Was I?

I stepped sideways, and Randy Reed swept past me, stumbling like a man who remains standing on an escalator without realizing he has reached the floor. The kids roared with laughter. As he turned around, trying to regain his balance, I stepped in to throw my first punch of the fight—a short right hand that I had to aim downward, since Randy Reed was stooped from his impromptu pirouette.

As I stood there, my fist poised to strike, a diorama flashed through my mind—mental snapshots of the school year that was coming to an end. The surfboards, the monkey bars, the fool's gold, the theater where I asked the lady for a box of FUCKS, the other FUCK, the one on the blackboard. And the dark turn in the story about how my father met my mother. They were there, all of them—scenes so vivid that I seemed to be reliving them. I marveled at the images, but just for a second, for they vanished almost as soon as they emerged. Gone. And when they left, I had to confront the boy who had been confronting me all year.

Randy Reed was in front of me, almost helpless, ready to be pounded. And then it happened. I started to lose my courage. *Ay Dios.* I remembered the humiliation and fear from the first incident on the monkey bars. The memory assaulted me, just as his fist had assaulted me all those months before, and I froze, my heart gripped by . . . what? More fear? More humiliation? I was not sure. I stood there, waiting—waiting to hit him or to be hit by him. And then he made my decision for me.

Randy Reed, already bent low, ducked lower, and as I aimed the punch, he clasped his hands behind his head, as if my hand were a hatchet about to chunk into a block of wood.

"No!" he screamed. "Don't!" He remained in the same position, waiting for the punch to land, for several seconds, but I never threw it. I just stood there, my arm cocked, wondering if this was how Johnny Risko felt.

"Randy Reed is a pussy!" Wendell Wilson yelled. "Ha!"

Randy Reed, finally straightening up, glared at Wendell Wilson.

"Oh, I am?!" he screamed.

Randy Reed lumbered toward Wendell Wilson, but he felt a tug on his shoulder, the same kind of tug I had felt on the monkey bars. It was Mrs. Chaney. Yanking him by the collar, she spun the boy around, his arms gyrating so wildly that he almost hit her in the face. It would have been his first solid punch of the day.

"You're in enough trouble, young man."

Then she addressed the rest of the students on the playground.

"Randy Reed has to go to a meeting—a meeting with me, Sister Francis Louise, and . . . his parents," she told us. "The rest of you can go home. The school year is over. But before you go, I want you to do me a favor."

Mrs. Chaney smiled. She smiled. We waited the whole year, but we finally discovered that her facial muscles could produce something besides a frown.

"I want you to leave the fighting and the dirty words to Randy Reed," she said. "He doesn't know any better, but he'll learn, trust me, he'll learn. But the rest of you . . . the rest of you . . . know better. Don't you? Have a good summer. Enjoy yourselves. And try to read a little poetry . . . okay?"

The kids roared. School was over. I sighed. School was over for me, too. *Gracias a Dios*. Thanks be to God.

"Okay!"

With Wendell Wilson leading the way, the kids streamed through the gate at the other end of the playground, stumbling as they executed their escape. Mrs. Chaney and Randy Reed headed back to the classroom, the executioner and the condemned. I stared until they disappeared into the classroom, two tiny figures swallowed up by the school building.

"Robert, I'm proud of you."

"Huh?"

"I'm proud of you. You didn't hit him."

It was Rachel Olsen.

"Oh," I said.

And, for the first time since the fight began, I was scared. Really scared. But not so scared that Rachel Olsen could smell the fear on me. No, not that scared. Would the old man be proud of me?

"Walk me to the gate?" she asked.

I blushed.

"Okay."

We sauntered to the bike rack, where I unlocked my bicycle. Then we walked to the gate, where Rachel waited for her mother to pick her up. I waited with her. It was hot, maybe 100 or 102, the hottest day of the year so far, and I struggled to find something to say.

"It's hot," I told Rachel, holding my bike by the handlebar.

"Yes, it is, Robert, very hot."

Silence ensued, entombing both of us. Then her mother drove up in a white, four-door Buick—the most beautiful vehicle I had ever seen. It shattered the silence.

"Bye, Robert!" Rachel said, hugging me. "Have a great summer. See you in the fall."

As I rode my bike home, I looked up at the sky, blinded by the crystalline brilliance of the sun. I raised my hands to shield my eyes. There were no clouds to chase—or to chase me. I could feel the sweat trickling down my sides. The sun would burn my skin brown, browner than it already was, but I did not care. *Ándale, pinche* Randy Reed. I was brown, and I did not give a damn. I did not whip Randy Reed, but he did not whip me, either.

I was no Johnny Risko, but I did the one thing my father wanted me to do. I slowed down. And for one of the few times that year, I was not going to lie to the old man. I was going to tell him everything. Everything. I would not be dishonest with him—not this time. I froze when I raised my fist, but I did not cower from Randy Reed. It was Randy Reed who cowered from me—me, the chili. I was not a *chingon*, a badass, but I was not a *cobarde*, a coward, either. I was something in between, *medio chingon, medio cobarde*, half badass, half coward, which suited me fine.

I could not wait to get home and tell the old man. Where would I start? With Randy Reed or Rachel Olsen? With the sun making my skin darker and me prouder? I pedaled faster.

## Afterword

There is a flip side to my opening line in this book. If time erodes the things that do not matter, it also underscores the things that do. That, more than anything, is what my year in Bakersfield taught me.

It was a surreal experience, riding my bike home on the last day of school, awash in emotions I had not felt in months. Randy Reed was gone, banished, his malignant presence evaporating into the atmosphere. God bless Alita, but I no longer needed her wise *consejo—No le hagas caso.* The advice was part of my DNA now, at least with regard to Randy Reed. I thought about him, every now and then, but he no longer haunted me, and it struck me that the word he was really trying to say all that time was *chile,* as in the jalapeño pepper. And whenever I heard the word *chili* or *chile* afterwards, I thought of that man in the television commercials, the one with the cowboy accent who hawked Wolf Brand Chili, his ecstatic voice conjuring images of the red glop the men were cooking in the hobo jungle that day.

I never saw Randy Reed again . . . or Wendell Wilson . . . or Gregory Bukowski . . . or Mrs. Chaney . . . or Rachel Olsen. But I thought about Rachel all the time, thoughts that were never suffused with romantic notions—the yearning for a lost love. I just missed her. As I got older, I would find myself wondering how she looked during the various stages of her life, how she aged, whether she retained that sweet, golden loveliness, both inside and outside, that marked her as a child. I was certain she had. There was no doubt.

We left Bakersfield that summer, my mother and I, just a few weeks after the last day of school. My mother was homesick, and we followed her malady back to El Paso. She could not take it any longer. The old man stayed behind, continuing his work at the *Bakersfield Californian,* but that little war in Southeast Asia had intensified, and as more men died, American as well as Vietnamese, he became more vocal in his opposition to the conflict. Some of his colleagues did not appreciate his, uh, attitude. One of them came at him with a pair of scissors one day—in the newsroom. When big wars start provoking little wars in newspaper buildings, something is wrong, the old man thought. He resigned a year later, rejoining us in El Paso.

Back in El Paso, my friends loved him. He was one of them—without trying to be. He and Alita picked up where they left off, savoring the sunsets as they sat on the porch of our duplex. We were lucky; the previous tenant had left, so we got our old place back. Pito Peterson was not amused.

I started shaving in the eighth grade, as a lark; my beard was no thicker than the lint on a suit, but once I started, I had to keep it up, and the old man got a kick out of it. He called me Billy Goat Gruff. My friends thought it was cool. When I went a few days without shaving, I looked older, so my buddies started asking me to buy them *Playboys* at a convenience store on Stanton Street, about two miles from the neighborhood. It worked. I looked depraved but legal, and the cashier sold me the magazines with no questions asked. I had a stack in my closet, behind my clothes, where I was certain no one could find them.

One afternoon, two of my friends barged into my room. Alita, our diligent sentry, must have been off duty at that moment, because the old man let them in, without the impolitic comments that usually signaled the arrival of my friends—"*Bobby, aqui esta el gordo.*" I was sprawled in a chair by the window in my bedroom, reading a *Thor* comic book (I had not outgrown them yet). One of my friends asked me where my *Playboys* were.

"Huh?"

"Your father said you were in here looking at your *Playboys*."

"*Nel*," I said.

"No, really, that's what he said."

"How did he know I had them?"

I should have known. The old man knew more than I thought he did. Of all the dads in the neighborhood, he was the only one who liked the Beatles, although he preferred the Brothers Four, the folk group that scored a minor hit with "Rock Island Line" in 1964. He also liked Wayne Newton—how someone could like Jorge Negrete and Wayne Newton was beyond me. How someone could like Wayne Newton, period, was beyond me, especially someone like my dad, who usually exhibited good taste. One evening, knowing that I was heading to the moonlight madness sale at Bassett Center with my friends, he gave me five dollars for a Wayne Newton album—any Wayne Newton album—with "Danke Schoen" on it. I came back with *Abbey Road.*

Alita never said anything bad about the Beatles, but she hated most of the other rock 'n' roll bands in the 1960s, especially the ones that appeared on cheesy TV programs like *Shindig* and *Hullabaloo.* She called the rock 'n' rollers *maricones*, queers, as if their very presence on the planet assaulted her sensibilities. The world was changing.

Alita died in 1967. She was ninety-four. Tía Maria blamed her death on me. I was a *travieso*, a prankster, as Alita herself acknowledged, and I was playing in the park one evening, about fifteen minutes past suppertime. It was one of those windy, blustery days common during the springtime in El Paso. Alita, already walking with a cane by this time, got worried, so she went out looking for me. The wind tossed her to the ground, breaking her hip. She never recovered, and it was my fault. If it had not been for me, Tía Maria said, Alita never would have ventured into the streets, a frail flower whipsawed by Mother Nature. It was not my fault, and I knew it, but the comment crushed me. The old *consejo—no le hagas caso*—was never more appropriate, and this time it applied to my aunt. The old man would not let me go to the funeral, and from that day forward, whenever he spoke of Tía Maria, he never mentioned her good qualities. The gene pool is a mystery. Alita was the one with the good qualities, but none—or very few—filtered down to my aunt.

My beloved Alita was gone. They say that when someone you love dies, a little bit of you goes with them. When Alita died, I discovered the legitimacy of that notion—not because my grief had wounded me, although it had, but because we behave with different people in different ways, our interactions specific to those relationships, from our conversations to our body language. And when a loved one dies, those dynamics, tied to a special person during a special time, are gone forever. Never again would I behave with anyone in quite the same way I behaved with Alita. She was gone. I miss her to this day.

My mother and I stayed in El Paso, and except for part of 1969, when he worked as a copyeditor at the *St. Louis Post-Dispatch*, the old man spent most of his last days with us. He focused on his short stories, and with Chicano studies programs gaining prominence in universities throughout the country, his work started to reach a wider audience. It was an irony he never discussed, but he must have loved it—nobody outside the family and a few close friends realized that the Amado Muro stories were written by an Anglo from Cleveland.

Four years after Alita died, my father followed her. It was 1971, just a few days after I turned sixteen. He and my mother took me to Furr's Cafeteria for my birthday. It was a weeknight. My father was a chain-smoker—his brand was KOOL—and while my mother and I sat at a booth in the cafeteria, he sat in a chair about two feet away, worried that the smoke would bother us.

The following Sunday, we got a call from Mr. Zamora, who owned Zamora's News Stand on Paisano Street. My father visited the shop every Sunday morning, coming back with an armful of Mexican newspapers and boxing magazines. It was one of his few vices—that and the cigarettes. He collapsed in the tiny store, falling on the stacks of *El Fronterizo* and *El Continental*, and when we got the call, my mother and I headed out to the county hospital in a taxi. We were too late. Dead on arrival. Heart attack.

My grandfather came for the funeral. It hit him hard. He felt what every mother or father must feel when one of their children dies. Why him? Why not me? The night of the funeral, he sat in the living room, going over the literary quarterlies that published the Amado Muro stories. He read "Blue" out loud, his tone calm and respectful, and the words—like a lullaby sung to a crying baby—

soothed me. And then he read another story and another. It was then that I decided I wanted to become a writer.

> Toward sidehills matted with chaparral, mesquite and gobernadora stood adobe homes with blessed palms hanging over their doors to keep evil spirits and lightning away. Stumpy cottonwoods, misted with grey veils woven by caterpillars, leaned before them. On fair days the gossiping housewives, whose doings gave the street its name, sat on rush-plaited chairs under the trees, where wrapped in thick mantas woven by High Sierra Indians, they patched *rebozos* in the sunshine. Their conversations were famous. They talked mostly about their husbands. Some said they wished they had gone into the convent instead of getting married. Others disagreed. "Ay, Madre, it's better to undress one-horned drunkards than dress plaster saints," they insisted. Sometimes Pug Nose and I listened until they drove us away. ("Sister Guadalajara")

Even as a child, I understood his love of words, but I had never known of anyone else who experienced the same mystical bond with the language. And then it came, the epiphany, and it was, appropriately enough, through a book. When was it? Aaahhh, yes, it was near the turn of the century—1999 or 2001—almost thirty years after the old man died. The book was three hundred pages of lyricism, a poem disguised as a memoir, *The Bend for Home* by Dermot Healy, one of those singular books that are lovely beyond description. The prose sent my imagination "on a wonder," as the old man might have said. Healy described his fascination with words—the excitement he derived from simple sentences. He described his relationship with his loved ones early on in the book:

> It was . . . a fondness for words that startled me. I can still remember the liquid feel of those words for rain. The words for rain were better than the rain itself. I wanted to type up words. . . .

I read *Portrait of the Artist as a Young Dog*. Then I moved on to Dylan's poems. The words shimmered on the paper and released themselves from the prison of the sentences they were in. They became things in themselves. A single word collected a myriad of meanings. Verbs bounced in open spaces. A noun was like a bowl of cream. It contained vast worlds. An adjective made an image infinite.

About a month after my father died, I was walking home from school, following a dusty trail of back alleys to our home near the gully. I was a senior at Cathedral High School, and my academic résumé, a little sparse up to that point, received a much-needed jolt: I made the Gold Honor Roll, a first for me. My dad would be proud, if not flabbergasted, I thought, for he saw me as someone with more brains than discipline, although he may have given me too much credit for one and not enough for the other.

As I walked home, my gold certificate tucked in my literary anthology, I thought about my dad, about how proud he would be of my achievement, and the more I thought about him, the more that horrible day receded from my memory—the day he died. It was a great feeling, a cleansing. Obsessed with the card—and his reaction to it—I walked faster, thrilled at the thought of how pleased he would be when I told him about my achievement. Then, as I saw our chimney poking above the last hill on my way home, it hit me: There would be no Dad waiting for me. I started crying; it was as if my father had died twice in one month.

My grandfather died eight years later. He was eighty-two, felled by the same cruel blow that struck his son—a heart attack. We flew up to Cleveland for the funeral, my mother and I. It was the first time I had seen the city that my old man—and his old man—loved so much. A part of me died when Alita died, but a part of Cleveland died when my grandfather died, because he had meant so much to the city for so long. They called him "Mr. Cleveland." I would never forget the day he told me "don't pay attention to him"—to Randy Reed. He was a great man.

"To his staff, he was the man who gave Christmas gifts to reporters' children, the playful fellow who jumped up on desks and tossed peanuts at people," Dick Wooten wrote for the *Cleveland Press* on June 17, 1982, the day the newspaper folded.

> But beneath it all he was a dynamo who practiced high-powered journalism and made the *Press* one of the best papers in the United States.
>
> Louie died April 2, 1980, at the age of 82. Today the newspaper for which he worked tirelessly died. God showed mercy by taking Louis first.

My mother had a stroke in 1996. It paralyzed one side of her body, left her unable to speak coherently. She remained in a rehab center for a year, and it was hard to see this feisty woman marooned in her own body, her arms and legs unable to obey the commands from her brain. My mother died in 1997. She was eighty, a woman who could be tenderhearted despite her volcanic profanity.

Forty-six years after I gave up on *Ivanhoe*—bedeviled by the arcane language that locked me out of a world I really, truly, wanted to enter—I tried again. What a difference forty-six years make. The edition—a $7.95 paperback—was shabbier than the rich, handsome "volume" the old man gave me, but its contents were no less glorious than they would have been if I had just hung in there almost five decades earlier. What a great read. It was not the violence that captivated me this time around, and no wonder—I had graduated from Marvel comic books long before, fortunately (or perhaps unfortunately). No, it was the gallantry, the nobility of spirit—and it was not the fairy-tale kind, either. These were real men and women, flawed but big-hearted, with the capacity to overcome their fears and weaknesses. My favorite character was not even a knight. It was Rebecca, the "dark Jewess," who explains, toward the end of the book, why she must leave England:

> The people of England are a fierce race, quarreling ever with their neighbours or among themselves, and ready to plunge

> the sword into the bowels of each other. Such is no safe abode for the children of my people. . . . Not in a land of war and blood, surrounded by hostile neighbours, and distracted by internal factions, can Israel hope to rest during her wanderings.

The old man knew what he was talking about. *Ivanhoe* was magnificent. And so was *The Futile Life of Pito Perez* by José Rubén Romero, the book he had recommended to me in 1964, the year Randy Reed assaulted my dignity. I read it about forty years later. As with *Ivanhoe*, I had to ask myself, "Why did I wait so long to read it?" I had no answer, no good answer. Perhaps I wanted to bury 1964, including all the good things that happened that year. If that was my reasoning, what a huge mistake. *The Futile Life of Pito Perez* was sublime. As I read it, I realized why the old man recommended the book. It was about an outsider, a man who, consumed with bitterness toward the critics and hypocrites he faced every day, possessed more nobility and charm than those who scorned him.

Reading the books was an epiphany, belated but no less glorious for its tardiness, the pages ablaze with an immense spirit. *Ivanhoe* and *The Futile Life of Pito Perez*. They were better than *And To Think That I Saw It on Mulberry Street*.

Thanks, Dad.

## About the Author

A native of El Paso, Texas, Robert L. Seltzer earned a journalism degree from the University of Texas at El Paso. He has worked for newspapers such as the *Houston Chronicle*, the *Philadelphia Inquirer*, and the *San Antonio Express-News*, where he is currently the public editor. He has won state and national awards for his news, feature, and sports reporting, including the Nat Fleischer Award for Excellence in Boxing Journalism.